THE PRICE OF RACIAL RECONCILIATION

THE POLITICS OF RACE AND ETHNICITY

Series Editors Rodney E. Hero, University of Notre Dame
Katherine Tate, University of California, Irvine

Politics of Race and Ethnicity is premised on the view that understanding race and ethnicity is integral to a fuller, more complete understanding of the American political system. The goal is to provide the scholarly community at all levels with accessible texts that will introduce them to, and stimulate their thinking on, fundamental questions in this field. We are interested in books that creatively examine the meaning of American democracy for racial and ethnic groups and, conversely, what racial and ethnic groups mean and have meant for American democracy.

*The Urban Voter: Group Conflict and
Mayoral Voting Behavior in American Cities*
Karen M. Kaufmann

Democracy's Promise: Immigrants and American Civil Institutions
Janelle S. Wong

Mark One or More: Civil Rights in Multiracial America
Kim M. Williams

Race, Republicans, and the Return of the Party of Lincoln
Tasha S. Philpot

The Price of Racial Reconciliation
Ronald W. Walters

The Price of Racial Reconciliation

❧

Ronald W. Walters

THE UNIVERSITY OF MICHIGAN PRESS

Ann Arbor

2011   2010   2009   2008   4   3   2   1

A CIP catalog record for this book is available from the British Library.

Library of Congress Cataloging-in-Publication Data

Walters, Ronald W.
    The price of racial reconciliation / Ronald W. Walters.
        p.   cm. — (The politics of race and ethnicity series)
    Includes bibliographical references and index.
    ISBN-13: 978-0-472-11530-3 (cloth : alk. paper)
    ISBN-10: 0-472-11530-8 (cloth : alk. paper)
        1. Racism—United States.   2. Racism—South Africa.   3. Blacks—
    Social conditions.   4. Reparations for historical injustices.
    5. Reconciliation—Social aspects.   6. African Americans—Reparations.
    I. Title.

    HT1581.W27   2008
    305.800973—dc22   2007036083

Grateful acknowledgement is given for permission to reprint "The Lynching"
by Claude McKay. Courtesy of the Literary Representative for the Works of
Claude McKay, Schomburg Center for Research in Black Culture, The New
York Public Library, Astor, Lenox and Tilden Foundations.

CONTENTS

PREFACE

I WOULD LIKE TO USE THIS SPACE TO ACKNOWLEDGE several influences that stimulated the writing of this book and, in doing so, to provide a brief history of the reparations movement. I encountered the subject of reparations, as did many who came to political maturity in the 1960s, through the audacious actions of James Forman, former executive director and strategist of the Student Nonviolent Coordinating Committee (SNCC). I met Jim in the early 1970s when I served as chairman of the Political Science Department at Howard University. He was studying for a Ph.D. from the Union University system and would come to my office and provoke rich discussion that deepened my understanding of the Black movement and other movements for social change. In short, he was one of my teachers in a relationship that continued until he died as this book was being written.

I had known of Jim Forman since I was a student at Fisk University at the height of the Nashville civil rights movement in the 1960s, as many of the leaders of SNCC, including John Lewis, Diane Nash, and others, were students there and carried out activities from that base. By the time I left Fisk and moved to Washington, DC, to enter graduate school, many SNCC workers had also come out of the South to the city, as SNCC was undergoing a transition from its Christian nonviolent roots, associated with the Southern Christian Leadership Conference, to become a more militant Black nationalist organization, headed by Stokely Carmichael and then H. Rap Brown.

My familiarity with the changing organization, however, did not keep me from being startled by Forman's bold demand for reparations when he took over the pulpit at the Riverside Church in New York City on the Sunday morning of May 4, 1969, and argued that $500 million should be turned over to Black organizations by the religious establishment in the United States because of its role in legitimizing slavery. It was a dramatic moment that brought home to many the question of redress and culpability for Black America's place at the bottom of its civilization. Having completed my master's degree in African Studies and with my approaching candidacy for the Ph.D. in international politics, I was armed with the intellectual knowledge to match the information of my cultural upbringing, which made Forman's challenge highly credible. Even then, I reached the conclusion that regardless of whether reparations would ever be given to Blacks, they should be demanded as an act contributing to the historical integrity of African people.

As an activist in the Pan-African movement, I was a charter member of the National Coalition of Blacks for Reparations in America (NCOBRA), founded in the mid-1980s. Although this organization was largely unsuccessful, it did carry forward the demand for reparations, largely unheralded by the major Black organizations, developing a legal approach that rested in part on treaty law and precedents set by Native Americans and the unfulfilled post–Civil War amendments to the Constitution. Although many Black leaders in the 1980s gave nodding approval to the formation of NCOBRA, the primary goals of the Black community in that era were protecting the civil rights agenda from the onslaught of President Ronald Reagan, mobilizing a challenge through the presidential campaign of Rev. Jesse Jackson, and helping to free South Africa from the grip of the white minority regime.

In the many meetings of activists in the Pan-African movement, which supported the renaissance of African countries, and of Black intellectuals in organizations such as the African Heritage Studies Association, I frequently met Queen Mother Audley Moore, long a fixture in Harlem who championed reparations for African descendants. At first, she was an oddity to me. But as I came to know more about Harlem, established a relationship with John Henrik Clarke, the venerable street intellectual of Africana history, and plumbed the lineage of this demand back to the pension rights movement, I grew to respect her unwavering demand that Black activists and intellectuals support this issue.

Despite these initiatives, reparations were never a popular cause among the Black middle class and their organizations, nor even among the most ardent Black activists, until the novel contributions of Randall Robinson in the late 1990s. Robinson was head of TransAfrica, a Black lobbying organization for Africans in the Diaspora that had led the anti-Apartheid movement in the mid-1980s, when NCOBRA was born. I had been an associate of his during the founding of that organization.

Robinson initiated a meeting in January 1999 that included veterans of the reparations movement as well as leaders who had not been previously active in it. By shrewdly including leading members of the Black establishment, Robinson did more to legitimize the movement for Black reparations than any other act in recent history. This meeting led to others, and to the formation of the Reparations Coordinating Committee. Illustrative of those involved were Congressman John Conyers of Detroit, who had sponsored a bill (H.R. 40, which would create a commission to study the issue of reparations) in each session of Congress since the 1980s; Black legal scholars such as Charles Ogletree of Harvard; Eric Yamamoto of the University of Hawaii Law School; and famous trial attorneys such as Johnnie Cochran, Willie Gary, Dennis Sweet, and Adjoa Ayietoro (longtime scion of the NCOBRA and the NCBL). Also in attendance were lawyers knowledgeable on reparations to Jewish, Japanese, and other communities, and academics such as Manning Marable of Columbia, Cornell West of Harvard, James Comer of Yale, Ali Mazrui of Binghamton University, and this writer. And Robinson included the civil rights leaders Dorothy Height and Wade Henderson, among others.

Then came Robinson's blockbuster book, *The Debt*, which brought reparations to the attention of national media, and to forums sprouting on university campuses, churches, and other venues. His book did not begin the task of educating the country about the role that slavery played in the construction of American history. We already had an intellectual legacy on slavery, with whole libraries of books by distinguished scholars who had contributed to this knowledge. Instead, Robinson's book politicized the subject by basing the demand for reparations on the dramatic foundation of the contribution of Black slaves to the building of America, even their role in the construction of the Capitol itself—and the Statue of Freedom, placed by them at the very top, ironically, as a symbol of the struggle for freedom by people all over the world. Robinson's book heightened public attention to the announcement of lawsuits by a recent law school graduate, Deadria Farmer-Paellmann, against major companies that had insured farmers and companies against the loss of their slaves. These events built a national discussion about reparations that reinvigorated NCOBRA's work and spawned a grassroots movement in the Black community led by activist organizations such as the Black United Front and others.

Robinson's book allowed me to consider writing a work that would explore a further question: if America owes a debt to Blacks for their role in the development of the country, a role with enormous historical, political, economic, and social consequences for the construction of American life, and if that role is recognized more by Blacks than by whites, how is racial reconciliation possible? Recognition of the Black contribution is the price of such reconciliation, and the politics of the lack of recognition—in each generation—will fuel the demand for reparations. As a foundation for establishing that price, I have sought here to summarize the cost to Blacks and the nation of their oppression, and identify the methodologies involved in previous historical attempts at repairing the social fabric.

As such, this book acknowledges two sources of debate about redress of the existing socioeconomic status of Blacks. First, if slavery and racism after slavery are important impediments to the social development of Blacks, to what extent could reparations change the structure of opportunity in America? Second, the conservative movement that has captured both the political institutions of American society and its cultural voice rejects the view that slavery and racism are ongoing factors in the subordination of Blacks. The conservative claim is that reparations would be unfair to whites, that racial reconciliation is immaterial to the further mobility of Blacks, and that America is already a fair, a truly democratic state. The conservative movement has ironically heightened the demand for reparations by attacking existing policies that have liberalized the opportunity structure, policies based upon the institutional and legal foundation of racial fairness constructed during the civil rights period and afterward.

This book is dedicated to deconstructing the fiction that slavery and postslavery racism are unrelated to the current socioeconomic status of Blacks in America, and that the past history of Black subordination is, or has ever been, without consequences to Blacks in the present, or to American society in general. It reemphasizes the demand for reparations by discussing issues that were confronted in the paradigm of racial reconciliation in South Africa, which led to the development of the Truth and Reconciliation Commission there.

For most of my teaching and research career I have been attentive to the power of comparative analysis, as illustrated in my previous work, *Pan Africanism in the African Diaspora,* and in a series of papers.[1] In 1998, I was invited to Australia by the Hubert Humphrey Center for Social Justice at the University of Minnesota, for a conference sponsored by the government-initiated Council on Racial Reconciliation. As I was leaving the conference, it struck me that I was returning to a country where President Bill Clinton had begun a so-called Dialogue on Race to stimulate interracial understanding and to reduce tensions, and that in South Africa, the long-awaited report of the Truth and Reconciliation Commission was about to be made public. My feeling was that all of these efforts, combined with the new interest in the reparations movement in America, created a dynamic environment within which to explore salient elements of the topic in a comparative fashion.

The last major influence on this study was the World Conference against Racism, Racial Discrimination, Xenophobia and Related Intolerance in Durban, South Africa, in July 2001, the initiation of which prompted debates about whether a discussion of reparations would be allowed. Through the diligence of Adjoa Ayietoro, many scholars and activists were made aware of these debates and were able to participate in the Durban conference, presenting the issue in a global forum. As a participant in the symposium of nongovernmental delegations at the conference and in the deliberations of the African and African Descendants Caucus, I was able to understand more acutely the breadth of the demand for reparations around the world.

These influences suggested to me that what would be useful was a discussion of issues that did not constitute a straightforward case for reparations, but an engagement with the "independent variables" necessary to construct a reasonable and powerful argument for reparations. If one wants an explicit history of the reparations movement, works other than this book may be consulted. But if one desires to investigate how any fair society might understand racial subordination, that is the work I have attempted to present.

◆

CHAPTER ONE

Introduction

History is fiction subject to a fitful Muse.
—Derek Walcott, *Memory*

AFTER A LONG PERIOD IN THE BASEMENT of the African American agenda, reparations have become a serious bone of contention among Blacks and others. Two events were especially important in making reparations salient. One was the lawsuit in 2002 by Deadria Farmer-Paellmann, a Black law school graduate, who found evidence that companies such as insurance giant Aetna, the railroad company CSX, and FleetBoston financial services had insured slaves for plantation owners or used slaves in their enterprises.[1] The second was the publication in 2000 of *The Debt* by Randall Robinson.[2] Robinson's message, that a debt remains unpaid to descendants of slaves—slaves who helped build the very Capitol of the United States, its surrounding city, and many other parts of the government's infrastructure—rekindled the debate over reparations. In this new climate emerged a group of highly visible lawyers and academics who attracted considerable press attention to their pursuit of a legal strategy to achieve reparations.[3]

The power of these events, coming so close to each other, stimulated a national discussion that generated new life in such organizations as the National Coalition of Blacks for Reparations, which was founded as an advocacy group in the mid-1980s. Moreover, it directed new attention to H.R. 40, legislation to develop a commission to study the issue of African reparations in America, which Congressman John Conyers has offered in every session of the House of Representatives for the past two decades.

In a pattern that resembles the grassroots movement against

Apartheid South Africa, several cities, especially those with large Black populations, such as Baltimore, Chicago, Washington, DC, and Detroit, have passed or considered resolutions affirming support for H.R. 40.[4] In addition, the state legislature of California passed a resolution requiring insurance companies that do business with the state to reveal historical incidences of insuring owners against the loss of slaves.[5] Vigorous discussion has been heard in the news media, on college campuses, and in conferences, especially the United Nations Conference against Racism, held in Durban, South Africa, in July and August 2001. Reparations are now a subject that registers in public opinion polls, and are a consensus topic among Blacks and their leaders, who at one time considered it unreasonable even to refer to.

This explosive and emotional issue is, therefore, a fit subject of inquiry, but it is necessary to state at the outset what this book does and does not attempt. It is not an actuarial calculation of the bill for slavery and its aftermath, tallied up in economic terms. Rather, it mines the underlying concepts of the moral claim to recompense and, in doing so, presents a view of the oppression that Black people have suffered in America, which determines the price of racial reconciliation. I compare the American case to the South African, an example of a process of racial reconciliation that involved reparations to victims of Apartheid. This example raises poignant questions for those who pursue reparations in the United States. That quest, we will see, is based on the memory of Black oppression and its relevance to the present.

Reparations are an explosive subject in part because they invoke two different histories, two different memories of past relations between Blacks and whites. The power of history is not only its description of events, but also its relation to the identity of those who shape it, and those who suffer from such shaping. As such, "history" comprises events that groups select as a resource to derive identity and meaning from the past, and to inform present understanding or action. The selectivity of such events politicizes history, for the powerful can determine an understanding of historical events consistent with a narrative they wish to advance.

Thus, memory is politicized, raising the question of what constitutes the "truth" of the past and how to reconcile the contentious perspectives of different versions. In this context, unpleasant aspects of the past, introduced as an alternative to a version of history emphasizing positive social harmony, may be viewed by some as an imposition. One story provides an example:

> It was as if the town were trying to erase the very existence of the black pioneers who settled this area [Priceville, Ontario, Canada] in the early 1800s. Hide the fact that some of the whites who came here later married some of the blacks. Hide the fact that many generations later, some white people still living in this town may not be white at all. Just a drop, they used to say.
>
> Eventually, the only trace that black people had ever been in Priceville, working the land and building homes and schools, was the cemetery. Then in the 1930s, a white farmer named Billy Reid bought the land, plowed over the cemetery and planted potatoes.
>
> That is what they say became of the history of black people in this part of Ontario. It was plowed over, buried and hushed up. But some of it survived, as when adults would whisper secrets, unaware that children were listening.
>
> Now, black Canadians—who make up about 1 percent of the country's 31 million people—are trying to put the broken tombstones back together, pick up the pieces of their ancestry and fill in the spaces that were left in the history books.[6]

A buried, now resurrected history has unpleasant aspects for whites who inherited the Priceville community from its original Black settlers. The injustice done to Blacks has survived in the memory of the community, demeaning the dignity of the descendants of both the inheritors of Priceville and those whom they oppressed, and so the descendants of those who were harmed have taken on the responsibility to achieve justice in their name.

As an step toward dismantling systems of oppression in which one cultural group dominates another, reparations are more than simply "payment" for past injury. They are a national question. If this is so, then a *broad view* of history must be presented and a broad demand must be made for restitution. Reparations address Black oppression, and in the context of a "grand narrative," this oppression is not merely damaging to Blacks but constructs the identity of America itself.

Here, my view of American reparations is affected by the case of South Africa, where the struggle to accomplish racial healing through a Truth and Reconciliation Commission addressed a grand narrative of oppression. This makes reparations a larger question than "race relations," a concept that prompts attempts to rectify injustices according to a paradigm of racial dominance and subordination. This level of analysis comprehends what may be called "petty race oppression," and is qualitatively different from the interrogation of the sources of power differences among cultural groups in their relation the state. Since the paradigm is not concerned with the total environment, including the historical and current socioeconomic and cultural statuses that shape neighborhood conflicts, it invites petty methods of redress, such as calls for cross-cultural dialogues, symbolic apologies, and memorials and museums—forms of what Eric K. Yamamoto calls "cheap reconciliation."[7]

In South Africa the consequences of Apartheid were acknowledged to be so serious that reconciliation through restitution became a legitimate goal of the Truth and Reconciliation Commission. In particular, its consequences were legitimized for those whose relatives and ancestors were victims of Apartheid. Yet in the United States, the consequences of slavery for the descendants of the enslaved are held not to justify restitution to the current Black population. In this view, the progeny of slaves—great-grandsons and great-granddaughters, granddaughters and grandsons, even daughters and sons—are unaffected by what happened in the past. But what happened in the past is indeed profoundly material, in part because organic components of the institution of slavery—the most persistent of them being the inferiority of Black people—poisoned Black communities long after the legal regime of slavery ended.

Therefore, this book reconceptualizes the basis of reparations as an organic phenomenon of oppression, taking into consideration slavery, but making no sharp break between slavery and other forms of oppression. Nor do I take the position that slavery and other oppressive practices ended abruptly in the nineteenth—or some would say the twentieth—century, but understand that they recur as supports for the supremacy of the dominant class, especially when, in different periods of history, the underclass mounts serious challenges to that supremacy.

Given that oppressive acts have been directed at African American life for centuries, the demand for reparations has also had a long history.

Without describing that history here, I note that this demand parallels the history of oppression for at least four essential reasons: the politics of the memory as reflected in different notions of how America was born; the tension between majoritarian democracy and justice for all; the differential treatment of groups in America with respect to payment of reparations; and the attack by the dominant class on the liberal regime of rights that were meant to make the Black underclass equal. I will briefly discuss these factors in the sections that follow, as a preface to fuller treatment of these topics in the rest of the book.

The Politics of Memory

The dominant group in a society is often shocked to find that subordinate groups remember the harms done to them, which often resurface as the primary basis of their attitudes and behaviors toward the dominant group. The dominant group often appears naive, surprised that the historical victory over the suppressed group did not buy them peace. And that is because the settlement of or compensation for the harm done is inadequate, or nonexistent. Indeed, one frequently hears that, since the harm happened so long ago, the tactic of peace desired by the dominant group is forgetting and "moving on." But forgetting is hard when the harm is lodged in the collective memory of a group. Such recollection may be termed "common memory":

> A common memory . . . is an aggregate notion. It aggregates the memories of all those people who remember a certain episode which each of them experienced individually. If the rate of those who remember the episode in a given society is above a certain threshold (say, most of them, an overwhelming majority of them, more than 70 percent, or whatever) then we call the memory of the episode a common memory—all of course relative to the society at hand.[8]

This powerful, shared memory means that simply "moving on" is impossible, and that any regime of reconciliation must have unresolved issues as a rationale for action. This is even more true when the imperative to remember is reinforced by ongoing experiences of harm, re-creating the political content of the memory in each age.[9]

Consider Memorial Day, a national opportunity to remember and preserve the supreme sacrifices made by soldiers and their families in wars. Blacks have not been the fuel for keeping these memories alive, but rather—just to name organizations that remember the Civil War— the Sons of Confederate Veterans, the United Daughters of the Confederacy, the Daughters of the Union Veterans, and the Sons of Union Veterans.[10] Memorial Day began in May 1868 as Decoration Day, when the graves of both Union and Confederate soldiers were honored, in a move that began the reuniting of the North and the South.

Critically, the memories of veterans of both sections of the country were passed on to their descendants. One such descendant was Garland Pool, who recalled that his father could not shake memories of the war, for example, when, during a battle, slaves were liberated and one slave was given a gun, which he used to beat his slave master to death.[11] These memories live on to such an extent that students at a middle school in Peoria, Illinois, having received visits and email from descendants of Civil War veterans in 2004, said that their exploits did not seem to have happened 140 years ago.[12] For some people, these memories color behavior today.

Some Blacks and whites remember the Civil War strongly enough to participate in reenactments of its battles. In May 2004, I arrived at a hotel in Fredericksburg, Virginia, only to be asked at the desk whether I had come to participate in the battle of Spotsylvania, which on its 140th anniversary was being re-created on the nearby Belvedere Plantation.[13] The event was not restricted to men who took the role of soldiers. The full-page spread in the local newspaper assessed the role of women, who also donned period clothing, attempting in every way to conduct their roles as authentically as possible. Indeed, there are thousands of such Civil War reenactments all over the country.

The vigorous desire to preserve memories of the Civil War is demonstrated in other ways as well. A political movement has emerged to prevent developers from destroying historic battlefields. For example, a coalition was formed in 2002 to save the Chancellorsville battlefield, threatened by developers who wanted to build expensive homes on the site; the coalition won its battle before the Fredericksburg Area Metropolitan Planning Organization.[14] Indeed, many of the Civil War battlefields have similarly come under the pressure of development. The fifty-thousand-member Civil War Preservation Trust is dedicated to preserving them, believing that "these battlefields are the last tangible reminders of the valor of those who donned the blue and gray. They must be preserved for future generations of Americans."[15]

Thus the memory of the Civil War and of the reasons it was fought is still strong in the American psyche. Preservation of this memory entails recollection of the atrocious harm done to African slaves and their descendants, an aspect of the past that cannot be detached and removed from the history of which it is a part. It is thus a prime impediment to any "reconciliation" that consists entirely of forgetting.

Part of the equation of American memory, however, is that slavery and its aftermath are sensitive subjects. The sensitivities in the racial memory of the white psyche may seen in the tortuous considerations that always arise when one looks at the posture of the founding fathers on slavery, and in the massive rejection of the legacy of miscegenation exposed by the story of Thomas Jefferson's slave mistress. Sensitivities notwithstanding, African slavery and the subordination and virtual extinction of Native Americans were bloody affairs, with many victims, much slaughter, and the debasement of the humanity of such peoples. This stigma has survived into the modern era. Reconciling such a history requires an admission of this inhumanity and these atrocities. They constitute a significant part of the moral legacy of the victorious group, and therefore must inform its intention to make recompense, or establish, as it is often called, "justice."

Contentious Perspectives on the Making of America

Mt. Rushmore symbolizes the idea that America was created by great white men—George Washington, Thomas Jefferson, Abraham Lincoln, and Theodore Roosevelt—and that the purity of their contribution should be preserved, enshrined in stone as the basis of their right to rule. The monument was forged in the early twentieth century, an intensely nationalist era of American history. In fact, the primary builder of the monument, Gutzon Borglum, named the monument "The Shrine of American Democracy," calling it "the mark of American civilization."[16] His quest was not just to create the scene of four American presidents carved into Mt. Rushmore, but to define the meaning of this colossal memorial to the greatness of American civilization.

Roosevelt's place in this pantheon has been often questioned, but he was a favorite of Borglum, who was enamored with his policies and raised funds for his campaigns. Indeed, Roosevelt himself characterized his policies as the product of a period of "new nationalism." Borglum's contribution to the dominant ideology of the era not only exalts the contribution of whites to the making of American civilization, but tries to exclude Blacks from the myth of America's new creation. Borglum's view of America was that of a white nation in conflict with other racial and ethnic groups, some of whom came before the Europeans, such as the Hispanics and Native Americans, and others, such as Africans and Asians, who were used as laborers to build the country's material infrastructure. Mt. Rushmore is set in the Black Hills of South Dakota in the home of the Sioux Indians, who regarded it as a desecration of the land of their ancestors. The monument to democracy was carved not only in a place where, but at a time when, Indians were being hunted down, slaughtered, and set on reservations. Thus, Mt. Rushmore stands as one of the greatest ironies of America.

In some ways, it is consistent that the builder of the monument was not only a white nationalist, but a racist who excoriated Jews at every opportunity, and of course, felt that Blacks were patently inferior. The irony deepens in that Borglum also worked on a monument to Robert E. Lee and other Confederate generals at Stone Mountain in Georgia, just outside of the city of Atlanta. While he believed that the justice of the Southern cause was made moot by the Civil War, he also thought that "the character, the high principle of these great men, should not be ignored."[17] What's more, he was a partisan and close associate of the Ku Klux Klan, which was reborn at a ceremony at Stone Mountain in 1915. As John Taliaferro points out, Borglum "attended Klan rallies, served on Klan committees, and endeavored to play peacemaker in several Klan leadership disputes."[18] But regardless of Stone Mountain's association with the terrorism of lynching and other violence against Blacks, Borglum agreed to place a Klan altar at the base of his monument there.

In the 1920s, Borglum said about Black people, "[W]hile Anglo-Saxons have themselves sinned grievously against the principle of pure nationalism by illicit slave and alien servant traffic, it has been the character of the cargo that has eaten into the very moral fiber of our race character rather than the moral depravity of Anglo-Saxon traders."[19]

Proof that Mt. Rushmore remains a symbol of American nationalism may be found in the survey at the site that asks visitors to name the greatest president. While one of the obvious choices, George Washington, Thomas Jefferson, and Abraham Lincoln, has come in at the top of the list each year, Ronald Reagan, a modern nationalist, has often placed second. In part, this was the result of a dedicated campaign by the Reagan Legacy Committee, which succeeded in having Washington National Airport named for Reagan, over the objection of Blacks who regarded him as a racist.[20] But a primary point of the committee's agitation was to have Reagan's face added as the fifth president on the surface of Mt. Rushmore!

Neither the original faces on the mountain, nor the attempt to place Ronald Reagan there, reflects the contributions of other groups to America. Rather, Mt. Rushmore is a monument to a myth of creation that rejected their contribution. The effort to add Reagan symbolizes recent attempts to undo what progress had been achieved to bring racial and ethnic groups to full equality within American society.

Black Oppression as a National Question

Randall Robinson artfully brings to the surface the point that concern with Black oppression requires acknowledging the use of Black resources in the construction of the American state. The immorality of slavery has been compounded by the modern failure to acknowledge that the grandeur of this country was based, in substantial part, upon the monumental resources made possible by African labor. The failure to acknowledge the contribution of Africans is an act of social theft, removing from the story its real heroic virtue. Moreover, it is a theft that has been repeated in each age, corrupting what passes for American history and the education upon which it is founded. It fosters cynicism and alienation among Blacks and precludes their full-faith acceptance of the institutionalized version of the American dream.

Traditionally, the contribution of Blacks to the building of America has been understood on the basis of the pallid notion of "contributionism," that is to say, a nod toward Black inventors, soldiers, cultural artists, and such. The case made in Robinson's book is that the real impact of Blacks on the American genesis includes a comprehensive contribution to the entire political economy, including the accumulation of monumental profits by private companies and massive resources by the government. So reparations are significant not merely to Blacks, but to the reconstitution of a fair perspective that respects the roles all played in the making of America, as a primary content of their own citizenship.

Democracy and Memory Justice

When Blacks advance a project of recompense for subordination, the response by the majority contributes to the definition of a democratic society. If restorative justice is unavailable to the citizenry, one can have no confidence that the society intends to pursue a democratic state for all. Therefore, we must confront the question of whether the goal is real democracy, defined by the sharing of power, or the maintenance of a notion of democracy that accommodates white dominance and Black subordination. The answer will provide us with the criteria according to which the society remembers its past, organizes its present, and designs its future. We allude here, then, to a potential tension between democracy and justice.

James Booth suggests that we should endeavor to live in a world ruled by justice as the basis of democracy, and memory, he writes, occupies the heart of justice.[21] Booth suggests that to achieve the kind of society we desire, the future must be freed from the pollution of the past, and that the only possible cleansing derives from a feeling among victims that justice has been done. So the modern state must establish an apparatus to free itself from the unfulfilled responsibilities of the past, fomenting justice in order that dignity may emerge. It is the dignity of the victims that restores the past, not as a concealed burden but as an acknowledged source of the present and the future.

The political problem here is whose version of reality will govern. Our sense of reality is generally seamless in sewing together the past, present, and future into a whole experience. Within it, the events that comprise different eras interact with one another in inescapable confrontation. Memory is social, not merely individual, and incorporates social interactions. If an attempt to forget obscures a history (a set of memories) that is important to a subordinate group, this is another form of oppression, and contrary to Booth's concept of "memory justice." Erasing the unpleasant past to evade the truth, making selective aspects of past realities disappear, is impossible so long as representatives of the victims exist in the present and future.

Commenting on competing senses of memory, Ueno Chizuko poses the notion of a "multivalent reality":

> When slavery was practiced in the American South, there was
> no law against it. But subsequently, after a change in the con-

sciousness brought recognition of what a crime against humanity slavery was, American history was re-written. Slavery and
the genocide of indigenous peoples became indelible smirches
on American history. What Anglo-Saxon Americans had
understood as a "noble conquest," native Americans remembered as a massacre. Only with the challenge of minorities'
opposing realities has American history come to be written
from a more diverse perspective.[22]

Blacks have asserted their own reality in an effort to endow it with a
moral force that will attract restitution. About that stage of the contest-
ing of realities, Chizuko says:

When the victims are bold enough to break their silence, we
have no choice but to embark from their own overwhelming
"reality." By "reality," I do not mean here the same things as
"facts." When this great a disparity exists between the experience of the perpetrators and the victims, how can one call the
incident a single "fact"? Rather, two "realities" exist.[23]

If a society's memories offer up two realities, or more than two, are
all realities equally true? Michael Kreyling raises the question of
whether there is such a thing as "false memory" and how it gets
recorded.[24] The "multivalent reality" of American slavery has been
established primarily by those who reside atop the power structure: the
dominant group has made a dedicated practice of forgetting about it,
and very often about modern racism as well. Kreyling implies that one
reality may be more authentic than another, and that the latter exists as
"false memory." He sheds light on the process of false memorization in
the contemporary United States: "We live in a society which fashions
itself post-traditional and we imagine that we remake our society everyday, that we are members of a highly mobile deracinated community."[25]
In such an environment, he asks, why do certain events, such as the
Holocaust, merit the "justice of remembrance"? On that question ultimately turns an important ethic of our society, our collective responsibility to remember.

When realities are multiple, when they are not woven together in a
seamless garment, what happens? Larry J. Griffin asks what white
Southerners should remember about the struggle in Birmingham dur-

ing the civil rights movement, or about the exclusion of Blacks from. Ole Miss (the University of Mississippi). Since Blacks "now insist that the overarching majoritarian story is not the only memory," memories held by the dominant class must be scrutinized. In fact, since post-traditional society must be more inclusive, "it is precisely because of the contestation over the dominant narrative, or the story, that there is room for this kind of insurgent use of memory by any numbers of people who felt themselves to be slighted or ignored or forgotten in the grand narrative."[26] Such an insurgency has been created over slavery and its consequences, memories of which will not die because they are material to the identity those who still live as victims, a legacy of slavery's original victims. Dignifying past victims is the key to dignifying those who from them inherit a present and future. As Booth has observed about the Nazi regime, here "the intertwining of . . . political identity, responsibility, and remembrance is plain to see."[27]

Official attempts by governments to be accountable to the memory of oppressed groups by devising programs of racial restitution are meant to foster reconciliation, as the means through which their societies may settle social dilemmas that have plagued them. And, doubtless, they have in the past believed that they were employing democratic values in the process of considering restitutive acts. Nevertheless, the attempt to use democratic means to devise systems leading to racial peace has fallen short because, as Booth points out, memory justice is a democratic value in both means and ends that should be at the heart of the enterprise. The issue has been one of naïveté, of whether those who have proposed solutions understood the complexity of the problem and had the courage to confront the difficult issues involved. The result of the failure to comprehend memory justice has been not only a notion that one can buy racial peace on the cheap, but that one can close the deal while ignoring difficult problems. (All of this leaves aside another issue, whether attempts to resolve problems facing Blacks have been genuine or a strategy of delay, a political feint to the oppressed groups, meant to reduce pressure from them while the dominant group pursued its own priorities.)

At all ends, racial reconciliation does not come about simply through the initiatives of the dominant group, but as an urgent imperative of the oppressed, driven by their socioeconomic conditions. Such are the politics of "memory justice."

The Justice Problem and American Reparations

Reparations Given

On the basis of their common memory of oppression, African Americans seek justice in the form of reparations. They have been encouraged toward this politics by U.S. government attempts to make restitution for harms done to subordinated groups. Yet many Blacks are perplexed by the disparity in results. It is difficult to understand the motivation of an American leadership that, while denying consideration of reparations for slavery and subsequent racial oppression, has offered compensation to Native Americans, Hawaiians, and Asians and facilitated reparations for Jews. Reparations by the U.S. government were awarded as recently as 1994, when the Colville Indians received a package worth $53 million for the loss of breeding grounds for salmon and other tribal lands when the Grand Coulee Dam was built in the 1930s.[28]

The Jewish Holocaust of World War II has resulted in reparations to Jewish victims by European states, bankers, and firms. For example, in June 2001, 10,000 Jewish recipients in 25 countries who were survivors of Nazi-era slave labor received from German firms checks of about $4,400 each, wired to their bank accounts. This amounted to $23 million for 5,400 survivors living in the United States.[29] In August 2004, a second round of checks totaling $401 million was sent to 130,681 survivors, averaging $2,556 each. And while the total of some $7,500 might appear small to the affluent, one recipient offered, "If you're poor, it's meaningful."[30]

Reparations were also paid to Japanese families whose land and houses were taken and who were incarcerated during World War II, and payments were made to Chinese "comfort women" who were forced to provide sexual services to the Japanese, also during World War II.[31] These well-known examples of payments for crimes of the past have reawakened the sentiments of African Americans, who suffered far longer from the even more insidious and heinous crimes of slavery and from postslavery racism, and continue to suffer today.

These groups I have mentioned suffered at the hands of the state, and a political coalition at a moment in history believed it was worth an attempt to rectify an acknowledged historical wrong. Why, then, does this country believe that it can stop short of that goal with respect to the oppression of African Americans, without fanning the flames of Black memory even higher, thereby elevating the price?

In many cases, the motivation for attempting to resolve these problems by the U.S. government was as simple as righting a wrong done to people who could be identified as victims. The Jewish and Japanese American examples were not intended to elevate their material status, since these groups were already above the norm in measures such as family income. Thus, they constitute a category where the major consideration was to rectify the moral and legal wrongs in which their racial integrity was violated.

To make a further distinction, Jewish reparations were not intended to reconcile Jewish citizens to America, since the crime against them was committed largely by Germans and other Europeans. It was an American problem only in the sense that Jewish Americans expected that their government should assist in the resolution of the international problem, an expectation to which it responded positively.

The case of reparations to Japanese American reparations is different in that their incarceration during World War II occurred in this country and was perpetrated by the American government. Thus, there was a direct issue of restitution, though again, it was not intended either by the Japanese community or by the U.S. government to elevate that community as a whole to economic equality. Rather the sum of twenty-five thousand dollars per family as payment for relocation and internment may be regarded as a symbolic replacement for lost property. Both of these cases, the Jewish and Japanese American, fall into the category of "moral amelioration," since the reparation was intended to correct past damage to the group.

The case of Native Americans is also rooted in moral considerations, but it differs in that it involved ceding land and according them a semblance of sovereign rights, as a people whom the European settlers had defeated in battle and largely exterminated. Nevertheless, the reconciliation sought on the grounds of "fairness" has not been achieved because the treaties in many cases were honored neither by the American government nor the states. This is in part because fairness has always been assessed by those whites who control the political establishment and who represent the vested power of the victors, whose interests have always been protected. Hence there is an ongoing demand for reparations from the Indian community.

Reparations Denied

The preceding examples have brought into the full view the complexity of motives for restitution, political power, and race relations. In light of the compensation made to other groups, one is struck by how far outside the realm of legitimacy reparations to Black people are judged to be by the American government and white public. In fact, that judgment itself may be considered a manifestation of racism: Africans are boldly rejected despite a just claim and despite efforts to deliver reparations to other groups. So, while other writers have researched such issues as the nature of African slavery and what is owed to African Americans and by whom, this book discusses the price that must be paid.

The denial of reparations by the state is a singular illustration of how racism works in America. The definition of racism contains the concept of unequal treatment by authority systems with an impact that is visited negatively upon racial groups of color. When governments provide reparations to one group of people and deny them to another, it means, first, that the group denied is poorer economically. Second, this is not only "unequal" treatment, but also the most pernicious form of inequality in its duplicitous treatment of groups that claim reparations.

Many suspect that the rationale for the denial of reparations to African Americans is based on race and is, therefore, a manifestation of the dynamics of racism. C. Eric Lincoln has suggested that attitudes toward "race" are often governed by "the fantasies of social preemption," which become "institutionalized as values [that] inevitably set the stage for the fear and alienation that fracture the society and torture us all with a pervasive sense of contradiction."[32] Many familiar incidents—so many that they need no listing—are created by the fantasies of the powerful and their ability to affect social preemption, rather than the facts experienced by less powerful racial groups. This confirms the existence of differing perspectives on racial problems that are shaped by the race and class position of the viewer. This distance between viewpoints leads to different judgements about the quality of fairness or justice belonging to an event or practice. For example, if whites now feel that they are discriminated against by civil rights laws originally meant to protect Blacks, their class position enables them to act on that proposition. While Blacks may also feel aggrieved, their relative lack of power prevents them from establishing their perspective as the basis on which to achieve justice. Differing perspectives and the actions that flow from them are the source of much of racial politics in America.

South Africa and Retrenchment of the American Regime of Rights

Comparative public policy is described as "the study of how, why, and to what effect different governments pursue particular courses of action or inaction." Certain issues of political significance are presented to the political system for authoritative resolution in the form of policy, and governments enact certain policies but not others. The choice of policies is in one sense the outcome of a "political class struggle."[33] African-descendant peoples, who as a political class have not fared well in this struggle, face the problem of how to obtain necessary "public goods" through governmental policy that would allow them to become viable social and economic actors, apart from the private resources to which their group has access. This brings into sharp relief the separate and collective activities, attitudes, and policies of governments and their perspective toward African-descendant peoples. Here, the common heritage of western European and American countries is vital to understand, in that it has yielded concepts of restitution based on a common history of involvement in the exploitation of African peoples.

The state as a host of the African-descendant community is the primary reference where race is concerned, understanding that "the state" is a composite that comprises the government in a dynamic interplay with the private economic and social sectors. Almond and Powell have addressed the "rule making function of government" in a comparative context as that produced by government bureaucracies and party structures.[34] This discrete function of government, however, must be challenged within the racial context, to conceptualize the entire state as an organism that gives support to "policy" through the political culture, since the state and its various agencies are often but the superstructure for the manifestation of the racial interests of the majority. Here it will not only be necessary to take the state seriously as a unit of analysis, but also to treat it as transparent in order to unearth the racial-ethnic interests of the majority, and thus, the real face of majority and minority competition.

In my previous work, *Pan Africanism in the African Diaspora*,[35] I found it useful to design a comparative race framework of analysis that consisted of two major variables involving, first, a comparison of governmental institutions that addressed race relations in different countries and, second, a reconstruction of the relationships among Blacks who interacted socially and politically, in order to assess the nature of Pan-Africanism in those relations. I will present in this work a brief sketch of the history of Black Americans and Black South Africans who maintained some level of interaction and especially of Americans who were resident in South Africa at the turn of the twentieth century. Because of the prominence of race in the United States and South Africa, and because the two countries share aspects of their racial histories, I believe that the project of restitution in South Africa yields principles that would be useful to racial reconciliation if a similar project were to arise in the United States.

South Africa is perhaps the best-known example in the global system of a state based on racism. When it sought to resolve its racial conflict as part of a general complex of issues—but perhaps the most vexing of them all—it devised a system of racial forgiveness in connection with restitution to the victims of Apartheid. My inference is that the racial situation of South Africa, though not identical to that of United States, contains lessons for the resolution of the America racial problem.

The first proposition is that the issue in the United States has been posed as one of the continuing impact of something known as "racism" but that a more sophisticated understanding of this term, bringing to bear the meaning of South African Apartheid, exhibits the entire history of Black people in the United States and the dialectic between their oppression and the result of that historic process. Michael Brown has ventured into an analysis of the differences between "racism" and the apartheid system.

> *Apartheid* . . . is far more than can be hinted at by "racism" at least as that term is traditionally used. It is something on the order of a state system that attempts to coordinate economy, polity, and community in order to maintain the systematic racialist division of the national population on which that state system depends. *Apartheid* is, in other words, a statist project

that attempts to subordinate the whole of its natural population and all aspects of "society" of that population to its self-reproduction as a state.[36]

Brown defines apartheid according to its role in the capitalist order, and especially in South Africa's links to other capitalist states in the process of trade. South Africa used race oppression not only as an internal ideology, but as a system to generate profits derived from its ability to export low-cost goods to international markets. The intensity of capitalist demands required the administration of the state on the basis of strict separation of the races and the oppressive control of the Black population. This structure prohibits the development of "society" in the normal sense, since it violates the very principle of society "in order to provide sufficient conditions for pursuing the project of a self-reproducing state, specified on its own denial of that principle."[37]

However, the function of "racism" in the United States is, in one respect, obscured by a comparison with South Africa, because those who perpetrate it are in the majority in the United States, while in South Africa they were in the minority. Given these demographic differences, the treatment of Blacks can take on a more benign appearance in the United States, where the goals of containment and control of the Black population are still evident, but where the consequences are not as drastic because Blacks and their demands upon society are not immediately threatening to the majority. Under this circumstance, the majority can even allow a modicum of social progress, given that it can still maintain dominance and avoid violent conflict. However, when the interests of Blacks are perceived to be threatening, the system responds by closing down further benefits to the Black community, as has been the case in the 1990s and beyond.

Conclusion

Having introduced the comparative context of this work in this chapter, including a preliminary comparison of relationship between Blacks in South Africa and the United States, I proceed with three chapters on South Africa. The United States and South Africa "changed histories" after a period of very similar circumstances because in the twentieth century there arose two different notions of the desired society, as will be seen in chapter 2. A "grand narrative of oppression" forms the crucible for the struggle for justice by Blacks in South Africa, leading to their assumption of power. Chapter 2 assesses their attempt to govern by forming the Truth and Reconciliation Commission as a mechanism of racial redemption. Chapter 3 examines the conceptual issues involved in constructing that mechanism, elaborating a template of theoretical concepts that will be useful in understanding how those who constructed the TRC believed it could be successful. Chapter 4 evaluates the success of the TRC process.

The extensive preparation by the South African government, intellectuals, religious leaders, and others for the Truth and Reconciliation process, and the participation by victims of Apartheid and perpetrators of its crimes, have left an indelible record of concepts, processes, and issues that must be broached by any country attempting to bind up the racial wounds of the past. This record helps us see why the past must be confronted, what victimization consists of, which contexts allow racial reconciliation, and how the dynamics of reconciliation, justice, reparations, and just war play out. It gives us a template of critical parameters by which one may measure the prospect of racial reconciliation elsewhere, and discern its true price.

The application of the South African template to the American racial situation makes it possible to tease out the factors that are necessary to achieving racial reconciliation in the United States. The chapters on South Africa are therefore followed by four chapters on the United States, three of which parallel those on South Africa. The additional chapter is chapter 8, "The Reparations Movement: A Liberatory Narrative," which considers the two principal parties in American's contentious historical racial relationship.

❧

CHAPTER TWO

A Grand Narrative of
South African Racial Oppression

A PROGRAM OF REPARATIONS IN SOUTH AFRICA was enacted in light of the long suffering of African people under a white minority culture, which through its control of the government instituted programs of harsh social control, dehumanization, death, and appropriation of African land—what came to be known as the system of apartheid. Despite the worldwide infamy of the South African regime, knowledge of the practices of apartheid was incomplete even with South Africa. Indeed, the Human Rights Commission of South Africa detected "a great deal of ignorance, puzzlement and now—as a result of the TRC hearings—curiosity within the South African public's mind about the gross violations of human rights that have been perpetrated in this country during the last 50 years."[1] Here I will summarize this history of this oppression, focusing on the period of the most intense application of oppressive methods, after World War II, meted out by the apartheid system and formally condemned by the international community as a crime against humanity.

Evolution of the Apartheid State

The system of control that led to Apartheid began with Dutch settlement at the Cape Coast beginning in 1654. Slavery was instituted almost immediately, as on April 28, 1658, a total of 174 Angolan slaves were offloaded at the Cape, and a few weeks later 84 more were brought in. But the experience of the Dutch farmers was not a good one. The West African slaves ran away and resisted harsh agricultural work, such that, ultimately, they were returned to the slaving company. The source of slaves shifted to Madagascar, Mozambique, and Mauritius.[2] Alfred Moleah gives us a description of their lives:

> The dominating feature of the lives of slaves was work, even more so in the lives of rural slaves. Their hours of work were long and arduous. It was much more than from sun-up to sun-down, especially in the peak seasons of planting and harvesting. Both rural field and domestic slaves were general workers who did whatever task was assigned, at whatever time for whatever duration. They were chattel and as such were the property of their owners to be used a they saw fit. Skilled slaves were in the towns and villages where they worked as smiths and carpenters, or were on a few large estates.[3]

Women were not used in the field, but cared for children and did house chores, while slave children worked the fields in certain seasons. In general, the company contractor, often connected to the East Indian Company, housed slaves in barracks, but minimal provisions and clothing were provided for them where they worked. Female slaves were greatly outnumbered by males, causing extensive competition with both white masters and other male slaves. Many were without female companionship, and marriages were forbidden to slaves until 1823. Slaves were brutalized by the master and the "Knecht," or overseer, an attempt to establish his dominance and to increase the responsiveness of slaves. Violence was visited upon slaves through the sjambock, which split human flesh on contact. Slave codes were promulgated in the early 1700, with a resolution of 1711 allowing whipping and branding on the buttocks for runaways. By 1727, the violence was so extensive that many Africans had scars or were missing limbs, evidence of their encounter with the social rules of the institution. The mortality rate was high.[4]

Many racist attitudes held by the Afrikaners emanated from the culture of slavery, as in other parts of the world where the dehumanization of Africans was intensive, the racial hierarchy was enforced as the legitimate social system, and manual labor became characterized as slave labor. In a system where the racial hierarchy was strictly enforced, work was also racialized. Whites expected to experience the fruits of Black labor, emerging as a privileged class of urban dwellers and farmers.

The influx of English and Dutch settlers in the region quickened with the discovery of gold and diamonds. Diamonds were discovered in the area of the Vaal River in 1867 and Kimberly in 1869; gold was found in the Witwatersrand in 1886.[5] The advent of a mining industry from the 1870s on intensified the pressure on Blacks through the need for a consistent supply of cheap labor. Large companies such as Rhodes Consolidated Gold Fields developed, along with subordinate operations. The large mining houses remained profitable by holding the cost of labor at a minimum and keeping production at a maximum. American miners controlled more than half of the mines for these companies through their superior possession of mining knowledge and technology.[6] This superexploitation of African labor led to both continued poverty and physical debilitation. The Masters and Servants Act of 1873 set forth the role of Africans and the growing group of "Coloured" peoples who lived among the Dutch and especially those who served them on farms and in various business enterprises such as the mines in the context of the rapid growth of capitalism. Coloured people were a distinct group by this time, a product of not only miscegenation between whites and their African slaves, but also the conversion of many of the Khoikhoi peoples, or "Hottentots," who remained in the Cape region, into servants who also intermarried and intermingled with whites and other Africans.[7] Of 12 to 15 million Africans at the turn of the century, estimates by the Native Affairs Commission were that 752,000 African laborers were needed in the four states of the country, but that only 350,000 were at work at one time.[8]

Africans anticipated some relief because of the political competition between the Boers and the English that led to the Anglo-Boer War of 1899. Africans not only sided with the British government, they participated in military operations, believing British promises of liberal treatment. Some faith was justified insofar as the British had followed a colonial policy in their conquests that made allowances for the support of native peoples who were subordinated. In most cases, however, as in southern Africa, Africans were left at the disposition of white settlers whose objectives were more aggressive and treatment of Africans more harsh. However, after the settlement of the war, Africans and many Boers alike found themselves in concentration camps, and nearly 116,000 Africans who had supported the British inhabited sixty-six such camps by May 1902.[9]

Another wave of measures of social control attended the development of the African Union in 1910, when the South Africa Party "dedicated itself to the reconciliation of Boer and Briton and to the creation of one South African white nation."[10] Attendant to the creation of the union was the continued assault on the supply of not only Black labor, but African land as well. In 1912 the president of the South African Chamber of Mines said, "What is wanted is surely a policy that would establish once and for all that outside special reserves, the ownership of land must be in the hands of the white race."[11] This pernicious sentiment resulted in the hated Land Act of 1913, called the "dispossession" by Blacks, the implementation of which gave 87 percent of the land in the country to whites and expelled thousands of Africans from their land, sending them wandering throughout the country. Further laws treated them as "squatters" and made the men subject to conscription to work in the mines.

The conditions in the mines for Africans was deplorable. The Mines and Works Act of 1911 contained specifications defining the more attractive and safe jobs as available only for white laborers, and the more dirty and dangerous as suitable for Blacks.[12] The Native Mine Wages Commission heard testimony in 1942 about conditions in the mines:

> The mine compound rooms were infested, overcrowded, dirty, windy, wet, ill-lit, had no storage facilities and had concrete bunks (sleeping coffins) without mattresses. Washing facilities were inadequate, as were latrines. The bad sewage brings swarms of flies to the compound. Fuel supplies were insufficient. Compound discipline led to victimization.[13]

For example, allegations of sodomy were rife, and other violence and death occurred. Strikes were initiated in this period because, as an example, while the mining company made 1.25 million pounds in 1943, workers were expected to live on relatively little money per week.[14] Appendix table A1 shows that even by 1967, the wages of Africans were still so inadequate that workers' weekly pay was 15 percent short of what it cost to purchase basic necessities.[15] While Africans in this period made 46 percent of the wages of Coloured workers and 39 percent of the wages of Asians, they only received 14 percent of the wages of white workers.

On the other hand, the attraction of South Africa to both indigenous and foreign investors was that low-wage labor yielded enormous returns from investments. As a result, between 1948 and 1975, the South African economy grew at a rate of 3–4 percent per year. Mining profits increased so fast that major firms such as Anglo-American, headed by Harry Oppenheimer, grew to control companies whose shares constituted half of those quoted on the Johannesburg Stock Exchange.[16]

Terrorism and the Nationalists

In 1948, the new National Party came to power with an ultranationalist program. Its ideology was openly represented in the folk culture of Afrikanerdom as a special people chosen to rule over the African, creating, as one author said, "God-created entities" to preserve the purity of their culture.[17] This perspective led them to institutionalize the practice of apartheid, meaning "apartness" in Afrikaans, and whites promptly began limiting further the life conditions of Africans. The purity of the culture had long ago been breached by the sexual union between whites and Africans, the product of which was the substantial "Coloured" population. Nevertheless, in 1949, the Mixed Marriage Act prohibited marriage between or among these groups, but explicitly between white and Africans, and the Immorality Act of 1950 went further by prohibiting sexual relations between them.[18] These laws terrorized certain families that had already culminated interracial unions or households and their children.

Additional punitive laws were passed, such as the Population Registration Act of 1950 that required all Blacks, Asians, and Coloureds to register, freezing their cultural identity at the official level of the state. The Suppression of Communism Act of 1950 outlawed the Communist Party in South Africa, but given the interlocking membership between the party and some members of the African National Congress, it sought to suppress internal dissent much beyond the party. The Abolition of Passes and Documents Act of 1952 voided all past documents and established a new uniform pass for all Africans to carry that would identify them and their residence and employer, qualifying them to work in the urban areas for whites. Not only did this recognize the substantial population of urban Africans, but legitimized their presence in the white areas. The Native Law Amendment of the same year held that Africans could remain in these areas if they had worked for the same employer for ten years or for different employers resident there for fifteen years.

The Apartheid government also tightened the administration of Bantu education as essentially education for labor. Much of this kind of education took place in the so-called tribal languages of the various groups, but some studied English. Only 30 percent of African children seven to seventeen years of age attended school in 1949.[19] Even though there were a few college-educated Africans, South Africa had a racial education system with schools in the rural townships for Blacks and urban institutions for whites. The Apartheid education system limited Black opportunities in the white-controlled economic system. In fact, the job reservation system held Blacks in both industry and government to menial jobs where higher education in English was necessary.

The ambition of the nationalist government, however, was nowhere more visible than in its attempt to create a majority out of their strategic position as a white minority in a sea of Blacks. The first step was the Bantu Authorities Act of 1951, which legitimized the tribal areas of the country as the legal residence of nonurban Africans, Coloureds, and Asians. Thus, for Africans, patches of the 13 percent of the land were drawn up into "Bantustans," that is, homelands.[20] The act gave powers to the tribal chiefs, who, for the white minority regime, were the linchpin of the Bantustan movement, invoking the cultural idea of separate development that was the focus of Apartheid. In fact, tribal chiefs were put on the payroll of the South African government in a move that made them an appendage of the Apartheid system and created for them the enmity of progressive Africans. The ultimate plan was uncovered in 1959 when, as a result of the proposals of the Tomlinson Commission (established to investigate economic development of the homelands), the Bantu Self-Government Act was passed, eliminating representation of Africans in the central parliament of the country and established nine regional parliaments for the ten Bantustans. Africans were represented in the Assembly by three white legislators, four in the Senate, and two in the Cape Provincial Council.

The 1959 legislation brought about another wave of terror by forced removals as thousands of African peoples were herded into the Bantustans, which many of the individuals endorsed out to them had never seen. Yet the government's purpose was to remove the "black spots," and thus these areas were to be their new homes and legal residences. Thousands of Africans found in violation of their passbook residences—often because of lack of employment—were put on trucks, sent to the Bantustan, and dumped out. They were often barren and desolate areas with the worst soil and, therefore, unfit for productive farming. With few resources, these areas remained unproductive and existed essentially as labor reserves for white areas. Africans traveled to them when there was work and returned when there was none, or evaded them and the authorities altogether.[21] One source suggests that between 1960 and 1979, 1.9 million Africans were resettled and nearly 6 million moved altogether as a result of the homelands scheme.[22]

The Freedom Movement Era

These moves by the government were designed not only to fragment the population power of Africans, by promoting separate and smaller identifies, but also to dissipate African nationalism, which required a unity among the various groups. The problem with this strategy was that there already existed an urban Black population that had forged linkages to urban whites, Coloureds, and Asians. The African National Congress began as the South African Native National Congress (SANNC) in Cape Town in 1898, formed by a small group of professional Africans. The creation of an African union in 1910 had been resisted by this group all along, by sending delegations to meet with the colonial officials to plead for an enhanced position for Africans. Failing this, they resolved to match the union created by Afrikaners with their own unity. On Monday, January 8, 1910, a conference was convened by Pixley Ka Isaka Seme, who opened the meeting with these words:

> We have discovered that in the land of our birth, Africans are treated as hewers of wood and drawers of water. The white people of this country have formed what is known as the Union of South Africa—a union in which we have no voice in the making of laws and no part in their administration. We have called you therefore to this Conference so that we can together devise ways and means of forming our national union for the purpose of creating national unity and defending our rights and privileges.[23]

This attempt to forge an African union resulted in the creation of the African National Congress, which became the center of African opposition between 1910 and 1950. The adoption of the Freedom Charter that set forth the future context of a nonracial South Africa was forged at a conference in Kliptown near Johannesburg in April 1955. Nevertheless, this objective was opposed by African nationalists at the conference, who perceived whites as an oppressive settler class and Africans as the original inhabitants of the land who should rule and be the sole possessors of legitimate citizenship. This group broke away from the ANC and in 1959 held an Africanist conference that formed the Pan African Congress.[24]

The ANC and the PAC constituted a threat to the white South African regime that, as early as 1955, began to arrest activists under the new Suppression of Communism Act, since it was clear that the Congress of the People, a conference held in 1955 that fostered the Freedom Charter, marked a new and aggressive mobilization of many groups to test the apartheid system. This meant that the confrontation between the white regime and Black-led activist movement would grow more intense. The pivotal event was the Sharpeville Massacre. In March 1960, both the ANC and the PAC planned protest demonstrations against the Pass Laws Act of 1952, but the PAC event was first, held on April 21, and demonstrators turned out at many sites around the country. Robert Sobukwe and other members of the PAC leadership were arrested at Orlando township.[25] However, at Sharpeville, a township south of Johannesburg near Vereeniging, demonstrators were met by the South African Police Force, which fired on unarmed people; many were hit in the back as they ran away from the onslaught. The human toll was 69 Africans killed and 178 wounded there. The killings set off demonstrations called by Chief Albert Luthuli. In response, South African police commandos and a citizen force were mobilized around the largest townships, detaining 20,000 people. Between March 21 and April 19, 83 civilians and 3 policemen lost their lives and 365 civilians and 59 policemen were wounded.[26]

The international reaction to the massacre at Sharpeville brought sharp condemnation to the South African regime and caused the ANC and the PAC to become more aggressive opposition parties. The ANC, for example, called a conference in 1961 to force the government to negotiate differences with the Black population under threat of renewed demonstrations. The government was not responsive, and Nelson Mandela, head of the ANC, called off the demonstration, planning instead to change strategies and convert the ANC into a revolutionary organization. In fact, the new direction of the ANC was announced in Botswana in 1962, when the armed wing of the organization, Mkhonto we Sizwe, was created.[27] When Mandela came back into South Africa shortly after the announcement, he was arrested and charged with sedition. He was imprisoned in August and sentenced to life in prison. In 1963, nearly the entire leadership of the ANC was arrested at Rivonia and, like Mandela, sentenced to life imprisonment.

The reaction to oppression by Black people in South Africa was one of responsibility, self-determination, and self-amelioration. As early as 1949, Robert Sobukwe, leader of the Pan African Congress, in his inaugural speech noted that the missionaries were fond of counseling moderation in the pace of change, opposing "naughty" African nationalism and highlighting what had been done for Africans, while "forgetting . . . that what they say has been done for the Africans the Africans have achieved for themselves in spite of the South African government."[28] Defining the reason for adopting a revolutionary method of change, Mandela and the leaders of this new ANC movement explained that they had tried civil approaches that required them to work within the system of Apartheid to achieve a dignified civil status. However, the repressive structure and function of the Apartheid state was antithetical to that objective and thus, they had to enter a movement to change the racial and political complexion of the system of governance in order for dignity and freedom to be achieved on behalf of all South Africans.

Umkhonto we Sizwe (Zulu for "Spear of the Nation") began to launch sabotage campaigns inside the country. In 1962, the Pan African Congress and its allies also formed Poqo, or "Standing Lone," to conduct similar operations. That year, the South African government passed the Sabotage Act, which authorized a penalty of death for such actions and a massive campaign of police and military repression that by 1963 had all but eliminated the activities of both Umkhonto and Poqo through mass arrests, imprisonments, killings, and banishments to the Bantustans.[29]

From that point on, both ANC and PAC moved their headquarters outside of the country, forming powerful alliances with progressive groups, countries, and international agencies such as the United Nations that legitimized their struggle globally. This strategy also helped the movement to develop financial resources to sustain the organizations and to finance guerrilla operations mounted inside South Africa against the Apartheid government and its supporters. Guerrilla campaigns often targeted the life and property of white farmers, critical transport, electrical and water resources, police stations, or other facilities considered strategic. The South African government, in turn, expanded its war against the ANC and PAC by launching strikes at their bases in the neighboring territories of Mozambique, Zimbabwe, Tanzania, Angola, and elsewhere. These incursions widened the theater of conflict and further internationalized the opposition to Apartheid state.[30]

Internal Repression

The Boers and British in South Africa were a 15 percent minority of the 30 million people in the 1980s, while Asians and Coloured constituted 10 percent and 2 percent respectively, with Africans comprising the remaining 73 percent. Whites, vastly outnumbered, controlled the rest of the population through a military infrastructure that included the internal security forces and police. The entire white male population had one year of compulsory military training for the citizens' militia, which was capable of rapid mobilization. There were no Blacks or Asians in the military. Through its relationship with the West, the South African government built a formidable defense capability composed of air-to-surface missiles with German support, submarines, highly mobile land craft and tanks, helicopters and Mirage jet fighters from the French, and even nuclear technology from the United States and probably Israel.[31]

Policing

Both military and police budgets increased in the 1960s by more than 100 percent. The police and Bureau of State Security Branch (or BOSS) benefited from their overwhelming firepower, used directly in repression of dissent. The police, in fact, exercised a paramilitary style of action, having a commando unit and street forces. In 1978, there were more than 35,000 police with 19,341 whites, 12,990 Blacks, 1,795 Coloureds, and 785 Asians.[32] Blacks, however, were concentrated in the lower ranks and were not permitted to bear arms. The Security Branch was responsible for investigations using intelligence, counterinsurgency, and other tactics. BOSS was most often the unit that ordered torture to extract information and conducted extensive surveillance on Blacks and their supporters, using a network of paid Black and white informants, electronic means, and surprise intervention into homes and offices to gather information. Through these units, the government could exact the most critical kind of social control over

> [t]he right to hold public meetings or public and private protests; what individuals may say, what they may read, where they can travel, who they can visit, who can attend a university and what can be studied there. The police may enter and search anyone's home at any time of the day or night without a warrant. They may arrest anyone without bringing charges against them. They may keep people in solitary confinement without allowing anyone, even a lawyer, to visit them. They may send people to live in remote parts of the country and may forbid people to either enter or leave an area. The police may forbid teachers to teach and prevent writers and journalists from writing. They may wiretap telephones, open and scrutinize all letters, and in countless other ways keep any given individual under close surveillance.[33]

The Suppression of Communism Act allowed the "banning" of individuals suspected of subversive or threatening acts from the general population. This practice, originating with the Riotous Assemblies Act of 1929, restricted both the movement of individuals to certain locations and their civil association with others.

The "Justice" System

The entire system of "justice" was influenced by the policing function of the state, to the extent that allegations of brutality or improper behavior by the police or Security Branch were honored only in rare circumstances and only when serious security issues were not at stake. And although Africans generally had access to the services of African and sympathetic white or Asian lawyers, judges consistently legitimized the charges of the police authorities. Such was the case in the Rivonia farm trial that delivered Nelson Mandela to prison for twenty-eight years. The police and courts worked tirelessly to criminalize and punish those who challenged the control of the white minority.

The result was that the prison population in South Africa in the 1970s averaged one hundred thousand, one of the highest incarceration rates in the world.[34] In fact, Albie Sachs, a progressive South African lawyer, estimated at the time that one in every three males would be arrested and spend some time in prison. Individuals committed to prison were often treated inhumanely, being forced, for example, to endure cold weather without clothing, or being whipped with a lash. Whipping could be meted out for the simplest infractions, such as traffic offenses or fishing illegally. Between June 1972 and June 1973, South African Department of Justice data indicated that 45,233 whippings had occurred.[35]

Prison

Those sentenced to prison often found that more brutality awaited them than they experienced at arrest and temporary confinement. A judge described conditions in 1944:

> In our prisons you will still hear the clank of leg irons, you will see a caged human being, half-starved, marching up and down a narrow isolation cell, with a hard and cold cement floor and no furniture, with hardly any ventilation, in a fetid atmosphere, with a minimum of light . . . you will still hear cries of pain and distress as the skilled operator, with a cat or the cane, takes a sadistic delight in hacking dead human flesh to shreds.[36]

Apparently conditions had not improved much in the 1970s, as a white former prisoner described Pollsmoor prison, on the outskirts of Cape Town, which housed hundreds of Blacks.

> Men in chains. Men with their buttocks raw and bloody from whippings. Yells and screams—these were commonplace sights and sounds in the isolation section. [I saw enough] of conditions at Pollsmoor to convince me that the possibility of death, the possibility of physical assault, of arbitrary and unjust punishment, is ever-present in the consciousness of black prisoners.[37]

From the 1960s on, the repressive force of the government intensified as both civil unrest and the guerrilla campaign of the ANC and PAC challenged the efficiency of the regime. For example, the sabotage campaign of the guerrillas put significant pressure on the government to know where such acts would be conducted and where their internal support was located in conducting counterinsurgency operations. In 1976, the student uprising in reaction to the forced use of Afrikaans in the schools found the police responding in military fashion. They wore camouflage uniforms, carried automatic rifles and shotguns, and rode in "Hippo" armored land vehicles, which were supplemented by air force supply and reconnaissance aircraft.[38]

Detention and Torture

In the 1970s a movement was initiated by a medical student, Steve Biko, that was devoted to promoting Black self-determination based on Black consciousness. The Black Consciousness Movement was another attempt to resist the repression of the state through its mechanisms of control over the identity, location, employment, and schooling of Blacks. It incorporated such organizations as the Congress of South African Students, the Azanian Peoples Organization, the Congress of South African Trade Unions, the Writers Association of South Africa, the Port Elizabeth Black Civic Association, the Azanian Students Organizations, and the Soweto Committee of Ten. The force of this new consciousness was one of the elements driving the 1976 rebellion by Blacks in a widespread movement that resisted the attempted imposition of Bantu education, which featured the Afrikaans language, upon Black students.

Between 1976 and 1977, the rate of detentions by the South African police rose by 900 percent and by March 25, 1977, 471 people were in detention with one-third having been in that state from six months to one year.[39] The threat posed by the Black Consciousness Movement led the government to track down and murder Steve Biko, its leader. Evidence that he had been brutally tortured while in police custody caused a denial by police authorities that torture was used. Nevertheless, a 1978 report by Amnesty International concluded: "The pattern that emerges, on examining the available evidence, is one of torture being used almost on a routine basis by the Security Police."[40] Between 1963 and 1983, at least forty-five persons died in detention at the hands of the security police. Torture was the main cause of death during detention, although police reports claimed that detainees hanged themselves, jumped from windows, or otherwise injured themselves by "accidental" means in the process of interrogation.⁴¹

Moleah indicates that white South Africans used the mechanism of the state security and police apparatus to execute Blacks, in the first place through summary street executions, many while Blacks were allegedly attempting to escape. Table A2 in the appendix illustrates that, in comparison to whites, Africans and Coloured faced the brunt of death at the hands of the South African police, though four to five times as many Africans were killed as Coloureds. Those wounded followed a similar pattern, although in this case the numbers grew substantially between 1980 and 1981 (see table A3). Table A4 shows that between 1975 and 1984, 1,015 people were hanged by the South African government and that the execution rate jumped 69 percent over those years, reflecting the civil unrest fostered by the challenge of the Soweto uprising. Death sentences were administered along racial lines. According to a report from Amnesty International,

> Death sentences were disproportionately imposed on Africans and Coloureds by an almost entirely white judiciary. Between June 1982 and June 1983, 81 blacks were convicted of murdering whites and 38 were hanged. During the same period, 53 whites were convicted of murdering whites, but only one was hanged. None of the 21 whites convicted of murdering blacks was hanged.⁴²

Blacks who killed whites were disproportionately executed by white South Africans, suggesting that Black life had less value and white life the ultimate value, since no white was executed for killing a Black person.

Repression of the United Democratic Front

In 1983, activists who had withstood the challenge of the white-led regime's repression following the Soweto revolt believed that there should be a locus of struggle inside the country on a persistent basis, with its own program and tactics, but with the possibility of a linkage to external liberation groups. The United Democratic Front (UDF) was born and quickly collected many organizations under its banner to form a substantial coalition, including the surging Black labor movement, which launched a "mass democratic movement" to express the power of

Black workers. The UDF struggled somewhat for two years after its beginnings, with protest spreading to most of the major centers, but yielding few national results because of the difficulty of coordination.

The UDF experienced a resurgence in 1985, adopting the slogan From Protest to Challenge. The executive committee observed the pressures placed on the regime by the growing but unorganized rebellion and understood its responsibility to organize a coherent approach at the national level.[43] This was the idea by which the UDF came to occupy a central position in opposition politics, having learned the lesson from the 1976 Soweto uprising that "mobilization was not sustainable without strong and widespread organization."[44] The idea of "people's power" eventually came to represent a union between the protest activities of various organizations throughout the country and the more disciplined objectives and approach of the liberation movements that were seeking to expand their base inside of the country.

From September 1985 to June 1986 dispossessed South Africans would launch yet another stage of internal resistance to Apartheid, followed by the predictable repression by the white minority regime. A revolt begun in the rural areas in 1984 provided the opportunity for the UDF to consolidate its organization in these areas, together with the ANC. By 1986, the UDF was so successful that it appeared the organization would provide the base for a formidable challenge to the white regime. In response, and leading up to the tenth anniversary of the Soweto uprising, on June 12, 1986, the South African police conducted raids in the townships and suburbs all across the country and detained twelve hundred people, including much of the leadership of the UDF and cadres of the ANC underground. By mid-August, the government had detained more than eighty-five hundred people, a number that grew to between sixteen thousand and twenty thousand by the end of the year.[45] The government declared a state of emergency and cracked down on suspected and known political activists with such force that the effects of living in a police state drew complaints even from white members of the National Party.[46] The crackdown by the government had the unintended consequence of further uniting elements of the UDF and other progressives, such as the Congress of South African Trade Unions, the largest Black trade union coalition, which made more effective the previously planned stay-away strike that year involving 1.5 million workers.[47] The strike affected 70 percent of the manufacturing sector and cost the economy an estimated 500 million rand.[48] By

February 1988, some twenty-five thousand people had been detained by the regime.

As this account of the force of the repression in South Africa approaches the 1990s, one finds that levels of repression from all sources began to diminish in anticipation of the coming change in regime structure, coloration, and philosophy. Nevertheless, the Human Rights Commission of South Africa collected wide-ranging statistics on political deaths in custody, political assassinations, political abductions and disappearances, and politically oriented massacres that provide a perspective on the comprehensive nature of tactics used against the Black population.[49]

Apartheid's Legacy: Corruption of Black Social Life

As we have seen, the white minority regime maintained the Apartheid system by various methods of control in order to achieve either long-term or momentary objectives of domination. This repression and control had both social and political consequences.

The Social Impact of Repression

Even after the fall of the Apartheid regime, South Africa exists as a grand contradiction. It is at once the most developed nation on the African continent, largely due to the tremendous profits created by slave labor, and yet contains one of the poorest populations as well. As an example, the contribution of the manufacturing sector to the gross domestic product was 25 percent in 1997, with trade accounting for another 16 percent.[50] At the same time, 33 percent of the 38 million people in the country were unemployed, with 45 percent of the total population living in abject poverty, 21 million without adequate sanitation, two-thirds without access to electricity, 12 to 14 million without access to portable water.[51]

Race accounts heavily for the disabilities noted in the population. More than 80 percent of the population is Black, Coloured, or Asian, who are predominantly poor, and the reverse is true for the whites employed predominantly in the business sector. Given this stark class structure, one understands the perverse behaviors that emanate from it and what must change if the disadvantaged are to have viable opportunities in their own country.

The Tradition of Political Violence

A vital aspect of the depravity of Apartheid is that it set Black against Black in the process of social control, promoting petty repressive acts by Blacks themselves as an extension of the policing function of the Apartheid system. Legitimate civil violence under Apartheid by Blacks was not permitted unless it was done in support of white objectives. As such, the more than eleven thousand Blacks who served in the police and in BOSS became targets of the liberation forces. But what was "political" to most Blacks was often a "criminal" violation of the established social order to whites, and what was "political" to them was, to Blacks, the assertion of the human right to resist tyranny. Thus, political violence in the context of guerrilla war and internal social struggle became a powerful dynamic in society.

The daily repressive acts of violence by the South African Police Force, such as harassment, jailing, torture, and murder, provided the basic context for more notorious events such as the massacre of unarmed Africans at Sharpeville, the killing of Steve Biko, repressive policing of townships, and the military incursions into neighboring states in a program of political "destabilization" in the 1980s.

Africans inside the country reacted to the political violence of the state by engaging in high rates of civil violence against each other and also used violence against persons seen to be collaborating with the Apartheid system.[52] For example, a common form of political opposition by militant Africans in the townships was "necklacing," in which those suspected to be collaborators were placed in a gasoline-filled tire and set on fire. It was not long before the targets of political opposition included agents of the state itself, including police and urban officials. There were also extreme forms of retributive violence:

> Four men from ages 34 to 63 were hauled in front of a Peoples Court in Soweto at three o'clock in the morning after ignoring a stay-away call which they had been told was optional. They were sentenced to 500 lashing each, stripped naked in front of 10 year-olds, spreadeagle over a drum and flogged. Some people who did not support the stay-away had their ears cut off.

A man in the Orange Free State was forced to swallow a bottle of tablets he had bought from a pharmacy during a consumer boycott. He died of an overdose. . . .

For allegedly breaking a consumer boycott, a mother in the Eastern Cape was stabbed at a bus shelter and her baby flung to the ground.[53]

Although internal and external leaders of the liberation movements formally disapproved such tactics, discipline nevertheless became ruthless, a counter to the tactics used by the state. In May 1985, Oliver Tambo, head of the ANC, in a radio address, directed "[o]ur people in the Bantustans to isolate and destroy the Pretoria puppets." Later that month, he testified before the Foreign Affairs Committee of the British House of Commons, "We are reaching a level of conflict where the innocent are hit. It is unavoidable. Now, there is going to be more bloodshed than ever before."[54]

Although the minority-controlled state was ruthless and efficient in suppressing the growing signs of revolt by the Black African majority, it could not effectively suppress the growing guerrilla activities of Umkhonto we Sizwe or the PAC's African Peoples Liberation Army. In fact, weapons such as AK-47s, used by the guerrilla armies inside the country, became available for use in civil violence. Many of their actions, such as sabotage bombings, attacks upon white farmers in rural areas, attacks upon Black political dissidents in the more conservative townships such as Kwazulu and Natal, while called crimes by the police, were political in nature.

Official government figures indicate that in 1995, South Africa had eight million "squatters" (referred to as the "homeless" in other societies), most of whom were Black and experienced a 48 percent rate of unemployment. This underclass is the source of much of the crime in any modern society. The concentration of Africans in South Africa was created by the Apartheid regime. Especially in the townships, they became the basis upon which the strong and organized preyed upon the weak and tribal groups made war against each other, for spoils such as advantaged position in the drug trade, for employment, or for petty favors linked to the Apartheid system.

When it took the reins of government, the ANC initiated an ambitious plan for the reconstruction and development of the country. The RDP focused on such elements as the building of one million units of housing in a country where there are approximately 8 million squatters, and at least as many others with subhuman shelter. Those areas where housing was to be built and other social services to be provided required peace and social stability. Likewise, those who promised to provide the resources from outside the government needed to be assured that the investment in social infrastructure would not be wasted in a sea of violent social disorganization. Thus, a supreme irony of Black majority rule is that it inherited the social legacy of the Apartheid state as a political problem to be overcome if its attempts to use the newly established government to serve the people are to bear fruit. The ANC is thus challenged to use the instruments of government to satisfy critical social and economic need rather than those of repression.

Conclusion

One reason that a white minority could rule for so long in a country where Blacks represented 75 percent of the population is that it possessed a monopoly of coercive power. While that power was rendered in the form of the military and police, it should be understood that there were important derivatives of that power. The aim of that power was social control, to maintain the people in such a status that they were totally dependent upon the government for their livelihood. Though horrible, the system worked "because South Africa's minority racial rule [did] not, at least in the twentieth century, rest[] primarily on coercion but rather on a highly efficacious structure of utilitarian compliance."

> The form of centralized control introduced by the National Party as part of its apartheid project made the Black population totally dependant on the state for the essential means of biological subsistence and social advance. Jobs, education, health care, housing and the ability to live where these were available, were all doled out by the apartheid apparatus. What was given could, of course, be taken away. To fall afoul of officialdom was to risk one's access to the city, which given the economic destitution of the homelands, could spell disaster for oneself and one's family.[55]

The success of the liberation movement was eventually to break the cycle of dependence of the Black population upon the Apartheid system psychologically, and thus politically and socially challenging the economic control of whites over them. Short stay-away campaigns, longer strikes, withdrawal from the economic system altogether, and participation in mass demonstrations meant that Blacks were willing to risk their menial status and to deny its origin.

The major feature of Apartheid in the twentieth century was that the sentiment of its practitioners hardened into an oppressive political system that was constitutionalized and made the basis of not only civil relations, but also of the entire social, political, and economic system. In fact, the radicalization of the system of Apartheid was the attempt by the white minority leadership to create a separate physical reality on the basis of its political regime in the midst of an overwhelming Black majority. This attempt required the kind of oppressive force, planned at every level from cultural subordination to the development of nuclear weapons, that would result in the deep and profound alienation of the Black population and revulsion among opponents of Apartheid abroad, ultimately stripping legitimacy from the practice and making the country ungovernable.

This summary of the history of the South African struggle up to and including the coming of the "new dispensation" establishes the predicate for South African reparations. And while the historical treatment of Black people in that country clearly indicates that all of the forces that participated in the scenario of domination—major institutions such as the church, the corporations, and the government—are culpable in the project of restoration of the dignity and well-being of the African people, still, it must take into consideration the changes that have occurred since the end of Apartheid. Those who ran the white minority regime have either been absolved by the Truth and Reconciliation Commission or will not be further held responsible for their acts as government officials. In any case, the government is now in the hands of the leaders of the Black majority. This leaves the major private white institutions such as the churches, social organizations, and especially the corporations as legitimate targets from which to demand reparations. In fact, it is possible to suggest that the coming of the "new dispensation" in South Africa will not be complete unless there is a more substantial transfer of economic resources from those who financed and otherwise supported the infrastructure of Apartheid and who, even now, continue to benefit from the establishment of legitimate government, through legal means.

꙾

CHAPTER THREE

The Persistence of Memory

O N A TRIP TO SOUTH AFRICA IN 1998, I accepted an invitation to visit some of the sites of revolutionary struggle that took place during the internal battle against Apartheid. The tour was conducted by the Direct Action Center for Peace and Memory, a serious group of former cadres in the military wing of the African National Congress, Mkhonto we Sizwe (MK). They took a small group of us visiting Americans out to the area where the Coloured and Black townships were located, known as the Cape Flats. There at the townships of Guguletu and Langa, in discussion with the former MK members, we heard of the assassinations by Apartheid police of young Black militants. At Crossroads township, we came to understand the massive protest by people in that area against the racial cleansing policy of the South African regime, which sought to move them farther and farther out, to places such as Kayalitsha and beyond.

Learning firsthand, in the brief interaction with people at these sites, what I had known through secondary accounts, I witnessed a theme that was evident in lives of people at all of the sites we visited: the theme of severe damage, yet the survival of their humanity. These people were living in the aftermath of legal Apartheid, locked in a struggle for survival that challenged their access to everyday elements of life—adequate jobs, living space, food, control of children, and other things. They were still dealing with the legacy of Apartheid. Some were winning that battle, but most were merely marking time, not much better off than before the new dispensation that ushered in Black majority rule. The question for some was whether the struggle had been worth it, and for others how could they acquire some of the things that would materially change their situation. One former MK cadre, Charles Meyer, said that he felt "bitter about how things have worked out for me."[1]

Clearly, the former MK guerillas were experiencing the irony of many who accomplish change after bitter struggle, which is that although they have paid the highest price, they are the last to benefit, precisely because the depth of their sacrifice has robbed them of the opportunity to gain the skills and resources necessary to participate effectively in the reformed society. This was not the fate of the leaders of any of the political parties, many of whom now hold seats in parliament or top corporate posts or are otherwise well off—some even close enough to serious resources to attract allegations of corruption.

A part of the legacy of the militant side of the Black liberation struggle is honored by remembering the uprising of June 16, 1976, when students took to the streets in several days of violent clashes with the Apartheid police and military, triggered by a policy of imposing the hated language of Afrikaans upon their education. By doing so, high school students, many of whom were leaders of the Student Representative Councils, shifted the battle against Apartheid from the guerrilla tactics of the ANC and PAC in the countryside to targets in urban areas and townships.

The reverberation of this event was the second shot heard around the world, the first being the massacre of Blacks in the township of Sharpeville in 1960 by the South African police. In reaction to the student revolt, South African authorities locked up top Black leaders, with the result of stiffening the anti-Apartheid movement in many Western industrial countries. One year later, Steve Biko, leader of the Black Consciousness Movement, was assassinated in a desperate attempt by the leaders of Apartheid to stamp out the most militant leadership of Black organizations in South Africa.

These were important events to be remembered as South Africans attempted to move "away from the discredited governing memory of the past" and build what Kader Asmal has called a "shared memory." This is a difficult accomplishment, however, because history is also the stuff of the identity of a people, as James and others note: "Collective memory constitutes the informal, widely accepted perceptions about past events in which the collective identity of a people is mirrored."[2]

By eventually ending settler colonialism through violence, Black South Africans entered a new period in which their collective identity status shifted from the politically dominated to the politically dominant—which established in the new government a responsibility to build a nonracial nationalism by redeeming the past oppressive state.

The Truth and Reconciliation Commission (TRC) was decided upon as that vehicle. In effect, the South African national question was achieving majority rule as a key goal in the elimination of Apartheid.

Preparing for the Truth and Reconciliation Process

When the South African Truth and Reconciliation process was initiated, it was one of the most scrutinized in the international community because of its novelty, audaciousness, and promise for helping to make possible the ambitious goals of the new government in fashioning a nonracial democracy. The process of dismantling Apartheid had been a global drama, in which many individuals and their countries participated, both officially and nonofficially. Now the focus on Apartheid continued in the bold attempt to rationalize the human pain it had caused. The instrument of healing was to be the Truth and Reconciliation Commission, headed by Bishop Desmond Tutu and launched in 1996, an effort that compares favorably with official attempts in other countries to strike an accommodation between the state and groups previously in serious conflict with one another.

What is important for this work is that the construction of the TRC was thoughtful, preceded by symposia that revealed the dynamics of the project of reconciliation between factions that had been engaged in an internal struggle for power and one of which had severely oppressed another. In this chapter, I will briefly describe the steps taken to initiate the TRC and review some of the major dilemmas pointed out in a series of debates at the Institute for Democracy in South Africa conference in 1995 and the TRC in 1997. In doing so, my assumption is that the responses to these dilemmas may be applicable to the search for reparations in America for Blacks.

Truth and Reconciliation Mandate

In 1990, negotiations began between the African National Congress and the National Party on the practical issue of the fate of ANC political prisoners. While South African law provided for a process of indemnity and release, there was no law covering individuals who were not in the penal system. On May 25, 1992, upon his installation as professor of human rights law at the University of the Western Cape, Dr. Kader Asmal proposed the development of a process of reconciliation in his inaugural lecture presented on that occasion. His view was that the future of the country would be dim indeed unless it reached a "conscious understanding of the past," as the product of a process of deliberate remembrance.[3] In a later volume Asmal and his coauthors summed up the reasons for proposing a process of reconciliation.

achieve a measure of justice for the victims of our horrific past by acknowledging the atrocities that they suffered;

provide a basis for collective acknowledgment of the illegitimacy of Apartheid;

facilitate the building of a culture of public ethics for the first time in South Africa and . . . make room for genuine reconciliation;

provide a basis for the necessary decriminalization of the anti-Apartheid resistance;

ensure a sound basis for corrective action in dismantling the Apartheid legacy;

lay bare the tools of the violence that still plagues parts of the country;

illuminate the longstanding humane values of the anti-Apartheid resistance, for so long distorted by Apartheid propaganda;

demonstrate the morality of the armed struggle against Apartheid;

place property rights on a secure and legitimate footing for the first time in our nation's history;

enable privileged South Africans to face up to collective understanding and, therefore, responsibility for a past in which only they had voting rights;

offer an acknowledgment of the wrongs done to the countries of southern Africa in the name of our country;

clarify the important international implications of Apartheid in the past and present; as well as acknowledging the correctness of international mobilization against Apartheid itself.[4]

These ideas were taken up by the National Executive Committee of the African National Congress as a response to challenges that it had also participated in the gross violation of human rights by its revolutionary activity. In November 1994, the new government introduced the Promotion of National Unity and Reconciliation bill in parliament. Having been passed by parliament, it was signed into law by President Nelson Mandela on July 19, 1995, and went into affect on December 1 of that same year.

The TRC was given a mandate that consisted of four major tasks:

1. Analyze and describe the "causes, nature and extent" of gross violations of human rights that occurred between March 1, 1960 and May 10, 1994, including the identification of the individuals and organizations responsible.
2. Make recommendations to the president on measures to prevent future violations of human rights
3. Restore the human and civil dignity of victims of gross human rights violations through testimony and recommendations to the president concerning reparations for victims
4. Grant amnesty to persons who made full disclosure of relevant facts relating to acts associated with a political objective

Theoretically, this mandate was straightforward: the period in question began with the Sharpeville Massacre and ended with the adoption of the framework for the majority rule government. The clear emphasis was on political acts for which people suffered, as opposed to civil criminal acts, even if they were racial in nature. As it operated, the commission was to consider applications for amnesty based on hearings and finding of facts by investigators that the individual involved was making full disclosure. The commission was to place equal weight on the harm or loss of the victim, and recommend means by which victims could be made whole through a program of reparations. This process would provide to the victims knowledge of the whereabouts of their relatives and friends, including the remains of the dead, and grant them some relief, as well as amnesty to the perpetrator in exchange for the truth. The process, it was believed, would foster healing and, thus, reconciliation.

Vetting the Concepts

The IDSA Conference

In February 1994, before the ANC government came to power, the Institute for Democracy in South Africa (IDASA) held a conference on the proposal to establish a Truth and Reconciliation Commission. In a keynote speech Aryeh Neier, executive director of Human Rights Watch in New York City, presented a rationale for the commission's work:

> There are two crucial reasons for confronting the past. Firstly, as a civilized society we must recognize the worth and dignity of those victimized by abuses of the past. If we fail to confront what happened to them, in a sense we argue that those people do not matter, that only the future is of importance. We also perpetuate, even compound, their victimization.
>
> The second reason has to do with establishing and upholding the rule of law. It is important to send a message to the effect that everyone is subject to the law. The rank and office of those who victimized others must not be allowed to immunize or insulate them from society's efforts to confront the past.[5]

In his first reason, Neier indicates that a society is a "civilized" entity to the extent that it upholds the dignity of the individual. Failing to remember and to correct past injustices done against a person is a sign that his or her dignity, and therefore his or her personhood, which is a reflection of that dignity, does not matter. Neier's position is that if the personhood of an individual or group of individuals can be ignored, this in itself constitutes another source of—and an extension of—the oppression of the group. The logic of this suggests that such an attitude toward a group is powerful evidence of the existence of a class attitude that would contribute, not only to this specific oppression, but to all of those oppressions a society may tolerate or toward the given group.

I take Neier's second point to be more conditional, because it suggests that to call for the accountability of those who have perpetrated a crime is to support the rule of law. But the Apartheid state erected its own laws, a race-oriented pantheon of legalities that elevated the white minority and maintained the racial hierarchy, which was the dominant feature of the Herrenvolk democracy. So a corrective regime of accountability for past crimes against a people would have to rely on the authority of a progressive regime of law, such as that enshrined in the Universal Declaration of Human Rights or established by a progressive government.

This is an important point to make because it highlights the nature of the regime in which atrocities occur; South Africa, as an example, found that a Truth and Reconciliation process was not possible until there was a political transition out of white minority rule. However, mere transition to Black majority rule government was not sufficient; rather, the fact that the transition was pursued as a "just" one required consideration of other areas in which justice must be established, if white oppression was not to be exchanged for Black oppression.

Jose Zalaquett, a professor of law in Chile who served on its Truth and Reconciliation Commission, extended Neier's notion of the just state by adding a moral dimension: the state must be seen to possess a moral center as the basis of justice, not a civil idea alone. In making restitution to victims of crimes against their humanity, the state was effecting a moral restoration that allowed citizens to perceive the order under which they lived as just.[6] This, however, brought into full view the nature of reparations and their role in achieving the moral consensus, which was at the basis of justice. Of course, moral restoration would be a negotiated solution, not like the Nuremberg trials or any other war that resulted in a winner's justice. Negotiated solutions are always imperfect, from the point of view of the negotiating parties, in that each side has to give up its ideal vision of what is fair.

Nevertheless, the idea of rightness in a broad moral sense—the idea that there should be some form of recompense that precedes what is fair, and is beyond the particularities of negotiation—emerges from an admission that a terrible wrong must somehow be corrected. If a state does not achieve that idea of morality, that justice for a victimized people, Neier suggests, the obvious conclusion is that they are not viewed as worthy of justice.

Concepts of Reconciliation

There were, as might be imagined, a great number of questions about each of the major assumptions and concepts that governed the construction of the TRC. So in 1997 the commission, once empaneled, conducted a series of six seminars with invited experts, most from South Africa, to consider some of the major questions involved, in effect continuing the IDASA discussions. And while the IDASA discussions were more theoretically relevant, the commission considered specific problematics related to the process of Apartheid, which we will consider in what follows.

The context. At the January 24 symposium, Pamela Reynolds, chair of the Anthropology Department of the University of Cape Town, noted an important point of departure, which was the nature of the social order within which reconciliation is attempted. She suggested that "reconciliation works within the context of a social order, an order that must be realigned with the demands of everyday continuity."[7] She inferred that the primary task was to institute a new concept of morality—one different from that of the Apartheid period—that would govern the process as the new controlling "everyday continuity." Acknowledgment of the loss and pain from Apartheid, she believed, was not yet accomplished. In fact, there was a moral cloud, the removal of which would require an admission of what was right and wrong, good and evil in what Apartheid had wrought. By inference, Reynolds's view was that the TRC process was about the transition from the Apartheid state to a more moral status, and that getting there required an assessment and admission of the costs.

In the March 12 seminar, Heidi Grunebaum-Ralph posed a substantial challenge to the process, wondering whether the TRC would be able to deal with the real victimization produced by "a trauma that has an overarching historical, political, and economic context; a paradigm of racialized power which is not neutralized nor contained by the sanitizing vocabulary of reconciliation."[8] She questioned whether a "historical relativism" was not being created in the memory and forgetting of who was wronged, was victimized, who suffered and why. Therefore, she appeared to suggest that in the reduction of this historical and social process to, in effect, a bureaucratic negotiation, the TRC might be unable to deal sufficiently with the trauma, but rather to facilitate a "traumatic repression of the past in its displacement of the relationship between the victimized and beneficiaries."

Grunebaum-Ralph's view implied that the TRC was not constructed to deal with the historical accumulation of the wrongs of Apartheid: if it were, then its mandate would have extended back in time to the promulgation of the Master and Servants Act of the colonial period.[9] Rather, the TRC had a narrow mandate that Mahmood Mamdani has referred to as "political reconciliation," which was to be achieved through negotiation and political compromise.[10] This direction influenced the way in which the white community entered the context of the majority rule state and, thus, determined the limits of whites' acceptance of the process of reconciliation. In other words, the fact that the white minority regime was forced to accept change by the internal force of the UDF, by the combined external force of revolutionary groups, and by the international community, meant that the white community that had supported Apartheid did not come to the table of reconciliation out of belief in racial justice but out of the political necessity of its own survival.

In fact, Mamdani suggested that most of the beneficiaries of the Apartheid state were not aware that they were "beneficiaries" in the terms used by the TRC, since they believed Apartheid was a legitimate basis upon which to order society. In this context their notion of benefit was limited to aberrant illegal benefits from crime or corruption, rather than from their status alone. Furthermore, recognition that their status itself defined the racial stratification of the state, and defined the material distribution as well, was being forced upon them because the Black majority who were themselves the victims of Apartheid now controlled of the legitimate processes of government.

Mamdani, noting Grunebaum-Ralph's idea of "historical relativism," conceived that at least two truths might be emerging: one like Martin Luther King, Jr.'s truth, which came from a creative tension between good and evil forces that illuminates reality, and another truth "that obscures, hides, veils, masks the unpleasant face of reality."[11] This leaves open the question of which truth would ultimately emerge from the TRC process—and whether they are even distinguishable.

On the basis of the interventions by Mamdani and Grunebaum-Ralph, Heribert Adams suggested that the TRC might be a vehicle for the creation of a "false consciousness" about the harm of Apartheid, "camouflaging racial privilege by leaving white property relations and racial privilege intact." Although this formulation was rejected by Mamdani, one of its implications was that achieving justice would require increasing the cost of reconciliation for whites, either by raising the level of reparation for Blacks or by levying a greater penalty on perpetrators. It appears that the TRC formula placed a much lighter burden on the perpetrator—deliberately so, as an incentive to yield vital information—than full reparation to victims would require. This left unresolved whether Adams's observation would be taken into consideration in the TRC process or not.

The grand narrative of oppression. As Demitrina Petrova suggested in the IDASA dialogue, a "grand narrative" of oppression, though obscured, is not lost since elements of it may be reconstructed from the memories of the victims.[12] I would wager that a memory of a "grand narrative" of oppression is the foremost impetus to civil unrest in the world. The fact that people believe that an injustice has been committed against them corrupts their view of the morality of their state, constricts their participation in it, and fuels their struggle against those elements of oppression that, if not resolved, result in a challenge to the state itself. This is one reason why many observers of the TRC process, as represented by Mamdani, had so little faith in the results.

> The assumption is that truth leads to reconciliation. But this is demonstrably nonsense. The divorce courts prove this every day. Biko's widow made it crystal clear in front of the TRC. There stood the murderers of her husband, shameless in their lack of remorse, trying to obtain amnesty on technical grounds. Why should we forgive them, even if they are telling the truth?"[13]

Without regard to the complexity of the Biko case, in general it was the fact that the pain and the truth of Mamdani's reservations would be exposed publicly that led to the South African narrative of reconciliation eventually being perceived as a somewhat inadequate instrument for healing. The American racial narrative, by comparison, causes persistent tension and is viewed as a source of division, in part because of the lack of accountability to the truth of Black historical oppression in the form of an effective instrument being developed for racial reconciliation.

At the IDASA conference, victimization was generally discussed as the most critical result of the grand narrative of oppression, a status that results when a crime is committed against a person or group. The individual persons or groups become "victims" as a result of the actions of an oppressor. However, this issue is seldom discussed from the perspective of the victim. This status may be conceived as the outcome of a process wherein the perpetrator of the crime of oppression commits an act that makes a victim out of a group or individual who are then consigned to live within that status, suffering myriad slights to one's humanity in every feature of life, as the price one has to pay for that status. Commonly referred to in Black America as the "race tax," it is recognized by the victim as the experience of various kinds of subordination that are visited upon a person or group because of race.

The corrective to victimization must take into consideration not only the crime as defined by law or politics, but also the perspective of the victim, in terms of the nature of the offense against his or her humanity, which is elaborated in the way that the victim has to sacrifice parts of his or her humanity in order to survive within the social order. This is why Aryeh Neier considers concern for the victim and concern for the rule of law as two sides of the same coin.[14] However, the aspects of humanity that are sacrificed are most intimately known by the victim and constitute the discrete parts of the collective demand for redress.

Justice. Mamdani implied that justice was more important than truth, since truth does not always lead to understanding and often leads away from reconciliation. This important observation meant that the formal process of reconciliation had to deliver "justice" in its treatment of both those who provided the truth and the victims about whom the truth was presented.

Following this line of reasoning, some observers believed that achieving justice in this way was complicated because the beneficiaries of the crime of Apartheid, who originally perpetrated the human rights violations, skewed the process of achieving justice because of the status they had already achieved in society—largely as a result of their crimes. This meant that they could receive amnesty for their crime, then take advantage of the "golden handshake" of social status and other benefits, which they received as a result of the negotiations to turn over power to the Black majority, while the victims had to go through the lengthy, uncertain process of achieving recompense. Who were the winners and losers in this process? Roy Brooks asks, "Does South Africa's style of total amnesty [and the qualifying conditions specified] the most important being that the human rights violation in question must have been guided by broader political objectives—ensure justice?"[15]

In fact, the lack of clarity on this issue is exceedingly risky to the success of the TRC process since it places the benefits of the process on the side of the perpetrators, not only forgiving them for their crimes, but also allowing them to maintain their exalted status in society. Then there is the additional protection that the TRC must provide: "The commission will have to be put in a position where it can facilitate striking a balance between the revelation of the truth and the shielding of the perpetrators of abuse from the vengeance which in a moral sense they actually deserve."[16]

Just war. At the May 5 IDASA seminar, one respondent noted that it was important to disassemble the perpetrator's rationale for many violations of human rights by understanding the "total war" concept and how it was used to destabilize the whole of southern Africa. This point exposed another complication, which was that the victims of Apartheid were not only South Africans, but Namibians, Angolans, Mozambicans, Zimbabweans, and so on. In addition, in a wider appreciation of the activities of the Apartheid state, one recalls that the effectiveness of its security apparatus required the collaboration of some Blacks. Were they not also victims and should not they also be forgiven?

In the May 6 seminar, there was a sharp clash between former general Constand Viljoen, who had been chief of the South African Defence Force, and other speakers.[17] He held, in essence, that the ANC and PAC groups could have obtained their objectives through peaceful means, since other groups inside South Africa had done so by promoting peaceful change through the church or civil action within the context of the existing laws of the state. Furthermore, he held that revolutionary struggle was seen as illegitimate as a means of change in the international system by most states and that terrorism targeted at civilians was absolutely outlawed. On this basis, he attempted to make the case that justice for the whites lay in the fact that they had a *legitimate* right to defend against the *illegitimate* concept of a "just war" pursued by the Blacks.

This discourse revealed the degree of difference of opinion about what had occurred, and Viljoen's justification signaled defensiveness and a lack of consensus about what constituted justice. Deputy Minister Ronnie Kasril disputed Viljoen on the grounds that the moral basis of this struggle—even between two armed Black and white combatants—was the imbalance of power and thus, in the ability of each side to possess and evoke a proportionality of violence. He suggested that unless there was a consensus about why the ANC and PAC went to war, reconciliation would be impossible.

This point repeats the question raised earlier, whether or not the

same version of the truth about the basis for individual actions is necessary before there can be reconciliation. In this process, not truth but justice is the cause of reconciliation. As Mamdani argued, justice is a product of both the truth and the manner in which the victims, revealed by
the truth *as* victims, are restored to their dignity. This indirect relationship of the truth to reconciliation is important, but it also suggests that
the process of amnesty does not require an exact consensus on the
nature of the truth, only that one person be willing to present the facts
at his or her disposal and the rationale for his or her actions.

If there are different perceptions of actions, does this override the
process? Yes, broadly, because, as indicated previously, the difference
between a political motive and a criminal motive is important to establish as a basis for actions that caused harm. In some cases where perpetrators alleged a political motivation such as terrorism or membership in
a banned party, and investigation found other motives for their actions,
no amnesty was awarded. But within the broad framework of political
motivations, there is apparently room for difference. Therefore, to base
reconciliation on the achievement of an exact similarity in perceptions
may appear too ambitious; given the context of the South African
attempt at reconciliation, perhaps a more tactical approach would yield
realistic results.

In the end, it was left to Andre du Toit to suggest that defensive
actions of an oppressed people favor the conclusion that the ANC was
on the moral side of the equation. Even within a "just war" framework,
where the killing of civilians is considered illegitimate, there could
never be equivalence between the two parties because of the massive
activity of the national security apparatus of the Apartheid state, which
was directed against both the revolutionary forces and people presumed
to be allied with them.

Reparation.   By implication, the grant of amnesty to the perpetrator is the outcome of the victim's being granted some form of restitution or reparation. This concept was presented with profound simplic-
ity in the March 12 IDASA seminar by Reverend Mpambani, using a
commonsense parable: John stole Peter's bicycle. Later John came to
Peter and wanted to reconcile, whereupon Peter asked where was the
bicycle. John said that the bicycle was irrelevant to his desire to reconcile. But Peter said that the bicycle was an important issue, since its loss
presented him with other difficulties and soiled his view of John as a

moral person. So when the bicycle was returned, or some other form of recompense made, then Peter would consider reconciliation.[18]

Here, it is important to note that the concept of making a victim whole is embedded in Western jurisprudence, but it is also not without status in tribal law, a fact that may ground Mpambani's example. For Alex Guma, a professor at the University of the Western Cape and a specialist in African culture, said that in the Ngoni language, the word *ukihlewa* means the rehabilitation of human life that is transformed and reintegrated into society after having done something wrong. The term *ukuhlamba* is related to cleansing of both individual and community defilement. The latter is often accomplished through the pouring of a libation and the expression of terms of acknowledgment and promises of corrective behavior.

Both of the above examples address a process for achieving reconciliation through reparations as societal issues and processes. The TRC process, however, was narrowly tailored to achieve specific outcomes for specific violations of human rights. The accumulation of these individual cases, however, could not have made a significant contribution to the amelioration of the impact of Apartheid upon most of the Black population. Most of the Black population was affected for much longer than the TRC time frame by the Apartheid practices that began in the nineteenth century and were codified beginning with the Land Act of 1913. Then a plethora of other laws were passed and implemented when the Nationalists took power in 1948. Those affected—87 percent of whose land was taken away, who were placed on "native reserves" or in "townships," who were brutalized and killed, who were not given the budgets to make their social development viable, who were worked in the mines for substandard wages—constitute virtually the whole of the Black population. There is the question of how or whether they will receive restitution outside of the TRC framework.

One questioner in the March 1997 seminar asked the new minister of finance, Terry Crawford Brown, whether the Reconstruction and Development Program (RDP) was "hamstrung by the debt that the new government inherited from the past, since much of it related to packages negotiated as a part of the transition. The interests payments on these pensions was R39 billion ($5.2 billion in 6/2000 dollars) in 1997 and R44 billion ($6.1 billion in 2/2000 dollars) in 1998."[19] By comparison, the questioner noted, since the Housing budget was only 4 billion rand, this was a massive redistribution of wealth from the poor to the rich. Heribert Adam agreed and also noted that 97 percent of that 320 billion rand debt was domestic, since South Africa did not have access to external sources of credit. The magnitude of this debt would appear to place a substantial responsibility for reparations upon international private parties, especially businesses in South Africa and other international sources of economic assistance.

Although there was no strong consensus on the exact nature of reparations, some, such as Wilmot James, rejected the "check in the mail" model, believing that reparations must be symbolic and collective, both honoring the largest number of victims of Apartheid and reserving the most contentious challenges to the resources of whites who continued to control the economy.[20] Albie Sachs agreed:

> [W]e must find ways of truly honouring those who fought for democracy and suffered as a result. A commission can expose all crimes on all sides but it can do much more than that. It can find appropriate means of acknowledging and honouring those who suffered—families, survivors, neighbours and whole communities. Some of it has to be very personal and individual, not statistics.[21]

Reconciliation.   The formula for the reconciliation process mounted by the TRC was that the exchange of truth for amnesty and the redemption of the victims would amount to justice. This justice process would result in reconciliation. This outcome would occur not immediately, but through the aggregation of the careful treatment of the cases, promoting a healing effect upon South African society as a whole. Reconciliation assumed forgiveness and remorse on a basis of mutual acceptance of the truth. This view equated the value of remorse and truth with the value of forgiveness and reconciliation. However, if truth was at the heart of the enterprise, then there had to be a consensus on what constituted the truth. This thought, similar to that of Reynolds, meant that whites had to acknowledge their action or inaction within the context of Apartheid state structures and practices and to conclude that they were wrong because they brought harm to fellow human beings who were Black.

One commentator added that it must be clear who needs to reconcile with whom. That is to say, inasmuch as Apartheid created a line within society, on each side of it was the oppressed and the oppressor, the stark reality of which necessitated the understanding that, anywhere in the world, oppression is wrong and that the moral balance was heavily weighted on the side of the line where the oppressed were found. An understanding of this fact, however, did not absolve the oppressed of responsibility to forgive the oppressor under certain conditions, in this case, under the condition that the oppressor made public his or her role in the perpetration of the wrong.

Conclusion: The Template

Based on this discussion, the template that will guide our examination of this subject is a loosely constructed set of concepts that begins with a description of the injury that has occurred to African descendants, which we will refer to here as the *grand narrative of oppression,* that treats the context within which the state authorizes actions against an African community, that examines the nature of the behavior that produces victims, that seeks to understand the consequences of victimhood for citizenship, that challenges the state to engage in restitution for the purpose of restoring oppressed groups to full citizenship and social viability, and that proposes reparations as one of the most powerful acts of the state to accomplish this aim.

◆

CHAPTER FOUR

Truth, Reconciliation, and Reparations

THE LEGAL BASIS FOR THE CONSIDERATION OF REPARATIONS, as seen in the previous chapter, was vested in item 3 of the mndate of the Truth and Reconciliation Commission. However, it was further entrenched in domestic law when Section 20(7) of the Promotion of National Unity and Reconciliation Act was challenged by AZAPO (Azanian People's Organization) and others who believed that to absolve a person who had been granted amnesty from further criminal liability was unconstitutional. The high court found that indeed Section 20(7) was constitutional, and the decision was rendered in part with the following thought:

> Reparation is usually payable by states, and there is no reason to doubt that . . . our own state [will be] shouldering the national responsibility for those. It therefore does not contemplate that the state will go Scot-free. On the contrary, I believe an actual commitment on the point is implicit in its terms, a commitment in principle to the assumption by the state of the burden.[1]

Thus, the state is committed through the TRC process to developing a program of reparation as a step in the procedure of achieving justice for victims who have become a part of its process. The various aspects of reparations as defined by the commission policy include the following:

1. *Urgent Interim Reparation.* This is a limited financial grant to enable people to access various relevant social services to provide quick relief.

2. *Individual Reparation Grants.* These are individual financial grants awarded to each victim of human rights violations, according to various criteria, paid over six years.

3. *Symbolic reparation/legal and administrative measures.* These are measures to facilitate the common process of remembering of the pain and victories of the past, by the erection of monuments, memorials, museums and a national day of remembrance and reconciliation.

4. *Community rehabilitation programs.* Since some communities were victimized in the Apartheid era, the TRC Reparation Division has prepared proposals for the relevant government ministry consideration to provide programs to promote healing and the recovery of individuals in those communities.

5. *Institutional reform.* These measures are devoted to rehabilitating institutions of government to prevent them from administering laws, regulations, or practices that violate human rights.

In the administration of these five functions, the Committee on Reparation and Rehabilitation was tasked to

1. establish the harm suffered;
2. determine the needs and expectations of the victims;
3. establish criteria to identify victims in urgent need;
4. develop proposals regarding long-term reparation and rehabilitation.[2]

As can be seen, this agenda involves both the development of policy in establishing various relevant criteria, as well as case processing, evaluating information, database management, investigation, and other complex and relevant tasks. Thus, the committee focused on both financial rewards and what it termed a "service package," in making the determination of who should receive what benefit. The expectation of the TRC was that the financial incentive would be the most frequent form of benefit, followed by investigations, compensation of other forms, shelter, medical care, provision of grave markers, justice prosecution, and perpetrator apology. Thus, the amount of the financial award was set at between R2,000 and R6,000 for Urgent Interim Reparations. The individual Reparation Grant was pegged to the median national income of R21,700 and a formula used to include other factors such as the cost of living in the urban and rural areas and the like. Altogether, the cost of paying reparations for the estimated twenty-two thousand victims who were certified by the commission amounted to R477,400,000 per year, or R2,864,400,000 ($400 million) over six years.

The Reparation and Rehabilitation
Committee Struggle

The TRC tendered its five-volume final report in October 1998 and from that time to June 2000, its staff was reduced from five hundred to one hundred, the remaining staff being focused on the issuance of reparations as a result of the prior deliberations and findings of victimization and the necessity for forms of recompense. Its mandate was to be completed within the time frame of the completion of the TRC itself in July 2000. By August 1999, there was little movement on the issue of long-term reparations; however, more than 4,500 victims had been given Urgent Interim Reparations averaging R3,500 each, but most of the others were held in abeyance for lack of action by the parliament. The minister of justice, Penuell Maduna, said that parliament would have to decide on long-term reparations, as it was a national issue. Parliament must finalize them and provide clear guidelines, whether through legislation or regulations.[3] The commission was also concerned with what body would be charged to continue its work because of the lack of completion of many issues and cases during its tenure.

One thread that potentially was responsible for the delay in government consideration of long-term reparations was voiced by Hlengiwe Mkhize, head of the Committee on Reparation and Rehabilitation, who believed that the government had adopted a "development-centered approach toward victims."[4] This was based on the fact that an interministerial committee had been created to address victims requiring access to services. A deeper question, however, was raised by her perspective, since it may also have meant that the entire issue of reparations, which placed a significant demand upon the national budget, was being considered by high government officials within the context of its normal programs for the distribution of services to the entire population. Nevertheless, Mkhize continued to bring pressure to bear upon government officials, as she indicated a month later that "the reparation process should be implemented as a counter-balance to the amnesty process" and in not doing this, the TRC process seemed to have benefited the perpetrators of human rights violations, who were granted amnesty over the victims.[5] She also called upon government to ensure that businesses, which benefited from apartheid, would contribute to the reparation process.

The Justice Ministry again said that it was were working on recommendations for the issuance of long-term reparations, which would be assessed by the interministerial committee, and eventually brought to the parliament for debate and final decision. However, other sources in the ministry, as reported by the *Sowetan,* said that the government was also concerned about the financial implications of the proposals, as the estimated costs were already estimated to be R3 billion.[6] The government was especially cautious inasmuch as funding from the international community, much of which had been promised by individual countries during the period of the first majority-rule elections, had dried up.

By October 1999, Mkhize believed that the most urgent need was for a structure to be established in the president's office to administer the expenditure of the funds allocated for long-term reparations.[7] The growing disarray in the process became clearer somewhat later, as the interministerial committee that had been set up to process the needs for services by victims failed to function, as it was reported by Mkhize that many victims who had been referred for surgery on old wounds were being turned away from hospitals, others who had initially been referred were rejected by universities, and others were being passed from one government agency to another, unable to get referrals for assistance at all. Mkhize said that one source of the confusion was that some government officials did not understand the process and "they fight with the victims . . . victims are being re-victimized all over again."[8] To make matters worse, the TRC offices had closed its process of taking applications for hearing cases and yet, individuals were still attempting to access the TRC regional offices amid growing frustration, disillusionment, and desperation that often led to anger. In addition, many who had received the Urgent Interim Grants believed that, in light of their suffering, the amount offered had not been worth their expenditure of effort.

Mkhize intimated that the process had come to a halt prematurely inasmuch as those who had been suspected of being informers were still being targeted for violence and that the ongoing persecution of these individuals was a hindrance to reconciliation within the Black community. Nevertheless, given the fact that the process appeared to have come to halt and had engendered such turmoil, she concluded, "[A]s a country, we haven't started grappling with the question of healing."[9] As a result, there arose the common criticism that the commission had been strong on truth and had little or no contribution to reconciliation. This sentiment had even been voiced in Archbishop Desmond Tutu's own book, when he noted the imbalance in the slow pace of attention given the victims of Apartheid while those who received amnesty have received their rewards.[10] Moreover, Mkhize, who believed that the government wanted to provide for long-term reparations but did not know how to proceed, believed that part of the problem was that it wanted to integrate this issue into the "big picture."[11]

However, the alienation caused by the failure to deal with the immediacy of this issue by those who have suffered serious harm under Apartheid may complicate the ability of the government to deal, in fact, with the big picture. This would include the families of individuals, such as former ANC and PAC cadres, buried in other countries who now wanted to reinter their bodies in South Africa. In fact, the budget for 2000 of the Finance Minister Trevor Manuel was criticized by the head of the commission, Bishop Desmond Tutu, as having "failed the victims."[12] Neither did the issue of reparations appear in President Thabo Mbeki's Address to the Nation in January 2000. President Nelson Mandela announced in 1999 that there would be a national summit on reparations, but the Mbeki government announced its own priority, a national conference on racism.[13] Again, the sentiment was voiced by Brandon Hamber of the Center for the Study of Violence and Reconciliation that "[i]t is only those whose lives remain unaffected by the past—including government officials who have 'transcended their victimization' through the benefits provided by their new offices, who seem eager to forget."[14]

Legal Actions

Small wonder then that the commission would be challenged legally to fulfil its mandate by a group of destitute families in Port Elizabeth whose three relatives, active members of the United Democratic Front, had been killed by security police. They alleged that the TRC process had resulted in granting amnesty to the perpetrator of "heinous human rights violations" while providing only a pension to one of the widows and an Interim Grant to another.[15] The attorney for the group, a well-known advocate, Mpumelelo Nyoka, challenged lack of effective treatment of this case by the TRC on the basis of Section 26 of their law, which gave "any person who is of the opinion that he or she has suffered harm as a result of a gross violation of human rights [the right to] apply to the reparation committee for reparation in an endeavor to restore the human and civil dignity of such victim." In light of this straightforward mandate, one would expect that there would be other legal challenges as well, especially in the void of government having rendered a definitive legal conclusion on the matter.

Moreover, a coalition of nongovernmental organizations had decided to file a class action suit against the TRC on behalf of the victims, since no action had been taken by late March 2000, aiming to "break the silence" over the issue. This coalition—or Working Group on Reparations—was convened by Michael Lapsley, director of the Institute for the Healing of Memories, and included such other organizations as Black Sash, Trauma Center for Victims of Violence and Torture, Center for the Study of Violence and Reconciliation, Institute for Democracy in South Africa, Catholic Justice and Peace, and the Khumbula Healing Center.[16] Lapsley went on to suggest that given the assumptions under which the TRC had worked and which had been approved by government to date, one could easily infer that government is in contempt of the judgment, which held that in exchange for the grant of amnesty, reparations would be paid to the victims. Of course, this conclusion could be reached in a number of cases where individuals had been paid neither the Urgent Interim Grant nor the Long-Term Grant.

The government response to this pressure was understandably frustrated, as one spokesperson said that the government was taking a "multifaceted approach" to this issue, considering the payment to communities rather than to individuals, a step that had been taken in some cases. Nevertheless, he also intimated that there was some reluctance within the government to pay the sums envisioned by the TRC to individuals, asking, "Where do you start and where do you stop? Where is the money to come from?"[17] Another spokesperson, media director for the Ministry of Justice and Constitutional Development, appeared to be even more defensive:

> This process is not as easy as people would want us to believe. It is daunting with considerable implications for the fiscus and will need careful debate and reflection when a full debate takes place in Parliament. The commission's recommendations regarding this process cut across the whole spectrum of our society. In one of the recommendations the commission said the process of national reconciliation and engendering a human rights culture should be the responsibility of all South Africans. In this context the commission recommended that the private sector non-governmental organizations and civil society as a whole be a part of this process.[18]

From the above statements it is clear that government was apprehensive about the costs of final reparations, or long-term grants, and, as indicated by Hlengiwe Mkhize, wanted to view them within the context of a much wider responsibility of society to make right the victims of Apartheid, where the private sector (especially businesses that benefited from Apartheid), nongovernmental organizations, and South Africans of all stripes would be seen to be responsible for the outcome. So they attempted to draw out a much wider context for this problem than the narrow legal issue of financial payments from government, perhaps in preparation for what surely would be other court actions attempting to assign government primary responsibility. In this sense, the spokesperson from the Ministry of Justice went much further than necessary in attempting to reduce the scope of government's sole responsibility when he "placed on the record" the striking proposition that "the majority of people never fought Apartheid in order to be paid. It is an insult to many of them for anyone to suggest they be paid or that they deserve to be paid."[19] The government spokesperson apparently was of the view that victim status derived from the fact of those who were actually engaged in fighting Apartheid in one way or another, an interpretation that is at odds with the victim status defined in the TRC mandate as any who suffered under the direct actions taken by perpetrators for a political objective. His definition would exclude most of the people of South Africa from victim status, when they clearly were, both subjectively and objectively, subjects of the most massive and dedicated campaign of the violation of human rights in modern history.

The Exemplary Contradiction

In the foregoing description, the contradiction is obvious between the aims of the TRC process and its results, as is the case with many public policies. This contradiction is exemplified in the following two cases. The first concerns the "Eikenhof 3," three men, Siphiwe James Bholo, Sipho Samuel Gavin, and Boy Titi Ndweni, who were cadres of the ANC and were arrested in 1993 for an attack at Eikenhof, an area south of Johannesburg in 1991. They were charged and convicted of kidnapping, attempted murder, and illegal possession of firearms and ammunition, and two were given life sentences and the last a twenty-year term. After five years in Pretoria prison, they applied for an appeal of their sentence, which was rejected, despite the fact that the former commander of the Azanian Peoples Liberation Army, the PAC military wing, Phila Dolo, told an amnesty hearing before the TRC that he had killed three people at Eikonhof. Nevertheless, in November 1998, a judge denied an order for the withdrawal of the state's opposition to bail for the convicted men, in what would seem to be a perpetuation of the justice system's ignoring the admission of guilt by a credible person.[20]

However, Craig Williamson, a major in the security police under the white minority regime, committed a number of atrocities against former ANC activists and guerrilla fighters. Williamson killed anti-Apartheid activists Ruth First and Jeanette Schoon with letter-bombs sent to Mozambique in 1982 and conspired to kill First's husband, Joe Slovo. Williamson testified before the TRC and was shockingly granted amnesty by the TRC. While Slovo's family lawyer expressed respect for the decision, the ANC secretary general, Kgalema Motlanthe, deemed the grant of amnesty "regrettable."[21] The two incidences manifest the way in which "justice" is working in South Africa, where those who perpetrated the most heinous crimes against individuals who were fighting for majority rule have been granted amnesty, while those who fought for their freedom find the justice system stacked against them. The situation of the three members of the ANC are particularly telling, because when Nelson Mandela was released from prison, one of his initial statements was that the armed struggle should continue, and in fact, it was not suspended until 1992, after the guerrilla action by the ANC cadres. The South African courts, however, under the Apartheid regime, did not recognize the ANC cadres as prisoners of war; rather they were accorded the status of common criminals who had been apprehended. Their continued treatment suggests that while a process through the TRC has been developed for the former perpetrators of violence against the freedom fighters, the it is an imperfect process for former freedom fighters, some of whom are still embroiled in the Apartheid-era attitude that governs some courts.

So the cost of the reconciliation program was often a bitter pill for many Black South Africans and others who had been wounded by the Apartheid system, but this was envisioned by its framers as the cost. In this case, an editorial in the *Sowetan*, the major Black newspaper in the country, said that this outcome was part of the negotiated political settlement that led to majority rule and that although it was bitter, the Amnesty Committee's decision should be respected.[22] On the hand, there was some hope for restitution, since the four policemen who in 1977 killed Steve Biko, leader of the Black Consciousness Movement, were brought to justice, despite concealing the political motive that led them to commit the act.[23]

Giving Back the Bicycle

According to Reverend Mpambani's metaphor (presented in chapter 3), the moral thing is for the perpetrator who stole the bicycle to give it back to its rightful owner, not to come to the owner seeking reconciliation without it, as though it did not matter. This is necessary both to restore the capacity of the owner to use the bicycle as a resource in his self-development and to signal to the owner that the request for reconciliation is sincere and merited because it restores the morality of the person who stole it. In this sense, the government is correct that reparations are not the sole responsibility of the government that is now led by representatives of the formerly disenfranchised and harmed victims who, despite their political enfranchisement, are still suffering from the harm done to them in the Apartheid era. In this sense, those who clamor for government alone to provide reparations participate in the revictimization process. However, the criticism may be correct that it is the responsibility of government to provide leadership in constructing a reparations program from the resources in society and in the international community. In doing so, government might take the internal attitude that reparations are an urgent national priority, and in the international system it might have to redefine "development" in ways that shape proposals for economic assistance to provide for debt relief, special grants (not loans), and other compensatory concepts.

The Internal Project

In the internal project of reparations, the clear responsibility of government is to involve those sectors of society that benefited from Apartheid and are in a position to continue to benefit as a result of the violation of the human rights of Black South Africans.

Taxation. Several prominent South African leaders have called for the levying of a special tax to provide the finances to carry out the TRC mandate. For example, the archbishop of the Anglican Church in South Africa, Rev. Njongonkulu Ndungane, who took over from Bishop Desmond Tutu in 1997, argues that there should be a "reparations tax," since very little has been done for the victims of Apartheid, such as the elderly, orphans, and those with disabilities. Placing a substantial share of the burden on the international community, he noted that South Africa had provided a model by canceling the debts of some of its neighboring countries. However, he deprecated proposals by the sale of gold by the Bank of England and proposals by the International Monetary Fund to send some gold to provide for for debt relief, since the step by the Bank of England reduced the gold price by several dollars, affecting the profits of South African gold houses and causing some unemployment in the bargain. Rather, he believed that the Swiss and German governments should "atone" for their participation in the crime of Apartheid by direct grants.

There have been other proposals for a general wealth tax to deal with the gross imbalance in wealth between the white and Black communities created by the process of colonialism and racial subordination. For example, Sampie Terreblanche examined the wealth differential and its impact at a business sector hearing in Johannesburg on November 11, 1977, at which he provided seven reasons why "political supremacy and racial capitalism impoverished Africans and enriched whites unjustly."[24] In any case, a powerful argument can be made for the fact that the socioeconomic status of the white community was achieved substantially through the ill-gotten gains from the process of subordinating the Black population and that, therefore, restitution requires that the "bicycle be given back." In this sense, if Reverend Ndugane's tax were implemented and levied upon the general population, the victims would be paying for their own restitution. The morally correct thing would be to exempt the victim and for those who caused the harm to pay the tax. Indeed, Cynthia Ngewu, mother of one of the Gugulethu Seven (young men from Gugulethu Township executed by police in 1986), expressed this sentiment in the TRC hearings: "I think the best way to demonstrate a truthful commitment to peace and a truthful commitment to repentance is that perpetrators of acts of violence would make a contribution, a financial contribution to the families of victims and, in that way, they would then cleanse themselves of their own guilt, and they would demonstrate with extreme confidence that they are sorry about what they did."[25]

What prevents this solution from achieving legitimacy is precisely the same view that was responsible for the formula under which the TRC operated, which held that amnesty would be sufficient for the perpetrator, that the perpetrator would not have to participate in making reparation beyond the provision of the "truth." However, when the victimization results in a material consequence, is it justice to weight the scales so lightly in favor of the perpetrator? Perhaps unconsciously, the leaders of the victims had in mind that their failure to demand that the perpetrator participate in reparations also was the currency that the TRC provided as incentive, not only to achieve reconciliation by having them come forward, but also not tipping the larger scales of economic viability of the country by provoking a situation where whites began to leave and withdraw their wealth. Thus, there is an irony and a contradiction at the core of this problem, which holds that full reparation by the perpetrator is impossible because of the view of the government and the perpetrator that their resources will be necessary to provide a generally acceptable standard of living.

The defense sector. South Africa is a wealthy country compared to others on the African continent. Its ability to afford reparations should be judged in light of the fact that while the Committee on Reparations and Rehabilitation of the TRC and the government, especially the Ministry of Justice, debated over the R3 billion and more that it would cost to fund the long-term reparations grants, the government was considering a R32 billion purchase of weapons.[26] A review by the Auditor General of this controversial deal for the purchase of a package of weapons consisting of four corvettes, four submarines, thirty-eight fighter aircraft, twenty-four lead-in fighters, 108 tanks, and sixty helicopters included the JAS Gripen aircraft made by the Afro-Swedish firm SAAB and British Aerospace revealed that the processes followed in the contracting were not transparent and reflected the pressure levied by the Swedish government on contacts inside Armscor, the South African military parastatal. At the same time, South Africa maintained thirty Cheeta aircraft, which had been modified for South African conditions but had only ten certified pilots for them, while it would require another R35 million to modify the Gripen once purchased.[27]

Reactions to the cost of the Gripen aircraft were pointed. One observer called the purchase "incomprehensible" and suggested that "the money spent on arms procurement could have built a million homes."[28] Meanwhile, a coalition of organizations known as the Cease Fire Campaign mobilized in November 1998 to demand a halt to the remilitarization program and the use of these funds for human needs.[29]

This sale was supposed to have been the government's reequipment program that had been announced in 1998. However, it is worth noting that the South African military has no peer in southern Africa, either with respect to sea- or land-based military capability. The only context within which South African National Defence Force troops have been used were peacekeeping operations mounted by the United Nations in the civil wars to the north in Sierra Leone and Rwanda. Otherwise, the Apartheid regime was never attacked in the mode of its theorized "total onslaught," and it is even less likely that any of the countries in southern Africa would challenge the majority rule in South Africa as well. Therefore, analysts who have looked closely at the South Africa defense budget have suggested that it

> could be redirected to meeting socio-economic needs and help to create the stability and social justice on which South Africa's security depends. The South African defense budget for 1997/8 amounted to R9,579 million, that is 5.2 percent of GDP (RSA, 1997 figures).
>
> Although this level is considerably lower than some of the militarized economies such as Russia, the United States, Israel and some Middle East countries, it is notably higher than the

most recent figures for such countries as Australia, Japan, New Zealand, Mexico and Brazil, as figures of the Stockholm Peace Research Institute indicated in 1996.[30]

Thus, the rationale that the government does not have the funds to afford a modest reparations program weakens in light of the evidence that it is prepared to spend an extraordinary amount of its budget (15 percent in 1998 rand) to remilitarize, against a highly questionable set of adversaries or peacekeeping projects that called for this expenditure, and against the background of external questionable pressures on the government to do so.

The private sector.   The TRC and its Committee on Reparations and Rehabilitation found that businesses had been heavily implicated in the structure and function of Apartheid and were therefore culpable as perpetrators and as beneficiaries of the oppression of Blacks. The TRC report stated:

> Business was central to the economy that sustained the South African state during the apartheid years. Certain businesses, especially in the mining industry, were involved in helping to design and implement apartheid policies; the white agriculture industry benefitted from its privileged access to land. Other businesses benefitted from cooperating with security structures of the state. Most businesses benefitted from operating in a racially structured context.[31]

At the TRC hearings in May 1998, the industrial company Dorbyl released a report that detailed the existence of past racism, which continued to have an impact upon personnel performance. As a response, the company established a corrective commission for change from within. The TRC believed that this was an exemplary step for the company to take on its own and encouraged others to do so.[32]

These factual statements are true historically, but in their historical truth affirm the fact the artificiality of the dating of the period of the TRC mandate, since many of the structures devised by the mining companies in order to extract precious minerals and stones date back at least to the discovery of gold and diamonds in South Africa in the last quarter of the nineteenth century. Indeed, the mining houses, in the exploitation of gold, for example, depressed the wages of Black workers, denied them medical treatment, and regarded their person as expendable altogether. As a result, today, AngloGold has achieved a position in the global market where it owns 60 percent of the world's diamond extraction process and thus could participate in a reparations program with the substantial financial resources at its command.

The international sector. It is also true that one reason for the prominence of the South African political issue in global terms is that it has consumed a substantial amount of the attention of both international institutions, such as the United Nations, the North Atlantic Treaty Organization, the International Atomic Energy Agency, as well as many individual governments. Some of these major powers participated in the transition of South Africa from white minority rule to a Black majority legitimate government and the carrot they offered was financial assistance from the West and Asia. As seen in the first development plan, they did not provide sufficient external financial assistance, and one of the results was the inability of the government to entertain the payment of reparations on the scale decided by the TRC.

The Land Question

To be fair to the government in the struggle with the TRC over reparations policy, the project of restitution of the victims of Apartheid, who comprise most of the population, was not approached as a comprehensive matter, as is evidenced by the separate mandates given to entities such as the TRC and the Land Commission, a government entity that manages land claims, when the majority-rule government came into existence. Moreover, both of these entities, to some extent, have a "development" oriented framework, which is surprising with respect to TRC, since it was conceived as a temporary body and had relatively specific, past-oriented restitution to implement. Yet land is a principal economic resource, and its effective use as a tool of reparations might suffice where financial resources are scarce.

Thus, the "Principles" section of reparation and rehabilitation policy in the TRC report declared, "This policy is development-centered. In adherence to this principle, it is essential to provide individuals with sufficient knowledge and information about available resources and to help them use resources to their maximum benefit."[33] Nevertheless, in the section on forms of restitution, there does not appear to be a direct link between the TRC reparation process and the Land Commission, except insofar as it is made through the interministerial committee. Otherwise, there is only the slightest reference to the ability of claimants to demand the return of their land, as displayed in the 1992 decision of the Skweyiya Commission on the complaints of former ANC prisoners and detainees, which held that they had the right to compensation for lost property.[34]

The Land Restitution Act of 1994, promulgated as the first act after the establishment of majority rule, shows the importance of land to the new government and the people it represented. Indeed, the act suggests that land was conceived as the principal form of restitution in the task, as one observer put it, "of undoing some of the grotesque injustices of the segregation and Apartheid eras in South Africa."[35] In practice, the process of land restitution is a complex one that rests with three entities, the Commission on the Restitution of Land Rights, an independent agency; the Land Claims Court, which is a special body of the judiciary; and the Department of Land Affairs, which is a ministry within the government. Unlike the TRC, the mandate of this process is tied to the Land Act of June 19, 1913, which effectively transferred 87 percent of the land to whites, leaving Blacks with only 13 percent—and the worst land in the country. All land claims are against the state of South Africa, and it may make restitution as the result of a complaint by ceding state-held land, or by purchasing or appropriating land for the complainant. The process is decentralized, as each province has a land commission, and it might be expected that the process is slow and cumbersome, dependent as it is upon uncertain and often missing documentation in cases of disputed rights to land. In addition, the terms of reference of the various bodies is still being decided in favor of a role for the Land Commission, as both a point where complaints may be lodged and as an investigative arm of the Land Claims Court (LCC). The courts will take on primary responsibility for deciding conflicts in both cases initiated by those who use the courts as the point of original jurisdiction and those initiated by the commission as well. One implication of this is that if legal proceedings are to become the primary process of issuing decisions on land claims, then it will favor those who have resources and it will be a long-term strategy for restitution.

In fact, the authors of *Land Restitution in South Africa* admit that the mandate of the land claims process does not address the wider issue of reparations:

The question of how to resolve the tension between the relatively narrow terms of reference of the [Land Restitution] Act and a broader moral or political need for restitution was put directly to those interviewed [by the authors]. Although no clear answer emerged, there was agreement among commission staff that when there was any possibility of the claim being valid it should be gazetted and the LCC should be responsible for adjudicating the matter.[36]

The possibility that claims may be drawn out and complicated by the processes involved may create some alienation because as the authors note, "[P]ublic expectations of the restitution process are high."[37] The restoration of land rights is seen as another basic development issue by the government, since it empowers individual families and communities to participate in the growth of the country on the basis of their use of this precious resource.[38]

The Zimbabwe Land Invasion Scare

However, the most serious result of the growth of alienation is that the few sporadic land invasions that have happened may occur on the scale of those that have occurred in Zimbabwe. The ending of the guerrilla war that changed Rhodesia into Zimbabwe in 1980 was similarly a negotiated political settlement, since the forces arrayed against the white Rhodesians did not win an outright victory. Like South Africa, during the process of colonialism, the British ceded to its settlers most of the productive land of the country, upon which they established a viable commercial farming industry that has held sway in the economy of the country until the present. Also similar to South Africa, the 1980 national reconciliation program of Robert Mugabe was based on the promises of Lancaster House agreement. The Lancaster House agreement, however, entrenched the rights, such as land rights, of whites in the constitution for a ten-year period, but even after that period, the Mugabe government failed to act on a credible land reform and distribution policy. Thus, in the 2002 elections the dominant issue was the independent activity of former guerrilla combatants to reclaim land, and Mugabe sided with the combatants in this process. The government has made some tepid moves in the past, targeting 8.3 million hectares of land for redistribution through which it identified nearly one thousand farms in 1997 and sponsored a 1998 donors conference. The government acquired roughly 3 million hectares, and under the new policy, the remaining five million hectares will be acquired.[39] The land takeovers in Zimbabwe caused a serious breach between it, Britain, the United States, and international agencies such as the United Nations, IMF, and World Bank and caused serious reverberations in South Africa. Therefore, a central issue was the question of the attitude of the Mbeki government toward Mugabe's actions. Mbeki shared a political alliance with Mugabe, since Zimbabwe had been a principal stronghold for the ANC during its guerrilla era and Mugabe and some of his colleagues shares the "old boys" ties to Fort Hare and other southern African institutions. So the white community in South Africa, many of whom are from Zimbabwe or have other connections, pressed the government to disavow Mugabe's policies. But while the ANC party leadership sided with Mugabe, Mbeki became the leader of a more conciliatory approach. Recognizing that many countries had reneged on the Lancaster House agreement to provide Zimbabwe with the financial assistance that would have made a smoother path to remuneration of white farmers possible, he began a campaign to raise funds for this purpose, having some success with the Scandianian countries. Still, he has not placated right-wing white South Africans nor the international community. In any case, the dynamics of the 2000 elections in Zimbabwe pointed forcefully to the role of land reparations in the process of restitution and reconciliation.

Land Restitution

Part of the intractability of undoing Apartheid is the question of land reclamation by Blacks whose land was taken under the Apartheid system. This issue was a prominent factor in the first majority-rule elections in 1995 and remains a problem for the government today. In response, the government, under the new constitution, has set up a Land Claims Court to adjudicate claims of land by Blacks against whites for the most part. As a mechanism of restitution, it demands that those who would issue such a claim must have documentation of ownership. In fact, the Restitution of Land Rights Act 22 of 1994 states that

South Africa's land restitution process was born out of the Constitution of 1993. This Constitution conferred upon per-

sons who were dispossessed of their land under racist legislation, the right to claim restitution against the state.

All claims must first be submitted to the Commission on the
Restitution of Land Rights, whose role is to investigate the
merits of claims and attempt to settle them through mediation.

Where a claim cannot be settled through mediation, the
Commission must prepare a comprehensive report and refer
the claim to the Land Claims Court for final determination.

The task of the land claims court is to decide which form of
restitution is appropriate and fair in each case. Restitution can
take the form of returning the original piece of land that was
taken (restoration). If this requires expropriation then the current owner is entitled to fair compensation. . . . The Land
Claims Court [decides] the amount of compensation.[40]

This system has thus far been slow to return much land to
claimants, but it has been supplemented by the fact that the government, which owns large tracts of land, has enacted a program of reset-
tlement to provide land for those who are able to make productive use
of it. Both systems are designed to reempower Blacks who were impoverished as a result of their disposition of their land and to recapitalize
their families to enable them to participate in the new economy of
South Africa and to reclaim their cultural heritage to the land as well.

The ANC Submission

The ANC submission to the TRC described its long struggle against
the Apartheid state dominated by a white majority and the countering
actions of the government in perpetuating violence and subversion of
the guerrilla warfare by deploying the security apparatus of the state.[41]
the ANC document queries, "Did ANC perpetrate any human rights
violations?" Then, in a striking admission of guilt, the document
detailed a series of incidents involving bombings and attacks of military
targets in which innocent civilians were casualties.[42] The document
goes on to say that the ANC accepted responsibility for these acts but
that their context and motivation should be considered in evaluating
the injury to the human rights of the victims in acts that ultimately were
designed to liberate all oppressed South Africans. It posited that these
actions were instituted as the outgrowth of a just struggle against an

enemy that had been declared by the United Nations as having perpetrated crimes against humanity through the administration of the Apartheid system. In this light, the ANC committed itself to the process of the TRC, suggesting that there needed to be restoration, restitution, or reparations within the framework of such resources that South Africa could afford. The suggestive list of actions included these:

> monetary awards, either by way of lump sum or monthly pension;
> other forms of material assistance and support;
> psychological support and provision of comfort and solidarity;
> steps to be taken to restore the dignity and honor as well as the good names of victims;
> steps to be taken to ensure that South Africa remembers.

Resulting Public Opinions of the TRC

In general, the process of transformation, which requires that whites accept their role either in the TRC process or within the changes in society as a whole, have not gone well. For example, a national survey of all South Africans found that the public generally held negative views of the TRC.[43] When asked, for instance, whether the TRC hearings "helped the country live together," 39 percent agreed, but 38 percent disagreed in a divided referendum on its work. Moreover, when respondents were asked whether the TRC made matters worse, a substantial majority of all groups indicated that it had:

Blacks	62 percent
Coloureds	62 percent
Whites	72 percent
Indians	74 percent

Supporting this trend data, one observer says:

> Pointing to the failure of accommodation, the President [Mandela] has openly castigated selfish and unrepentant whites for impeding the progress of the "new" nation. These criticisms are a telling admission that accommodation has failed miserably to persuade whites, particularly politicians and business barons, to join in the work of eliminating the vestiges of Apartheid.[44]

With the relative failure of the TRC to achieve its objective of healing through voluntary admission of crimes, there will now have to be another process of long-term duration to achieve both the aims of continuing the racial dialogue and making meaning material restoration to the formerly oppressed people of South Africa. And while the government is controlled by representatives of this group and one would theoretically believe that such restitution can take place through its actions, the fact that so much of the wealth of the country is still invested in the white population means that the majority must have the cooperation of whites to achieve this goal without the outright appropriation of that wealth, which is the surest route to the revival of civil war.

Challenging the Mbeki Government

The belief in the potential of the Mbeki government to resolve the reparations dilemma faded with the winding down of the TRC when the government refused to commit itself to the payment of full reparations as called for in the TRC's final recommendations. In a private discussion between the author and Minister of Justice Penuell Maduna, he expressed the belief that while the TRC had fostered a process that was widely legitimate in the sense of conceptualizing a process that brought together perpetrators and victims in a system of restitution, the essential answer to the question of who was a victim was a "national question." As such, this question of victimization was only partially addressed by the TRC in that it surfaced and treated the most egregious cases and then only at a minimal level. Thus, the promise of restitution through reparations was an issue that would eventually have to be resolved through the mechanism of government and folded into the general program of national development.

While Maduna expressed an important view, events outran the government when progressive activists such as the Institute for Democracy in South Africa, the Institute for Justice and Reconciliation, Black Sash Trust, and church groups such as the South African Council of Churches and the Jewish Board of Deputies began a campaign, as the Working Group on Reparations, to seek a forum for redress and reparations wider than the government. The group addressed a letter to the government in August 2002, noting that the victims of Apartheid and survivors are expecting financial reparations and that if they not received, the credibility of government would be wounded.[45] Father Pasley, chairperson of the Working Group, noted that reparations would amount to approximately R4 billion and that the government was planning to spend R60 billion on the refurbishing of the military.[46] Bheki Khumalo, spokesperson for the president, dismissed charges that the government was not moving quickly enough to live up to the terms of the TRC promise of reparations, and said that the government had set aside R800 million for this purpose.[47]

Although over the seven-year course of the TRC, twenty-two thousand people testified, six thousand applied for amnesty, and more than nineteen thousand victims had been certified, reparations had not yet been paid by the spring of 2003. Meanwhile, the Khulumani Support Group had engaged Ed Fagan, a lawyer active in the Holocaust suits, to pursue legal action against twenty-one U.S.-based companies, such as J. P. Morgan Chase, IBM, Caltex Petroleum, Ford, and General Motors. The suit was brought in U.S. federal court in Brooklyn, New York, claiming that the defendants "acted with deliberate indifference to the well-being of the African population" under the U.S. Alien Tort Claims Act of 1789, which was used successfully in the Holocaust survivors suits against Swiss banks and German and Austrian companies.[48] Suit was also brought in South Africa by Jubilee South Africa, a group of progressive organizations, against an Anglo American mining company for $6 billion, suggesting that government reparations were not sufficient and that far more was owed by private corporations that benefitted handsomely from Apartheid.

President Thabo Mbeki was angered by the suit against the businesses, holding the position that reparations would compromise the economic viability of these businesses, elaborating a position that was welcomed by the South African business sector.[49] His position was subsequently articulated by Minister Maduna, who also opposed the suits on the grounds that if they were successful, the funds would come from shareholders who, in turn, would order cuts in employment, penalizing Blacks, and "the same people that you pretend to be so concerned about will pay the price."[50] President Mbeki offered a one-time payment of R30,000 in a proposal tendered in June 2003 to the National Assembly.[51] This amount, however, was rejected by both Khulumani and Jubilee. The position of Jubilee in a meeting at Technikon SA from July 18 to July 19 was that the TRC was not able to consider the full scope of the need for reparations because of the limited nature of its mandate, and therefore the suits against foreign and domestic companies were reconfirmed, "in order to secure reparations at a level able to redress the damage of Apartheid and racial oppression in all its manifestations, for all those affected."[52]

Conclusion

South Africa is embroiled in an internal conflict about the scope and propriety of sources of reparations payment in a scenario that has both government and the private sector under challenge by groups representing Apartheid victims. This is as it should be. Both the government and the private sector in that country, as in other countries, have roles and responsibilities in repairing the damage done by the historical process of oppression. One could make an argument that now that Blacks are in the majority, government should be exempt from this charge and that it should have the freedom to do other things with the financial resources of the state. However, one could also argue that the government should indeed have the central role in using both the collective resources of the state and those from the private sector—especially because government resources are inadequate—to address the demand for general compensation. This demand, as in the United States, should not exempt government from the normal course of dealing with the problem of everyday life for the citizens in that country, but should instead be considered an attempt to provide resources above and beyond those normally available for such purposes in recognition of the suffering that the Apartheid program engendered.

In any case, this discussion reveals that the political conflicts engendered over issues of restitution and racial reconciliation, at least in the South African context, are exceedingly complex and that the TRC experiment in particular may exist as a well-meaning, though deeply flawed paradigm. Perhaps, then, its real value is that it exposes the complexity in important ways such that it may inform attempts of other societies where racial history is a prominent consideration to social stability and to the moral quality of the regime.

CHAPTER FIVE

୶

A Grand Narrative of Black American Oppression

Over a hundred years ago, they gave my grandfather a shovel and told him to dig a hole, a big hole. He started digging and went down—down—down. When he asked how deep to go, they just told him "keep digging." When they thought the hole was deep enough they took the shovel from him, pulled it up by rope. They never pulled grandpa out the hole—they left him there. He tried digging his way up with his finger-nails and the dirt just got under his nails so that couldn't work. They threw him just enough to keep him living—and left him in the hole. All his children and their children— were born in the hole. All of us were born in the hole and mister, when you born there, that's the only place you know. You sort of feel you belong there and for a hundred years the white man ain't brought the shovel back.[1]

THE HISTORY OF BLACK AMERICAN OPPRESSION takes into consideration three categories of maltreatment that in the view of this author have maintained Blacks in a hole in relation to whites in American society until this very day. The first is slavery, the second is the extension of slavery and parallel forms of discrimination such as ghettoization, and the third is modern "Black Codes." In this chapter, we will be concerned with the oppression of slavery and its extension. Chapter 5 will end the description of oppression with a brief survey of postslavery racial ghettoization and modern Black Codes. The point, as in the South Africa case, is that the state was the constant arbiter and legitimizer of the choice of citizens to conduct various forms of subordination of Black people. As such, it is at the level of state power that reparations takes on their most decisive focus as the arena for redress.

There is the feeling voiced in the seminal work *An American Dilemma* that although there is discrimination in America toward other groups, such as Jews or Hispanics, Asians and Arabs, discrimination against Blacks has a different quality.[2] But a comprehensive understanding of the nature of that victimization and its acceptance by the majority culture is suppressed by its own view of the condition of Blacks and its power to circumscribe the Black perspective to a marginal role in the description of their own victimhood. The result is that Black victimization is still so pervasive, in part, because a mythical perspective substitutes for the reality that continues to constitute this as a "qualitative" feature of Black life.

In the twenty-first century, American-style racial victimization is couched within the soft covers of what might be termed a "civil oppression," difficult to imagine as oppression because of the overlay of public policy justification, which carves out a rationale presented by Dinesh D'Souza of what might be considered rational racism.[3] That is to say, the policy rationale has formed a consensus that the oppression is justified by the behavior of those receiving it.

In addition, the absence of the feeling that there are any American victims, Black American victims in particular, may be explained by at least two other perceptions. The first one is that the test of moral reconstitution has been met. One function of the perennial image of Martin Luther King, Jr. calling forth the moral project of civil rights as the mechanism for Black restoration is that it evokes in the mind of many a feeling that America, in a previous era, faced the test of historical condemnation for the wrong to Blacks. The nation has, thus, gone through the heroic period of struggle through the civil rights and Black Power movements and even came close to the edges of the revolutionary struggle that Black South Africa undertook to win the right to majority rule. This experience gave white Americans an opportunity to acquire some moral absolution through their own participation in opposing the worst forms of victimization.

Second, the Black movement also gave to the whites of that generation some linkage to the broader civil rights successes with others such as the women's movement, the disabled movement, and elderly movement, which were mostly white movements. The feeling that the Black problem has been solved to the extent possible may also be part of the personal experience of whites with their own generational participation in civil rights struggles that had nothing to do with Blacks, but which they view as an effort of moral political purity that has come and gone. The titanic struggle against the Vietnam War that arrayed the morality of right and wrong, good and evil on the side of protesters and the American government, respectively, was a clear-cut moral issue for most Americans, the restitution for which, in one form or another, through remembrances on the Memorial Wall, a "Rolling Thunder" Memorial Day, immigration policies that allow Vietnamese to enter the United States, restoration ceremonies with Vietnam itself, and other activities, is still being done.

Therefore, it is possible to understand the psychological frustration of many Americans, especially white Americans, with a condition that many feel they have attempted to make right, but that will not go away. This may merely mean that they have miscalculated the severity of the problem and the complexity of the corrective necessary to resolve it.

The State and Black Subordination

The historical fact of official slavery in America is only five generations away from most Blacks, and there are those living today whose grandparents and great-grandparents experienced other forms of group subordination in the twentieth century. So the social fact of racial oppression is nearer to us than has been presumed by the utter silence on this question among most Americans—Black and white. But as a review of this phenomenon shows, it plays a fundamental role in the lives of African Americans today.

Slavery was the product of "state action" as enacted by the colonial governments, the Articles of Confederation, and the United States in lending official sanction to the subordination of Blacks. To begin with, between 1619 and 1640 the institution of slavery was codified in many colonies; Virginia developed more laws than any other colony. Indeed, in 1662, Virginia used the word *slave* in laws that institutionalized a social and economic phenomenon that had already been common practice. Slavery was also referred to legally in the Carolinas in 1663 and in Maryland in 1664, and by the end of the century, it was affirmed in New York and New Jersey as well.

As slavery became a feature of English colonial law in the Americas, it was regulated by the local territorial assemblies. One source of alienation of the colonists that led to the 1776 Revolution was that when they became alarmed at the growing number of Africans in their midst and attempted to curtail their importation, the British vetoed their action. Antislavery measures began to be passed by the Massachusetts Colony in 1771; Pennsylvania levied stiff tariffs for bringing in Africans in 1773; and three southern colonies also passed measures restricting the importation of Africans: Virginia and North Carolina in 1774 and Georgia in 1775.[4]

Nevertheless, by 1792, British policy began to change as a response to antislavery agitation in Britain itself, and in 1807 Parliament voted 230 to 85 to abolish British participation in the slave trade. This decision appears to refute the allegations of conservative scholars such as D'Souza, who opines, "Slavery was a practice that seemed entirely reasonable" and "contradicted no important social values for most people around the world."[5] Although D'Souza felt that the Spanish and Portuguese enslaved other human beings without conscience, slavery always apeared reasonable to those with the power to subdue other human beings and extract their labor without cost for the sake of profit. But the abiding question was whether it was the right or moral thing to do. There is abundant evidence that both Spanish and Portuguese slavers and plantation owners were challenged with the issues of rationality and morality, as slaves declared their humanity by resisting slavery, by taking their liberties in escaping, and by petitioning these heads of state for their freedom and justice. Indeed, Ann Pescatello says that in response to petitions by slaves to the Portuguese royalty, "the Crown was not deaf to . . . appeals and fully realised the appalling conditions in which the slaves were brought from Africa and then employed on the sugar plantations. Numerous decrees were issued to protect the Negro, such as those aimed at reducing the mortality in the slaving ships" and to lessen other aspects of their discomfort.[6] However, the fact that plantation owners were usually powerful enough to avoid such decrees did not eliminate the moral question. In fact, the growing sensitivity of the British, a major naval power with ties to the Spanish and Portuguese, to this question caused them to eventually confront Spain and Portugal directly in policing of the prohibition of the slave trade in the early nineteenth century.

In the debate on the night that British participation was abolished, one of the points at issue was the clear knowledge that human subordination was the predominant feature of the practice. In fact, the head of state, William Pitt the Younger, said after the vote:

> I therefore congratulate this House, the country, and the world that this great point is gained; that we may now consider this trade as having received its condemnation; that its sentence is sealed; that this curse of mankind is seen by the House in its true light; and that the greatest stigma on our national character which ever yet existed is about to be removed! And, Sir, (which is still more important) that mankind, I trust, in general, are now likely to be delivered from the greatest practical evil that ever has afflicted the human race—from the severest and most extensive calamity recorded in the history of the world.[7]

Moreover, the moral issue of the rightness of holding human beings in involuntary servitude was a fact that William Pitt considered to be a "stigma" on the British national character. Indeed, it is also noteworthy, considering the extent of the British Empire, that he considered slavery to be an extant holocaust of that era, "the severest and most extensive calamity recorded in the history of the world." It is this perspective bound by the factual testimony of the oppressed themselves that defies historical forgetting and that continues to make fertile the rationale of slavery as a linkage to national race problems in each age of American history.

The Continental Congress first legislated on slavery when it began a war in which the colonists' ranks were outnumbered by the British, and it had to consider conscripting Blacks to serve in the army. Thus, by 1777, Blacks had earned a modest role in the army of 755 soldiers distributed over fourteen brigades, with a quota set per state. So, a country that began a revolutionary war had to confront the institution of slavery immediately and to adjust the status of some Africans from that of slave to freedman on the same terms as President Abraham Lincoln, who would design the Emancipation Proclamation originally as an order "upon military necessity."

The Legal Framework of Repression

Once the war was over, the status of slaves had to be addressed by the Constitution, which permitted the slave trade to be continued for twenty years, although it established a tax per head, partly as a compromise to exact some pressure with which to restrict the domestic importation of slaves. In any case, revenue from the slave trade flowed into the federal coffers. Nevertheless, Congress would pass legislation ending the slave trade in 1809, while permitting slavery itself to exist.

The fact that America is a state with extensive origins in the institution of slavery means that extent to which the Constitution was influenced by the practice of slavery has been underplayed. For instance, the word *slavery* itself is mentioned only in the Thirteenth Amendment, abolishing the practice for all but penal servitude. Nevertheless, Paul Finkelman[8] points out that other aspects of the Constitution were predicated upon the existence of slavery:

Article 1, section 2, paragraph 3 contained the infamous three-fifths clause, providing for counting slaves as three-fifths of a person for direct taxation.

Article 1, section 9, paragraph 1 prohibited Congress from banning the importation of slaves before 1808.

Article 4, section 2, paragraph 3 prohibited states from emancipating fugitive slaves and required that they be turned over to their owners on demand.

Article 5 prohibited any amendment of the "slave importation and capitation clauses before 1808."

Article 1, section 8, paragraph 15 empowered Congress to suppress slave rebellions.

Article 1, section 9, paragraph 5 and Article 1, section 10, paragraph 2 prohibited the indirect taxation on slavery by prohibiting taxes on exported goods produced by slavery, such as tobacco, rice and cotton.

Article 2, section 1, paragraph 2 counted slaves using the three-fifths clause for the purpose of counting the votes in the Electoral College, giving the South a significant influence in the process.

Article 4, section 4 promised to protect states from domestic violence, including slave rebellions.

Article 5 by requiring that any changes to the Constitution must have a three-fourths vote gave a perpetual veto to the Southern states on the abolition of slavery.

In fact, Finkelman says, "[T]he structure of the entire document ensured against emancipation by the new federal government because the Constitution created a government of limited powers . . . to interfere in the domestic institutions of the states." Finkelman quotes General Charles Cotesworth Pinckney, a delegate to the Philadelphia Constitutional Convention from South Carolina, who made this case straightforwardly. The extent to which the Constitution was a compromise that ensured the human property of the South led directly to the Civil War, and yet the constitutional flaw has seldom been held up as its cause.

Paul Finkelman has been one of the few observers to understand the reach of the three-fifths concept in providing a foundation for the South to participate in the life of the new Republic in political and economic matters. The *proxy power* given to white southerners constitutes the missing resource that disempowered Blacks then and is the source of Black underdevelopment today and thus is at the heart of the reparations project.

Cultural Inferiorization

The humanity of the slave was an issue inasmuch as, in order to legitimize the subordination of Black people, whites had to pretend that they were a subhuman species unworthy to enjoy the privileges and responsibilities of citizens in a free society; they were fit to be put into bondage and kept as slaves. Both those for and against slavery held such views. For example, Cassius Marcellus Clay, a cousin of Henry Clay and the editor of the *True American* in Lexington, Kentucky, was a prominent antislavery politician. He was also an early proponent of the economic inefficiency of slavery. But his view of Black humanity was illustrated thus: "I have studied the Negro character. They lack self-reliance—we can make nothing of them. God has made them for the sun and the banana." This view was apparently shared by a proponent of slavery, Hinton Rowan Helper from western North Carolina, who wrote the popular *Impending Crisis of the South* in 1859. His view of the humanity of the African slave was expressed as follows:

Every feature of the Negro, however large, or however small, whether internal or external, whether physical or mental, or moral, loses in comparison with the white, much in the same ratio or proportion as darkness loses in comparison with light, or as evil loses in comparison with good.[9]

The process of dehumanization is important as a preliminary step to the attendant process of subordination and has been an interactive variable with subordination at every step of American history and the hidden justifier of oppressive acts against Blacks.

Today we are reminded of the connection between the past and the present in the content of the Black memorabilia shows that capture the special memory of this period. It was clearly evident that many of the items from our past indicated the progeny of a Black slave culture: the slave collar; hand and ankle chains; crude hoeing tools; pictures of "pickininnies" and "Aunt Jemimas" with coal-black faces, bulging eyes, and huge red lips; along with other items. It has often caused me to think that individuals who could render such grotesque features of other people must have not only believed in the myth of their inferiority, but that they were inhuman to such an extent they would not react negatively to such stereotypes. In some sense, the audacity to construct and use these symbols of Africans represented both a tool of subordination and an affirmation of the victory and superiority of white culture. These figurines, which represented the dehumanization of Africans, reflected the presence within slavery of a bold, raw racism that has receded to the point that in public opinion polls today, 25 percent of whites admit that they believe Black people are inferior. How many beyond 25 percent would there be if all of the responses were truthful marks the current prevalence of negative racial stereotypes as significant and indicates the linkage between the past and present. The modern form of this legacy of Black inferiority has been presented to the American people in the form of the argument that Blacks are intellectually inferior to whites. A well-known work, *The Bell Curve,* advances this thesis and upon it concludes that Blacks cannot benefit from affirmative action and therefore it should be eliminated.[10] W. D. Wright, however, has criticized the Murray and Herrenstein approach, which devalues environmental factors that are central to high performance on tests that purportedly measures "intelligence." For example, he says:

[T]he environment that Herrenstein and Murray really played down in regard to Whites was the historical environmental factor, or what I call the *h* and *e* factor. That historical environment went back to the seventeenth century. It was an environment that said that white people were godly or godlike; that said that they were the only Americans and that America was theirs; and that gave them most of the opportunities in American education for jobs, occupations, and high incomes, as well as opportunities for good housing, good neighborhoods, good public services, and good health and medical care, and the most opportunities for power, prestige, and social position in America. That environment has kept evolving in America to the present day.

Wright goes on to analyze the impact of the racial hierarchy as a major factor in the composition of the tests used to measure something called "intelligence." His major thesis is that there is no scientific basis upon which to assert that there is anything known as intelligence and that such instruments measure various forms of "intellectual ability" that are culturally determined, rather than objective intelligence.[11]

The issue of Black intelligence is also present as an underlying thesis in the frequent displays of "race-gap" in test results between Black and white youth in both primary education and college. The innocent but subtle presentation resides in the "discovery" that Blacks do not score as high as whites on such tests as the LSAT or K–12 instruments that supposedly measure intelligence. The problem here is that such tests are not constructed out of the cultural framework of Black people or their youth, but by those who control the intellectual establishment and who, thus, predominantly construct such tests from a Eurocentric framework, sprinkled with a few aspects of Black life. This accords with the one-way socialization process that has been the experience of Black people in that white culture has been considered superior, since it has been the dominant source for the development of American civilization. But while that is true as a *political* fact, it does not suffice as a rationale for the innate intelligence of whites, a question that has not been resolved because there is no generally acceptable definition of intelligence, and there is, consequently, no instrument that can measure it.

In fact, the presumption that such tests are a meaningful measure of an intelligence gap flows from the erroneous view that the environmental and cultural conditions of Blacks and whites are comparable and can thus be amenable to comparative measurement on the same scale of values. What is measured, however, is the exposure of Black youth to certain experiences, and their lack of exposure to the experiences the tests presume is as much a feature of their oppression in America as any other. Thus, the test-makers argue, for example, that mathematics is an objective determinant of intelligence in that field. However, if the test-taker has not been exposed to mathematical concepts, by what right is the conclusion reached that the results of a test measures his or her "intelligence?" A test might be said to measure similar capacities only if Black children had been exposed to mathematical concepts in the manner and with the intensity that white children have been exposed to them—and even then, one does not know whether "intelligence" is being measured or something else.

The Making of Paupers

Slavery had an indelible impact upon the states that authorized it. Writing in 1857, George Weston described in precise detail the manner in which slavery impoverished whites by their inability to compete with slave labor.[12] Weston argued that whites were either forced to work for less than standard wages to compete with Africans, or had to leave the area altogether. White out-migration and the lack of skills of those who remained led to the general lowering of the wage base, making it necessary for those whites to supplement their livelihood by living off of the land, a pursuit that was also complicated by their inability to compete with the planters' agricultural products produced with slave labor.

Therefore, as slavery expanded, poverty in the region expanded, fostering a great divide in the distribution of wealth not only between whites as a whole and Blacks, but between the rich white planting class and the vast majority of poorer whites. In an 1862 work, Elliot Cairnes put it succinctly: "[T]he tendency of things, therefore, in slave countries is to a very unequal distribution of wealth."[13] Poor whites in the South, then, were ripe for racial manipulation of the planter class for a considerable time to come. For, as Frank Tannenbaum observed about slavery in Argentina, there was not a white "however miserable" who would not put on "a wig and a sword," joining the reality of membership in the racial class of whites, pretending to share their class interests as well.[14]

The Erosion of Black Citizenship
by State Action

After the Civil War several amendments to the Constitution enhancing rights were adopted. The state declared, through the Congress, that Blacks were freed from servitude (Thirteenth Amendment), for all purposes, with the exception of the commission of crimes; that Blacks were citizens (Fourteenth Amendment) and enjoyed the equal protection of the laws with other citizens; and that no state could prohibit the right of citizens of the United States to vote (Fifteenth Amendment). These amendments suggested some progress in institutionalizing the citizenship of the former slave.

The citizenship of Blacks was devalued, however, and by the 1876 Hayes presidency bargain, federal troops were taken from the South, exposing Blacks to a reign of terror by state action. The result was that whereas twenty-three Blacks served in the Congress of the United States in the Reconstruction era, by 1901 all had been eliminated from the Congress, and from legislative bodies in the lower levels of government as well, through violence and intimidation directed at Black voters.

The Fifteenth Amendment. After the Civil War, seven hundred thousand Blacks voted in the South under the protection of Union troops, and were important in electing Republican presidents from 1873 to 1885. As a result of the infamous Hayes bargain of 1876, however, Union troops were removed and the resurgence of white power and authority began to eliminate Blacks from the polls.

Despite the promise afforded Blacks by the Fifteenth Amendment in the late 1860s and early 1870s, attitudes had changed by 1876, when the decision in *United States v. Reese* found the Supreme Court devaluing the Constitution by declaring unconstitutional portions of the Enforcement Act of 1870 that established penalties for preventing Blacks from voting. The Court argued that the Fifteenth Amendment conveyed no positive right upon anyone to vote, but merely prohibited the state and federal governments from denying to anyone the right to vote on account of color, race, or previous condition of servitude.[15] The case *United States v. Cruishank* in 1876 also devalued the Fifteenth Amendment, by deciding that it did not apply to private actions of discrimination (where whites broke up a meeting of Blacks to prevent them from voting in Louisiana elections) but only applied in cases where the issue at stake was the participation of Blacks in national elections.[16]

In fact, by the turn of the century, Blacks had been effectively excluded from the franchise in most areas of the South. This led V. O. Key to say: "The disfranchisement movement of the 'nineties' gave the Southern states the most impressive system of obstacles between the voter and the ballot box known to the democratic world."[17] Dayton McKean said, "[T]he Southern states have a kind of defense in depth against the would-be Negro voter. If one barrier falls before courts or legislature there is another behind it."[18]

Another important case, *Williams v. Mississippi* (1898), concerns a Mississippi scheme that had been in use since 1890 for depriving Blacks of the ballot, by poll taxes, literacy tests, and residency requirements. This scheme was soon adopted immediately by South Carolina in 1899 and by other southern states soon thereafter. In 1902, the Supreme Court, in a decision by Justice Oliver Wendell Holmes, approved the practices in Alabama that disenfranchised Blacks by restricting voting to persons having education and regular employment, property worth three hundred dollars, ancestors with a war record, "good character" (which had to be vouched for by a white person), and an understanding of the duties of citizenship by a test. One observer said: "There was an increasing feeling in the North that it had been unwise judgment to try to force Negro suffrage on the South so quickly after the war, and that also suffrage was a local problem in which interference from outside could only have unhappy results."[19]

The Fourteenth Amendment. Richard Bardolph clearly delineates the decline in state protection of the newly won rights of Blacks:

> [The Supreme Court] decreed that the amendments applied only to measures taken by the states themselves or by their agents; that if a law was not on the face of it clearly discriminatory, the Court would not presume to determine whether it was in effect more burdensome to blacks than to whites; that the police power of the states took priority over less pressing considerations like the enjoyment of the equality promised by the nation's organic law; that while *discrimination* might in some circumstances be forbidden by the nation's fundamental law, racial distinctions were not.[20]

The Radical Reconstructionists in Congress were able to pass the Civil Rights Act of 1875, which was supposed to strengthen the Fourteenth Amendment, offering both social and civil rights to Blacks. But the promise of Black participation in society on the basis of equality was voided by the state action of the Supreme Court in the subsequent reinterpretation of these laws beginning in the 1873 Slaughter-House Cases that ended in the Civil Rights Cases of 1883. The decision in these cases concluded that citizenship was divided between the state and federal entities and that "the [Fourteenth] amendment forbade *state* impairment of the privileges and immunities that persons enjoyed as citizens of the United States; that most civil rights are attributes of *state* citizenship and therefore beyond the reach of the amendment."[21]

Bardolph argues that the driving force behind the new mood among whites to reempower the white South was the belief that the reconstitution of the initial racial compromise was necessary to achieve national harmony.[22] This meant that Blacks had to be resubordinated to the interests of the white South.

Thus, the decision of the Supreme Court in *Plessy v. Ferguson* in 1896 was a further action against the citizenship of Blacks that merely codified the various forms of racial subordination already being perpetrated against them in the South and in other parts of the country. The *Plessy* decision held that Homer Plessy, who was asked to leave a white train compartment for a Black one, suffered no devaluation of his citizenship because racial segregation could be justified if facilities provided for Blacks were equal to those provided for whites. This decision legalized racial separation on a national scale.

The Thirteenth Amendment. Despite the widespread impression that slavery ended in America with the Emancipation Proclamation, two mechanisms were created to extend it long into the twentieth century. Slavery was ostensibly ended by the Civil War and the Thirteenth Amendment to the Constitution. However, the Emancipation Proclamation was not a universal prohibition on slavery, but as indicated earlier, was a field order to commanders to liberate slaves who were in the territories under rebellion. It would be left to the Thirteenth Amendment to establish the principle abolishing slavery. However, that amendment had a loophole that excluded servitude for the punishment of a crime, and a mechanism that came to be known as the convict lease system took the place of the old chattel slavery. Thus, the criminalization of Black people became necessary to whites resuming their territory and privilege over Blacks to subordinate them using penal institutions. Blacks were routinely charged with crimes and placed under the supervision of penal officers, who promptly leased them out to plantation owners, who practiced the same discipline of slavery over these "convicts." The racialization of the penal system was accomplished as a new mechanism through which the practice of slavery could continue to operate.

The sharecropping system was the companion to the convict lease system. It became a mechanism to chain Blacks to certain plantations under the guise of hiring them, extending them credit to work the fields with the promise of a wage at the end of their term, but making certain they were in debt to the plantation owners. This debt became a legal obligation, which had to be worked off before the sharecroppers were permitted to leave the employ of the farmers, plantation owners, mine owners, and so on. While in the employ of these individuals, they were often in old-styled slavery, treated as little more than chattel and brutalized to deliver productive work.

How long the unofficial period of slavery remained viable is indeterminate from the records of the Justice Department. Nevertheless, evidence of restriction of movement was found in a case in Fort Worth, Texas, wherein Mettie Ann Strong was prevented from leaving the plantation to join her husband, Will Strong, and children in Little Rock, Arkansas, in March 1939.[23] Forced labor was also a widespread practice in this period, as noted in a case where Nellie Echols was forced to chop cotton for A. Leslie Wilkes for payment of a debt of $4.85 in Jackson, Mississippi, in October 1943.[24] Finally, violence and intimidation were still evident in the reported beating of Woodrow Wilson Tisdale in Georgetown, South Carolina, for a sharecropping debt owed to plantation owner Royce Green in 1943.[25]

Len Cooper, investigating the subject for an extensive article in the *Washington Post*, discovered a letter in the National Archives recorded in 1950 from a Black person complaining that he was not allowed to leave a plantation in the South. Cooper discovered that one case prosecuted by the Justice Department involved the Dial brothers, who owned a farm thirty-five miles outside of Birmingham, Alabama, and who had killed a Black man whom they kept in slavery.[26] Cooper's assertion that the longevity of slavery was a "secret shame" is correct: most Americans are not aware that aspects of this institution, in some areas of the South, lasted until the era of the civil rights movement. Indeed, Daniel Novak says the following:

> When the *New Republic* published an article on peonage in Florida in 1969, the description of the status of the peon could easily have been taken from reports in the days of the Black Codes. Through the tumultuous sixties, in the teeth of the "civil rights revolution" peonage continued as before—perhaps reduced in magnitude by changing economic conditions, but still alive and kicking its victims as brutally as ever.[27]

All of this means that in some places, especially in the South, the civil rights movement, which in the 1960s fostered the intervention of nonsouthern elements such as civil rights workers, law enforcement officials, sensitive white administrators and politicians and others, literally broke the back of the vestiges of old-styled slavery, whether defined as legal slavery or not. It also means that there were many more Black people held in this condition than the official version of history has admitted: how many and for how long is unknowable. In any case, this gives the lie to those who fervently believe that slavery ended in 1865.

Lynch-Law Brutality

His Spirit in smoke ascended to high heaven
His father, by the cruelest way of pain,
Had hidden him to his bosom once again;
The awful sin remained still unforgiven.
All night a bright and solitary star
(Perchance the one that ever guided him,
Yet gave him up at last to Fate's wild whim)
Hung pitifully o'er the swinging char.
Day dawned, and soon the mixed crowds came to view
The ghastly body swaying in the sun;
The women thronged to look, but never a one
Showed sorrow in her eyes of steely blue;
And little lads, lynchers that were to be,
Danced round the dreadful thing in fiendish glee.
—CLAUDE McKAY, "The Lynching"

The word *nadir* in astronomy means the point below the observer, or the lowest point—the opposite of the zenith. One of the lowest points in the history of the Black community was the reign of violence and intimidation that became the ordinary condition of life, especially in the South, beginning in the last twenty years of the nineteenth century and continuing through the first forty years of the twentieth century. Lynching became frequent, as the most authoritative statistics show that between 1892 and 1951, 4,730 people were lynched in the United States, 3,437 of them (or 70 percent) Black and 1,293 white.[28] The hatred of Blacks was so palpable that it drove the use of this violence as a method of social control such that even some whites were harmed. In this process, oftentimes criminal charges were levied against Blacks, the most common of which was "felonious assault" and the second being the rape of a white woman (much of the research on the causes of lynching was contained in a report by the NAACP, *Thirty Years of Lynching in the United States, 1889–1918*). Gunnar Myrdal suggests that the manner in which Blacks were perceived to have violated social norms made "getting out of place" for any reason the most common of motivations.[29]

No more authoritative account exists than that compiled by Ida B. Wells-Barnett in her work on the lynching of Blacks between 1892 and 1900. She observed in May 1892 at one lynching in Memphis, Tennessee, that "the leading citizens met in the Cotton Exchange Building the same evening, and threats of lynching were freely indulged, not by the lawless element upon which the devilry of the South is usually saddled—but by the leading business men, in their leading business center."[30]

The rationale that was often used for this type of heinous treatment of Blacks ranged from the favored allegation of the rape of a white woman, to impudence toward whites, as a punishment for a crime, or for the general purpose of racial intimidation. Thus, it became legitimized by the leading class of citizens as an acceptable way to visit the ultimate punishment upon Blacks. Ida Wells-Barnett described the typical method:

> They go into town where everybody knows them, sometimes under the gaze of the governor, in the presence of the courts, in the presence of the sheriff and his deputies, in the presence of the entire police force, take out the prisoner, take his life, often with fiendish glee, and often with acts of cruelty and barbarism

which impress the reader with a degeneracy rapidly approaching savage life.[31]

Wells-Barnett describes the famous February 1892 case in Paris, Texas, where the four-year-old daughter of a white man named Vance was brutally murdered and it was alleged that Harry Smith, described as weak-minded Black roustabout, was the perpetrator. The rage in the white community and surrounding states was such that ten thousand people came by every conceivable means to witness Smith, without a trial, being hoisted upon a platform, tortured, and burned with hot pokers to the roar of the crowd:

[T]he white Christian people of Paris, Texas and thereabouts had determined to lay aside all forms of law and inaugurate a new form of punishment for the murder. They absolutely refused to make any inquiry as to the sanity or insanity of their prisoner, but set the day and the hour when in the presence of assembled thousands, they put their helpless victim to the stake, tortured him and burned him to death for the satisfaction of Christian people.[32]

The extent of lynching matches complaints of peonage in the twentieth century. The distribution by year is shown in table A6. The list of Black people who were lynched by whites in the period 1940–65 is purely suggestive in that it has not been corroborated for accuracy. However, the probability is that it is a conservative count inasmuch as it includes figures from Tuskeegee Institute that were known to have been somewhat conservative.[33] In any case, there is little awareness that lynching, widely regarded as an phenomenon of the era before World War II, persisted with relative vigor long past into the 1960s.

Another way we conclude that the data are merely suggestive is from records kept of police brutality by the Justice Department. One common feature of the peonage system was the close cooperation of county sheriffs and justices of the peace, who worked with plantation owners to administer the system in a way that would ensure an adequate supply of labor for agricultural tasks. Police brutality established the control necessary for law enforcement officials to perform their function. And yet the data show that of the 461 cases of police brutality against Blacks reported to the Department of Justice in the period 1958 to 1960, there were no referrals by state authorities, and that most (83 percent) of the referrals were made to the Federal Bureau of Investigation.[34] This is illustrative of the leniency in the relationship of state police officials and the FBI in such cases. Moreover, data were apparently not received by the FBI for states such as Alabama, Georgia, Mississippi, North Carolina, South Carolina, Tennessee, Texas, or Louisiana.

But quite apart from a review of the data involved in this heinous practice, the point here is that degree to which Black people were dehumanized, in some respects perhaps even more than in the era of slavery, reaching a nadir that made it possible for seemingly ordinary whites to perform unspeakable acts against the body of Blacks. The festivities that often attracted people to a lynching made it a community event, especially in some small towns. This mood of celebration defines how far outside of the pale of society and democratic rights Blacks existed. But it also raises questions about the Christian civility of those who participated, especially given that lynchings were committed after Sunday morning church services.

A pamphlet published in 1901, written by the distinguished Black journalist John Edward Bruce, that reviewed and analyzed the record of lynching from 1893 to 1901 was entitled by the publisher *The Blood Red Record: Review of the Horrible Lynching and Burning of Negroes by Civilized White Men in the United States*. One wonders whether the reference to "civilized white men" in this manner was a defense of the barbarity they visited upon Blacks or a continued assertion of the status of whites in that time. Rather, it seems to convey his shock that this practice was perpetuated by the most upstanding citizens in some communities.

Disgust at the capacity of human beings to perpetrate such cruelty was felt not only by Blacks, but by whites as well. For instance, John Jay Chapman, a writer and Harvard Law School graduate, whose father, Henry Grafton Chapman, was president of the New York Stock Exchange, became involved in the campaign to bring justice to those who lynched Zach Walker in Coatesville, Pennsylvania, in August 1911. He had read in the *New York Tribune* that an apparent exchange of gunfire had left a white guard of the Worth Steel Company dead and a bullet wound in Walker's head. He was taken to the local hospital, but a mob came and dragged him out and set his body on fire. For hours it burned until only the torso was left, which was kicked around by children.[35] Since the NAACP investigated and discovered the names of those responsible, but the authorities never charged them with the crime, Chapman went to Coatesville out of conscience to do penance for all whites. For him this included not just those who committed the crime but those who watched as well. The method he devised was to make a public speech and cause citizens of the town to think about what had happened and perhaps correct this horrible event that had rippled through the country. Like Ida Wells-Barnett, he noted the appearance of crowds, but went on to say what he believed was the cause:

> The failure of the prosecution in this case, in all such cases, is only proof of the magnitude of the guilt, and of the awful fact that everyone shares in it. As I read the newspaper accounts of the scene enacted here in Coatesville a year ago, I seemed to get a glimpse into the unconscious soul of this country. I seemed to be looking into the heart of a criminal.
>
> The trouble has come down to us out of the past. The only reason that slavery is wrong is that it is cruel and makes men cruel and leaves them cruel. A nation cannot practice a course of inhuman crime for three hundred years and then suddenly throw off the effects of it. . . .
>
> On the day of the calamity those people in the automobiles came by the hundred and watched it—and did nothing. On the next morning, the newspapers spread the news and spread the paralysis until the whole country seemed to be watching this awful murder.[36]

This cruelty feeling of enmity against Blacks that accompanied their treatment during slavery was meted out, not only against individuals, but against entire Black communities. The so-called Red Summer of 1919 has been viewed as a special year when uppity Black soldiers coming back from World War I who attempted to assert their manhood rights were brutally relegated to "their place" in the social order by the use of force by white mobs. Riots against Blacks occurred in Little Rock, Harlem, Washington, DC, Baltimore, New Orleans, Chicago, Knoxville, Charleston, Omaha, and many other cities. Fueled by the same allegations that inspired lynching, whites accused Blacks of sex crimes or other fiendish acts against whites. Black former soldiers in Washington, DC, for example, who had fought in the First Separate

Battalion in France were attacked by four hundred whites in a period of violence that lasted four days. This violent and brutal period lasted much beyond 1919, in a pattern that carried on into the 1920s and 1930s.

For example, Black tenant farmers in Arkansas organized the Progressive Farmers and Householders Union in 1919 in order to protect themselves from exploitation and, as James Cassedy, a founder, said, "to advance the intellectual, material, moral, spiritual and financial interests of the Negro race."[37] In 1919, the Union was destroyed in the "Elaine Massacre" in Phillips County, Arkansas. White sheriffs and vigilantes from nearby counties attacked and killed an estimated one hundred people, including the targeted union officials and members.

In the infamous Tulsa riot of 1921, whites attacked and destroyed Greenwood, the Black neighborhood, including its commercial center known as "Black Wall Street" over a false report that Dick Rowland, who worked in the Drexel Building downtown, had tried to rape a white female elevator operator.[38] When Blacks of Greenwood marched to the courthouse to prevent Rowland from being lynched, a full-scale race riot occurred. It resulted in the death of over three hundred Blacks, the wounding of seven hundred, driving many from the area and obliterating the commercial center of the Black community.[39]

A similar fate was to befall the Black community of Rosewood, Florida, which was attacked in 1923, leaving eight dead and scores of injured in days of violence. The reign of terror did not end even with the coming of World War II, as race riots occurred in Detroit in 1943 and also in Beaumont, Texas, and Harlem.[40]

The brutal violence against Blacks was articulated as a theory of white power, not privilege, not merely white supremacy, but a raw and unmitigated power that gave them the ability and the right to destroy Blacks. An illustration of the intellectual basis of this mood was seen in the 1897 lynching of "Click" Mitchell in Urbana, Ohio. Comments about this murder were carried in several newspapers of the day:

> The state can do nothing to those persons who informally executed the Negro at Urbana. It has not the power; it derives such power as it has from the people, and the people determined in other tribunal than that which the law creates that for his heinous offense the Negro should suffer. Sympathy with the Negro, condemnation of what may be called a mob will be lost.

There can be no punishment of those people. The thing is impossible.[41]

Another commentator said:

There is a feeling in the white man's mind that whoever of the race not his own who attempts to defy this race instinct, and violently upset the physical line which nature has established, does by that act take his life in hand. Death must be his portion, whether legally or illegally matters not; and from that decree there is no appeal.[42]

This is a revealing window into the kind of humanity that allowed and indeed encouraged a sector of white society to become involved in the destruction of Black people; a dismissal of the line between legality and illegality in a celebration of the fact that right lay in the overwhelming power of the white cultural consensus, beyond the dream of democracy or racial civility. It is this history of the twentieth century that has been lost to memory and that the civil rights movement interrupted. In that context, this movement can be considered to have, in some cases, broken the final linkages of Blacks to the old system of slavery, a dynamic that occurred as a monumental challenge to lynch-law rule that happened not in 1865, but in the second civil war of the 1960s.

Conclusion

Although the first half of the twentieth century was a period of despotic oppression for Blacks, this treatment nevertheless existed in the context of a forward movement, especially in the North. There Blacks were making strides in education, the professions, and in generally enjoying some of the fruits of a semiliberated people. What made the twentieth century appear to be more democratic for Blacks in the United States in comparison with those in South Africa is that there was a brief moment in time that fostered the Thirteenth, Fourteenth, and Fifteenth Amendments to the Constitution, which gave Blacks and their allies who fought the Civil War to preserve the Union the vision to bring about a unified nation based on the absence of slavery and second-class citizenship. About this comparison, George Frederickson has said that

> the Civil War, Reconstruction and the promise of equal citizenship in the 14th and 15th amendments, made for significant differences in the long-range prospects and expectations of blacks in the two societies—African Americans had the Constitution potentially on their side and South Africans did not.[43]

Therefore, this reality developed in the nineteenth century, shaped the character of the grand narrative of race relations in the twentieth century as an encounter between Blacks and whites where Blacks were seeking to bring substance to the promise of equality in the Constitution in ways that would become the predicate for the expansion of rights in society. The hope was that this would change the paradigm of racial hierarchy and the practices of racial discrimination and oppression and achieve the equality that was the dream of those held in bondage, as the antithesis of slavery.

CHAPTER SIX

⤝

The Grand Narrative and the
Legacy of Modern Subordination

IN THE PREVIOUS CHAPTER, THE "GRAND NARRATIVE" ends around World War II, but after the war, America entered into a period of social reconstruction that included the civil rights movement and laws designed to affect that narrative. The question this chapter raises is whether the focus of that effort to achieve equality and the longevity of that struggle to the present era has achieved the desired results. The fact that it has not done so provides one of the strongest predicates for the consideration of reparations.

The process of slavery and postslavery subordination sealed the nature of the opportunity for Blacks and their place in social structure for some time to come. To this end, strategies were devised to end subordination, such as racial integration, the civil rights laws, the Great Society economic program, and political empowerment. And while the accumulation of these strategies have made a significant contribution to equalizing the income of a segment of Blacks and opened up their access to some of the material resources of society, the comparative social structure is still largely in place. These strategies have been crippled to the point of defeat in the twenty-first century.

Racism has foiled the attempts to effect a set of liberal strategies of integration, affirmative action, race dialogues, and so forth, to conquer inequality, and thus it still shapes the opportunity structure of America, determining the life chances of Black Americans and other peoples of color. At all ends, it is possible to conclude either that the evidence of racism has escaped societal leaders such that they are oblivious to its pervasiveness, or that they are dedicated to an ideological direction of strengthening the legal and practical regime of white racial privilege. Racism has changed to the point that many of its manifestations are not obvious, but there are still very visible aspects, so effective as to constitute modern "Black Codes." The Black Codes of the nineteenth century were instituted by many states as instruments of social control of Blacks after the Civil War. This period gave way to the vilest forms of oppression, as limits were set on Blacks in every direction in scenarios that marked, in some cases, the reinstitution of slavery. In the twenty-first century, the attempt to reinstitute a regime of social control by the conservative movement is taking place amid the gains made possible by the "second civil war," that is, the civil rights movement of the 1960s, and threatens to limit the material progress of the Black middle class and to intensify the poverty of poorer Blacks.

Frank Raines, former chief executive of the Fannie Mae Corporation, a national quasi-governmental housing finance agency, in a speech to the National Urban League in August 2001, presented a picture of what Black equality would look like, in comparison to their present status. Blacks would have:

3 million more homeowners with $780 billion more in equity;
700,000 more jobs than in 1991;
$190 billion more in income (or a 56 percent pay raise);
$1 trillion more in wealth;
31 billionaires;
2 million more high school graduates;
2 million more college degrees;
500,000 master degrees;
180,000 more doctorates
2.5 million more Blacks insured; and 620,000 more children;
3 million more households with computers; and internet
     access;
1.5 million more automobiles;
33,000 fewer juveniles in detention; 600,000 fewer Blacks
     overall;
600,000 more businesses with $2.7 trillion more in revenue;
62 Fortune 500 CEOs; with 590 more board members;
approximately 1,500 more congresspersons since 1789;
14 Supreme Court Justices since 1790;
5 presidents since 1790.[1]

This extensive list gives us a proportional perspective on what African Americans would have achieved without having been prohibited by the fetters of oppression. The list has confirmation from another authoritative source. The National Urban League, the oldest and largest African American social service organization, issues an annual report known as *The State of Black America,* and in 2004, it began to structure, as a part of that report, an "Equality Index." The index measures the well-being of Blacks relative to whites in the following categories:

Economics (wages and wealth differential)	56 percent
Education (educational achievement)	76 percent
Health (health gaps)	78 percent
Social justice (equality under the law)	73 percent
Civic engagement (voter registration, volunteerism, etc.)	108 percent

The overall average difference in the quality of life measured by the NUL is 73 percent.[2] Thus, the fact of Black progress is that while Blacks' status has grown, it has not achieved that of whites. We will discuss why that is the situation in the early part of the twenty-first century.

There is an interesting similarity between Blacks in the United States and Black South Africans in that there is a grand division of function between the political and economic aspects of life. Blacks in South Africa have achieved political dominance insofar as their numbers have allowed them to gain access to the political system and to acquire the majority of seats in the national, regional, and local legislatures. Whites, however, control the economy: the industrial companies, the financial institutions, the services, the technological sector, in short, the commanding heights in society that produce the things and services that determine the material quality of life.

In many American cities and counties a similar division exists between Blacks and whites. Where Blacks are the dominant population, they have elected Blacks to school boards, city and county councils, mayorships, and so on. These leaders have in turn appointed Blacks to high-level positions as fire chiefs, heads of police departments, cabinet officers and and other top administrative posts (even though they are also elected, one exception is often judges who are subject to the appointment of higher officials in the state). In these circumstances, Blacks essentially dominate the political systems, and citizens look to them for the services that flow from government. In these majority Black locales, Whites have recently fallen out of power—within a generation or two. But in their former dispensation, they worked with the white business class to create the social, economic, and political infrastructure. Now out of control of political offices, whites retain control over the financial sector. Blacks are functionally excluded from either significant influence over, or control of, this sector.

This division of function often marks the character of the politics in such places, where an often unstated but persistent racial conflict occurs. That is, the decisions of political systems dominated by Blacks are contested by whites who control the newspapers, banks, malls, and other private economic interests. Many of these financial interests are linked to national networks, which have further linkages to national politics and economic interests and even to global commerce as well. They give whites enormous bargaining power over issues such as local development and governmental fiscal decisions through quasi-governmental organizations such as chambers of commerce, zoning boards, development committees, and the like.

Since Blacks lack economic resources, sometimes even to finance their campaigns for elective office, whites are able to influence these elections and the decisions that flow from the elective bodies, thus setting limits on what is achievable through the exercise of Black political power alone. The irony of this is that the necessary interface between political and economic power means that whites, though out of political power, still have the ability to influence what occurs in that sector, making them primary political actors in any case. Thus, although Blacks in each instance have gained a measure of political access, they are still subject to the control of whites. This makes suspect the achievement of the nominal Black equality and self-determination by this means.

The question often asked is, why aren't Blacks able to compete? The answer to this has always been understood as the foundation of the decision of the Supreme Court in the cases involving *Brown v. Board of Education* in 1954. The NAACP was in the decision successful because it attacked the "separate but equal" logic of the *Plessy* decision of 1896, by showing that the provision of separate facilities for Blacks in the various fields of life was inherently unequal—largely because the quality of such facilities mirrored the stark difference in the socioeconomic status of Blacks in American society. Therefore, if the Court recognized this in the 1950s and continued, on this basis, to promote integrated education for the next fifty years, when did this logic become invalid? In fact, the continuation of inequality in the socioeconomic status of each race today makes the failure of integration and the enhancement of racial isolation revive the disparity that drove the *Brown* decision.

Thus, the principal reason Blacks are unable to compete is that they have not had the opportunities to amass wealth through incomes alone—even by having substantial and stable incomes over a long period of time. A second reason, however, is because Blacks are victims on an individual level, and therefore weakened individually . Thus the whole group is weakened, not only by the overall dearth of economic resources, but by the absence of *widespread* resources in the group. This weakness happens not only through the passive relations of whites with Blacks, but through the active daily intervention in every sphere of life where Blacks are overwhelmed by the competition and victimized in the process.

The previous chapter ended with the thought that the major reason for the difference in the fortunes of Black South Africans and Black Americans in the twentieth century was that different constitutional systems afforded the latter a different avenue to pursue social justice. And although the first twenty years of the twentieth century were marked with a lawless period of disrespect for constitutional equality between Black and whites and fostered a pernicious reign of terror against Blacks in America, a series of legal victories slowly opened up a fissure in the pattern of complete racial segregation, one that was widened by World War II and its aftermath.

The progress made by Blacks during this period led to strategies designed to achieve Black equality in society—a goal, however, that should be evaluated against the freedom and self-determination that were the goals of many Black thinkers after slavery and well into the Harlem Renaissance period. These strategies, however, proved deceptive, not because of conspiracies that led to their demise, but in the main through the major conspiracy of the power of the white community to limit the opportunities for Blacks in every conceivable area of American life.

The Failure of the Paternal Restitution

The limitation of opportunities for Blacks was strongly suggested by Carter G. Woodson, who in his seminal observations on the Black leadership of the early twentieth century saw that Blacks had no "vision"—that they had no control, that in their education and social life they were largely "mimicking" the behavior set for them by whites. Even more, although they pretended to the exercise of leadership, they led in the direction that whites wanted them to go.[3] With this in mind, Woodson's frustration appeared to be that Blacks were largely acquiescent in their social condition of stark segregation and did not plan ways to break out of the mold established for them by white power. I would argue that Woodson's view was largely correct (and correlated by individual scholars such as Ralph Bunche's observations on Black leadership, especially southern Black leadership in the 1930s). Although he died in 1950, much before the period of revolt against the dominant oppression of the white community's leadership, Woodson's assessment has since then become more relevant.

The "Great Society": An Incomplete Paradigm of Restitution

There have been many modest attempts at resolving what Gunnar Myrdal called in his classic work, *An American Dilemma,* a concept that defined race relations in America. Most recently, the Great Society programs and the civil rights laws of the 1960s built the framework that largely guided the formal approach for the past thirty-five years. I will suggest that these approaches, though well intended, have largely failed to provide equality and will not do so, as long as sufficient personal resources are not provided to African Americans within a context of their control and direction.

For a key to what was intended by the Great Society, we should investigate President Lyndon Johnson's paradigm. In his commencement speech at Howard University on June 4, 1965, anticipating passage of the Voting Rights Act, he remarked:

> Freedom is the right to share, share fully and equally, in American society—to vote, to hold a job, to enter a public place, to go to school. It is the right to be treated in every part of our national life as a person equal in dignity and promise to all others.
>
> You do not take a person who, for years, has been hobbled by chains and liberate him, bring him up to the starting line of a race and then say, "you are free to compete with all the others," and still justly believe that you have been completely fair.[4]

Looking at Johnson's paradigm with a keener vision, although he posed freedom as sharing "fully" and "equally" in American society, his enabling set of propositions, "to vote, to hold a job, to enter a public place, and to go to school," appear related to the opportunity to have equal access and status to public accommodations, but not to broach the fullness of that opportunity, most of which is couched in the realm of private production, wealth, privilege, and leadership.

When President Johnson gave us this paradigm, which referred to the impossibility of expecting a Black man who had spent his life with his hands tied behind his back, though now untied, to run the race of life as successfully as a white person who had always been fetter-free, it should be recognized as well-meaning, though also deeply flawed. It was his attempt to rationalize the passage of the 1964 Civil Rights Act, which prohibited discrimination in public accommodations, and it also gave impetus to his legislative program known as the Great Society. In effect, however, it would provide only partial restitution to Blacks because these programs were all designed to help Blacks attain access to jobs that—if everything worked out fine—would provide only relative paycheck equality and small business parity. However, the resources were never fully delivered, even to accomplish this, since much of the funding appropriated *did not flow to the Black community directly, but to corporations for job training, and so forth, and to other services often provided by organizations controlled by whites.* Thus, only the wages provided should be calculated in the sums that some use to tally up the government funds provided to Blacks since that time.

Integration: The Ultimate Solution Destroyed

Originally, the strategy of integration was tied to the existing socioeconomic paradigm of strict spatial, social, political, and economic segregation in which African Americans existed. The first aspect of this originating strategy was bounded in the scientific approaches of those scholars who were interested in race relations in the early part of the twentieth century and who conceptualized "status inconsistency" as a major problem. The thought was that if the status of the disparate groups within society could be equalized, this would constitute the basis upon which they could be integrated into society.

Notwithstanding the fact that this was a naive concept because of the problematic of culture and the dynamics of majority-minority group relations, it became a practical reality to early civil rights leaders, whose people faced real barriers to their social advancement through the restriction of Black people to a tightly segregated society and their exclusion from the mainstream. The practical solution for such a condition was to break down the barriers to entry into society and participation in every facet of American life; thus integration came to be the practical concept that described this objective. By the 1930s, it was firmly planted in the rhetoric of the speeches of major civil rights leaders such as Walter White and James Weldon Johnson of the NAACP.

At one level, the definition of integration was meant to be the desegregation of social facilities of all kinds, including social relations necessary to participate fully in American life. At another level, however, integration was set in a philosophy of the American dream and, thus, held out the possibility that if it could occur, it would give African Americans access to the material elements and political participation necessary to be identified as full Americans. Thus, the acquisition of the bourgeois value system of Americanness was to be the end result of the process made possible by integration. These concepts restate Philip M. Hauser's definition: "integration is viewed as more than mere desegregation; rather, it is seen as social interaction, effective communication, and a sharing in activities that fill one's life. In this sense, integration is a social process that may be considered one form of acculturation— social interaction embracing members of diverse racial as well as cultural backgrounds."[5]

These ideas became the objective of most phases of the civil rights movement: in the 1940s it was expressed in the push for integration in the war industries by A. Philip Randolph's March on Washington in 1941, the push of the NAACP for integrated education that led to the *Brown* decision of 1954, the development of the southern civil rights movement that called for the integration of public facilities, and the explosive demands of the 1960s for integration of every facet of American life.

St. Clair Drake assessed the progress of integration in Chicago when he suggested that the "controlled integration" of some Blacks into housing projects in order to maintain "racial balance" and the integration of the "Negro middle class" into various aspects of American life had the effect of intensifying the racial concentration of other Blacks in the ghettoes and the "creaming-off" of the middle class. He concluded, "This would result in a kind of victimization of the Negro masses which would be permanent unless the conditions of life for the lower classes were drastically changed."[6] Given the withdrawal of federal support for many low-income peoples and their neighborhoods, the process of integration by skimming has become implicated in the deteriorating socioeconomic condition of the Black masses.

The expectations upon which the struggle for integration was based—which were necessary for it to work—were rarely stated, but might be extrapolated as the following:

1. Whites would accept the moral rightness of integration based on the clear demonstration of the past harm done to Blacks from slavery and racial discrimination, based upon shared notions of the redemptive myth of Judeo-Christian religion and the objective of liberal democracy.
2. Thus, they would assume that the policy steps enacted from this acceptance were legitimate and would be implemented long enough and in ways that would permit integration to occur.

The integration strategy, however, was challenged strongly by the emergence of the Black Power movement in the 1960s as inadequate to achieve the comprehensive objectives of the Black community. Ultimately, the integration movement and its instruments of implementation were dependent upon the acceptance of whites and the governmental structure they controlled. Black Power challenged Blacks to depend upon the autonomous generation of resources and legitimacy through group consciousness and mobilization.

History followed the course of integration because of the persuasive power of the civil rights movement with its appeal to the moral conscience of America, its use of normal institutional methods of social change, and its tentative successes at integrating individuals into various aspects of American life. History did not, however, legitimize the objectives of the Black Power movement because of its threatening challenge to racism within the social order, the notion of the hypocrisy of the application of the tenets of democracy, and the perception that it was intertwined with violent urban rebellions.

Nevertheless, it is also clear that it had had an impact because the political objective of Black leaders began to change. Speaking of the responsibility of the Black intellectual, Kenneth Clark, a strong proponent of the integration strategy, said,

> [R]acial integration in America must mean more than the right of the Negro to share equally in the moral emptiness, hypocrisy, conformity, and despair that characterize so much of American life. To be truly meaningful, integration must provide the Negro with the opportunity, the right, and the obligation to contribute to our society and resurgence of ethnical substance, moral strength, and general integrity. Specifically, the Negro can contribute to our society an ability to face and accept the fullness of life and the ability to dare the depths of life and enjoyment and even suffering and pain unafraid. In an integrated society the Negro can help to free our society from the tantalizing frustration that is its worship of materialism. The Negro can help our society to accept the totality that is man with minimum conflict, shame, guilt, or apology.[7]

Martin Luther King, Jr. often spoke of the ethical rightness of integration. King distinguished between integration and desegregation, the latter being negative and short-ranged, leading to "physical proximity without spiritual affinity." Integration, however, "is genuine intergroup, interpersonal doing" and, as "the ultimate goal of our national community," is the "commitment to the democratic dream."[8] Though desegregation laws should be enforced, true integration would be achieved only when all people were "willingly obedient to the unenforceable obligations" of harmonious social interaction.[9]

Nevertheless, at the end of his career, King began to confront the internal development challenges of the Black community. In this, he considered that the elimination of poverty within poor Black communities was a more complex task than merely integrating housing, buses, or lunch counters.[10] The immorality of the Vietnam War meant that Blacks might be integrating into a "burning house" that exhibited immoral values, materialism, and the neglect of poor people. For both reasons, therefore, he believed that the original objective of integration was insufficient, nor could it be easily achieved because of resistance by whites.

In any case, the integration model marginally triumphed, and the internal developmental agenda fostered by the Black Power movement has yet to be achieved. Moreover, the prescience of St. Clair Drake's vision has been confirmed in that the integration process, focused on upward mobility for the Black middle class, has resulted in the loss of autonomous power through the weakening of the collective Black community's resource structure. This has occurred more obviously in the social disorganization of the Black community, illustrated by the adoption of harmful and antihumanistic values by many youths.

What has now challenged even this modest application of the integration model is the destruction of its underpinnings by the steady growth of the white resistance movement of the 1960s to a full-fledged white nationalist movement that has seized policy power. It has proposed or enacted laws that accomplished the following:

Challenged the access of Blacks to continued upward mobility by proposing wholesale reduction of the supportive power of government and the elimination of many of its programs for social development

Attacked legal rights, especially in the civil rights area, that facilitated access to employment, education, and relief from white supremacy operative in many aspects of Black life

Profoundly changed public attitudes toward the moral basis of the debt of society for the subordinate status of Blacks, shifting toward a perception of the immorality of Blacks for participation in crime, the drug culture, teenage pregnancy, welfare dependence, and so on.

The Clinton Race Initiative

In January 1997, President Clinton initiated a yearlong dialogue on race with the observation that the racial demography of the United States was changing and that Americans had to learn how to live together in a multiracial society of the twenty-first century. He pointed out that 73 percent of America was white, 11 percent Hispanic, 12 percent Black, 4 percent Asian/Pacific islander, and 0.7 percent American Indian, but that by the year 2050, the white population would be reduced to only 53 percent, while people of color would increase to 47 percent. Although he stated that he had begun this dialogue in an atmosphere where there was not urgent conflict over race, he was badly mistaken in his estimation of the racial divide and the reasons for its persistence.

In a speech at the University of California, San Diego, in June 1997, Clinton posed the question of whether America would become a "multiracial democracy," noting that the Kerner Commission warned that America could become two Americas, one white, one Black, separate and unequal. He continued:

> Today, we face a difference choice. Will we become not two, but many Americas, separate, unequal and isolated? Or will we draw strength from all our people and our ancient faith in the quality of human dignity, to become the world's first truly multi-racial democracy? That is the unfinished work of our time, to lift the burden of race and redeem the promise of America.[11]

Black Americans welcomed the initiative as necessary, but were skeptical about its adequacy, since the roots of the racial divide were so great. They raised many questions about the thrust of the initiative; many believed much more was needed, not just an apology for slavery, but a dialogue about racism, and economic reparations for the past injustices.

In June 1997 a Race Initiative Advisory Board was established by the president, with seven members of various descriptions, lacking either a white female or a Native American member. The group was headed by distinguished Black historian John Hope Franklin, and it had the following mandate:

> Promote national dialogue on race issues
> Increase the nation's understanding of the history and future of race relations
> Identify and create plans to calm racial tension and promote increased opportunity for all Americans
> Address crime and the administration of justice

The board held meetings around the country to stimulate a dialogue on areas such as employment, higher education, and health. Its final report to the president contains a modest set of recommendations, including the following:

Creation of a permanent body, which would be known as the President's Council for One America, to promote harmony and dialogue among the nation's racial and ethnic groups

Development of a government program to keep the public informed about race in America

A presidential call to arms to leaders of government and the private sector to make racial reconciliation a reality

Engagement of youth leaders in an effort to build bridges among the races

Reactions to the report, even from "right of center" intellectuals, indicate that the advisory committee squandered an opportunity to make bolder recommendations that would capture the attention of the nation.[12] The committee, tightly controlled by the White House, was prevented from entertaining many serious topics, such as the configuration of white privilege, the damage by the white conservative movement to public policy affecting peoples of color, the degree of racism in American society, the relationship of the past to the present, the relevance of an apology for slavery, the contribution of reparations to improving the socioeconomic conditions of Blacks, the dimensions of multiculturalism (in education, employment, social life, etc.) and its contribution to the goal of "One America." Moreover, committee members indicated that they did not have the time to cover many areas pertinent to the racial crisis.

The root of the failure lay in the expectation that the Advisory Board would both consider the vexing questions involved in the racial problem and make recommendations that would be considered seriously by Congress. This was a reasonable assumption, but perhaps naive in the context of the rise of a radical conservatism that controlled Congress. Moreover, action is something that Clinton could have proposed himself, rather than propose a mere dialogue. His own approach to this problem—a dialogic approach as the least that could be done that might bring the races together—was itself an admission that the problem was beyond dialogue.

Therefore, I argue here that the liberal regime that has pursued the goal of equality has, at the beginning of the twenty-first century, failed. The instruments of that failure were inherent in the lack of a radical vision for social, political, and economic change by the managers of society, who assented to the destruction of these very measures by allowing both the continuation of racial discrimination and raw racial oppression, meanwhile joining the conservative movement to reconfirm their cultural hegemony through the promotion of conservative public policies. Below I summarize some of the deficits faced by Blacks as a result of the long postslavery period and the failure of the recent policy to mitigate the essential status of Blacks relative to whites.

Modern Black Codes: The Continuing Structure of Subordination

Restricting Black Mobility

Blacks were nominally involved in the modernizing phase of America that was a product of the westward expansion into new territories, sharing in the development of new industry and the building of an economic system from the wealth they helped to produce. Slavery kept them largely bonded not only to the plantation, but to the region of the South, the least modern region in the nation.

The fact that slavery occurred most predominantly in the South meant that 90 percent of the Blacks who lived there did not have the benefit of the metropolitan influences that liberalized the nation, such as compulsory education and participation in industrial and small enterprises, which occurred in the urban areas, not on the plantation. Blacks did not begin to move out of the South in large numbers until the twentieth century, when 750,000 left in the first large wave in the 1920s. So the present distribution of the Black population is relatively recent (see appendix table A7.) In 1910, only 27 percent of Blacks lived in urban areas, reaching 49 percent by 1940, and 62 percent by 1950.[13]

Slavery, therefore, delayed and inhibited the rapid modernization and acculturation of Blacks and their access to resources with which they could have developed their communities and themselves. And although Blacks later began to take advantage of the industrialization in the North and West in larger numbers, the restriction on their geographical mobility was a decided factor in the comparable advantage of whites, who prospered much earlier as free laborers in the automobile, railway, steel, and other industries, and in the educational systems that would lead to professional growth and development and the more rapid accumulation of wealth.

This demographic pattern has profoundly contributed to the concentration of Blacks in the largest cities of the country. Even though there has been substantial suburbanization of Blacks, the concentration of Blacks in the inner cities has resulted in patterns of racial segregation consistent with those that existed prior to the civil rights movement. Thus, in the 1990 census, Blacks were concentrated in such cities as Cleveland (87 percent), Dayton (79 percent), Pittsburgh (73 percent), Buffalo (71 percent), Newark (71 percent), Boston (69 percent), Indianapolis (68 percent), Cincinnati (66 percent), Fort Wayne (65 percent), Columbus, Ohio (64 percent), Grand Rapids (61 percent), Joliet, Illinois (61 percent), Providence, Rhode Island (60 percent), Hartford (58 percent), and Rochester, New York (54 percent).[14]

At the same time, these high concentrations of Blacks virtually assured that there would also be high concentrations of poverty. William Wilson found that in the 1970s, the number of census tracts with rates of poverty of at least 20 percent, increased by 20 percent, and while white poverty tracts increased by 24 percent, Black poverty tracts increased by 148 percent. Moreover, the concentration of Blacks in the central cities has been correlated with a number of social problems, from the facility of "redlining," to health problems, low levels of educational achievement, high levels of environmental pollution, drug markets with the attendant targeted policing and violence, loss of jobs, and high levels of poverty.[15]

One of the results of slavery is analyzed by Benjamin Bobo as the "locking effect" in that the exclusion of Africans in America from acquisition of open land and their ghettoization had disastrous economic consequences because it prevented them from participation in the market for land and housing, prime economic resources. In fact, those inside the ghetto are excluded from favorable economic rates on insurance of all kinds, high-quality schools, good health care, and employment, since the best facilities of all kinds are located at a distance.

Land Loss

One of the greatest barriers to Black progress was the loss of their land. In fact, some Blacks did receive "forty acres and a mule" just after slavery. In June 1865, General Sherman, who was in charge of the southern theater of the war, gave about forty thousand former slaves four hundred thousand acres of land in Mississippi, divided into forty-acre plots, but some months later, he was persuaded to rescind the titles given to the former slaves and return the land to white owners. Bobo has calculated that if Blacks had been able to hold on to this land, valued at seven hundred dollars per acre, in 1990 farm prices every Black would have four hundred acres and 550 mules![16]

With the protection of the Union army gone from the South, there was wholesale theft of the land owned by Blacks, through intimidation, bureaucratic sleight-of-hand, and outright violence. The latter came to be known as "whitecapping," most often practiced between 1900 and 1929, in which vigilante nightriders took vulnerable land at night by forcible removal. Indeed, Raymond Winbush suggests that a significant number of those Blacks who were lynched were killed so that their land could be seized.[17] In the 1990s, the Federation of Southern Cooperatives established an emergency fund because of the rapid loss rate of Black farmland, finding that the 15 million acres in 1910 owned by Blacks had fallen to just 2.5 million. In addition, Black farmers were engaged in suite against the U.S. Department of Agriculture, which had systematically aided white farmers and participated in the disfranchisement of Black farmers by denying them credit, loans and grants, skill training, and other economic resources.[18]

Illiteracy and Education

Slavery did not place a value on educated Africans, but on their physical labor. In fact, most slave owners found that education was antithetical to the control that the institution demanded. Blacks suffered tremendously in obtaining access to education to become as acculturated as other immigrants to English ways. Nevertheless, after slavery, Blacks placed a high value on learning to read and write English, such that between 1890 and 1910 the illiteracy rate dropped from 61 percent to 33 percent. Yet the educational deficit still was serious. While in the nineteenth century one could find among "free" Blacks some who had not only gone to high school, but to Harvard and Oberlin, for the general population it was vastly different, since the plantation system required children to work alongside their parents.[19]

Thus, by the middle of the eighteenth century, only 10 percent of the 3.5 million Blacks five to nineteen years old attended school with any regularity. By 1890, 58 percent of white youths were enrolled in school, compared to half that rate among Blacks. As late as 1940, only 11 percent of the Black population had completed four years of high school. At that same time, 40 percent of whites had done so. At a similar period, only 2 percent of Blacks had completed four years of college or more, as opposed to 7 percent of whites. Even today, educational equality between Blacks and whites, as measured by high school or college completion rates, has not been achieved.

Appendix table A8 shows the distribution of higher education. The data indicate that higher education among Blacks has not reached "equality" since it does not match their representation among the the population (12.3 percent) in any category of degree. Parenthetically, this means that inasmuch as whites are 75.5 percent of the population, the decreases in white graduation rates at all levels should be seen as a function of increases in the nonresident alien access to American higher education, rather than increases by Blacks or Hispanics, given the relatively low numbers shown in the table. Thus, while Blacks were 95 percent as likely as whites to complete four years of high school in the 1990s, they were only half as likely to complete four years of college. Both numbers decreased from the 1990 census, but the college completion rates decreased more due to the downturn in the economy and the rising college and university tuition.[20]

Housing Discrimination

In 1989, a study of thirty-eight hundred realty offices located in twenty-five major cities, conducted by the Urban Institute and Syracuse University for the U.S. Department of Housing and Urban Development, found a systematic pattern of high levels of discrimination.[21] Blacks experienced a 56 percent rate of discrimination in renting housing and a 59 percent rate in the purchase of housing, such that 60–90 percent of the housing units shown to whites were not available to Blacks. When the Bush administration was presented with the evidence contained in this study, it attempted to repress its release and took no action.[22] But nearly thirty-five years after the Fair Housing Act was passed in 1968, the Department of Housing and Urban Development received over twenty-five thousand complains of housing discrimination, an increase of three thousand over the 1999 level.[23] One victim said: "It makes you feel like you are not a person, that if you are black you do not deserve a home."[24] A study by Gregory Squires indicated that while whites believed that the problem of housing discrimination had been solved, "almost every indicator contradicts that."[25] His study found that 33 percent of Blacks say they were unable to acquire their first choice in housing in the suburbs, compared to 20 percent of white counterparts.[26]

Mortgage lending. A study by the Federal Reserve Bank of Boston (1992) of forty-five hundred applicants involving 131 lenders found a 170 percent greater loan rejection rate for Blacks and other minorities than for whites. It said: "for the same imperfections, whites seem to enjoy a general presumption of credit-worthiness that Black or Hispanic applicants do not" and that "lenders seem to be more willing to overlook flaws for white applicants than for minority applicants."[27] This confirms a survey of 1,521 households by the National Mortgage Association (NMA) that suggests that Blacks pay more and consequently sacrifice more (because of lower average incomes) than other groups for home ownership.[28]

In the NMA survey referred to above, Whites were reported to believe, by 57 to 33 percent, that minority purchasers have the same chance as themselves of getting a home they can afford. Yet actions by the Justice Department against banking institutions such as Chevy Chase Bank in the Washington, DC area, the Barnett Banks in Miami, Florida, and others for discrimination in banking practices—such as the paucity of loans and banking facilities in the case of Chevy Chase or lending bias in the case of Barnett—support the accumulated data in this regard.[29]

In July 1995 another study by the Chicago Federal Reserve Bank, based on 1990 mortgage data collected by the Boston Federal Reserve Bank, likewise found disparate patterns of lending. However, unlike the other studies, which alleged the probability that racism was partially responsible, this report found that "cultural affinity" between white bank loan officers and white customers explained the difference, rather than a negative attitude toward Blacks. This is appears to be an attempt to change the terms of debate away from racial discrimination.[30]

Home insurance. A study of insurance policies written by insurance agents in twelve cities and the District of Columbia in 1991 by ACORN, a social action group, found that inner-city Blacks were quoted prices for home mortgage insurance as much as two-and-one-half times the normal rate for whites. A separate study of five cities found that, perhaps as a consequence, Black neighborhoods were 48 percent less insured than comparable white neighborhoods.[31]

Economic Condition

Slavery also established the structural distance in the economic status of Blacks and whites. Between Black slaves, who earned no money, and free Blacks, who earned very little, the composite was low earnings in comparison to whites.

By 1947, census data revealed that the relative median family income was as follows:

Blacks earned $3,200
Whites earned $7,000.

This pattern of 1:2 Black/white ratio of earnings has been substantially the same over time. For example, the ratio in 1947 was similar, at 49 percent of white earnings for Blacks. For the next twenty years the ratio only increased by ten percentage points, remaining relatively constant for the next twenty-five years.

The earnings level also reflected the kind of jobs open to Blacks. By 1940, one-third of Blacks were farmworkers, and others (40 percent) were concentrated in service jobs or low-pay industrial jobs. In 2000, one in two Blacks earned less than twenty-five thousand dollars annually, while only one in three whites did. In addition, Black household net worth amounts to $7,500, while white household net worth amounts to $84,000.[32]

As late as 1959, more than half of Blacks were below the poverty level at 52 percent, while only 18 percent of whites were. However, census data shows that while median family income increased from $27,311 in 1991, to $34,616 in 1999, it declined 3 percent by 2001 due to the decline in the economy. Consequently, this caused a rise in the poverty rate. The Black community experienced a dramatic decline in the poverty rate during the 1990s, from a high of 31.3 percent in 1991 to the lowest rate ever, 19.3 percent in 1999; then it grew in the following two years to 20.7 percent.[33] This record shows the lack of stability in Black income, with the consequence that severe fluctuations in household income keep large segments of the Black community off balance, unable to plan long-term. When the economy does not perform, they do not have accumulated wealth and, thus, are not able to continue to fulfill their economic needs. Poverty still exists as a factor for Blacks twice as often as for whites, with the white rate at 13 percent early in 2007 and Blacks at nearly 23 percent.

Employment

Labor force participation rate of Blacks was high after slavery. Blacks worked mostly at low-wage jobs, and their employment rate decreased only about ten percentage points between 1910 (88 percent) and 1947 (77 percent). The level of menial jobs taken by Blacks has decreased over time such that in the 1990s, 20 percent of Blacks hold professional or managerial jobs, while 30 percent of whites hold such jobs. In any case, with the decrease in the industrial base of the American economy, Blacks have suffered substantially from unemployment, which they have experienced, as a structural feature of life, at a rate twice that of whites for a period stretching back to the 1930s.[34]

Studies by economists such as David Swinton found substantial disparity between the Black and white labor force participation rates, much of the difference being accounted for by racial discrimination in the labor force.[35] Likewise, in a longitudinal study Samuel Meyers, Jr. and William Darity, Jr. found that racism levied against the Black male accounted for the persistent margin between Black and white family wage structure over time.[36] Others who have discovered and analyzed employment discrimination specifically have repeatedly documented the phenomenon of racism in the labor force, and have generally approved of the mechanism of affirmative action to fight it. Paul Burstein documents the development of the Equal Employment Opportunity Commission and its administration of employment discrimination complaints.[37]

As of July 1995, most of the more than ninety thousand cases of employment discrimination filed with the EEOC had been brought by Blacks. A study of discrimination in housing by the Urban Institute in 1989 and 1990, using Black and white testers in several major cities, having equal qualifications and dress, found that there was "entrenched and pervasive levels of discrimination," inasmuch as Blacks and Hispanics were systematically denied access to employment.[38] This was confirmed not only by complaints by Blacks in the private sector, but by suits filed in the Department of Agriculture, the Department of State, the Justice Department, and the Department of Treasury in the 1990s.[39]

In addition, evidence of discrimination in federal employment exists in the data from the Office of Personnel Management (1994), which finds that Blacks are fired at 2.5 times the rate of whites. Asked why the rates are disparate, the study director replied: "I think that there is a reasonable suspicion that a good part of this gap is due to various forms of differential treatment . . . If you prefer, a good part of this gap is probably due to discrimination."[40] The source of the discrimination took various forms, such as the mere use of an African-oriented name, such as Tamika, Aisha, or Keisha, names that Black Americans in the previous African-conscious generation gave to their children. Researchers Marianne Bertrand of the University of Chicago and Sendhil Mullainathan of MIT found, in a study involving thirteen hundred people in Boston and Chicago, that applicants with "black sounding names" were 50 percent less likely to be invited for job interviews.[41]

Using federal employment data on two hundred thousand medium and large employers, Fred and Ruth Blumrosen found that at least one-third of employers appeared to have discriminated against women and minorities in the same industry in the same geographical area.[42] These researchers, who helped to establish the Equal Employment Opportunity Commission in 1965, concluded that about 2 million workers were affected by "intentional discrimination" in 1999 alone.[43]

Business Ownership

Perhaps the most important area where the impact of slavery has been felt is in the development of business ownership. It was not, contrary to popular opinion, that Blacks did not develop businesses, since between 1863 and 1913 the number of Black businesses went from 2,000 to 40,000. But most were single proprietorships, and only 2 percent were organized as corporations. This was largely due to the fact that the capital base of all of them was extremely low due to lack of access to capital, since white-owned banks were not responsive to Black applications for large sums of money, and only ten Black-owned banks were in existence before 1975. Many of the larger Black businesses were actually farms located in the South. Black businesses, however, grew during the 1980s, going from roughly 250,000 at the beginning of the decade to more than 400,000 by the end. Yet it was not until 1986 that the first company owned by a Black person grossed over $1 billion of sales—Beatrice Foods. It is striking that while Black businesses in America clearly lag those of whites, they also lag other minorities, such as Asians and Hispanics. The pattern of low capitalization and single proprietorships with few employees still obtains (see appendix table A9). Although whites have over 5 million firms and 7 million financial establishments, among this group of firms, Hispanics have the largest number, but Asians have the greatest sales and receipts. Then, it is striking that the two groups that have suffered most in the United States, Blacks and Native Americans, have the lesser number of both firms and sales or receipts.

Health Status

The very bodies of Blacks in America bear the mark of slavery inasmuch as their health status is related to the physical deprivations suffered from that condition, although little or no research has been done on this. For example, the life expectancy of Blacks was well below that of whites in the first decades of the twentieth century (see appendix table A10). This was important, not just as a matter of quality of life, but inasmuch as people who live longer are able to accumulate more resources and to transfer them to succeeding generations. Thus, the low life expectancy of Blacks kept them from living long enough establish stable patterns of wealth accumulation. Between 1910 and 1920, Black life expectancy increased thirteen years for males and nine years for females. However, it did not begin to narrow the overtake whites significantly until 1950, when the gap between Blacks and whites was 7.5 years.

Much of the discriminatory social structure that was established for Blacks as a result of their oppression was already set as they entered the twentieth century. The point one makes is that the comparative condition of Blacks and whites largely conformed to this structure and persisted throughout that century, with slight exceptions. The cause was both a continuation of the remnants of the old-styled oppression and the new interpretations of white superiority in the new types of output from the public policy system and in the racial etiquette of social relations.

Below we will discuss what factors have perpetuated this oppression in the twentieth and now in the twenty-first centuries, that encompassed the failure of the attack on "inequality" especially with respect to the racial gaps in health. A study in the *Journal of the American Medical Association* indicated that Blacks have less access to medical care, are examined less aggressively by doctors, and get less aggressive treatment for heart diseases, organ transplants, and other illnesses.[44] This was confirmed by Louis Sullivan, secretary of Health and Human Services:

> There is clear, demonstrable evidence of discrimination and racism in our health care system. Each year since 1984, while the health status of the general population has increased, Black health status has actually declined. This decline is not in one or two health categories; it is across the board.[45]

These findings were confirmed by the Institute of Medicine, which in 2002 released a survey of one hundred studies conducted over the previous decade, concluding that the disparities in health care contributed to the untimely deaths of Blacks from cancer, heart disease, diabetes, and HIV infection.[46] The causes support a charge of racism; minorities are less likely to be given appropriate medications or to undergo appropriate screenings and receive the least desirable treatments for illnesses. Medicare records find, for example, that Blacks are 3.6 times more likely to have limbs amputated than whites for diabetes or advanced treatments for the onset of HIV/AIDS. Martha N. Hill of Johns Hopkins Medical Center, said, "The differences are pervasive. It cuts across all conditions of health and across the entire country, and we think this is a very serious moral issue."[47] Moreover, the differences persist regardless of the possession of health insurance.[48]

Health care is a moral issue because it contributes to the death and mutilation of Blacks through the official auspices of the national health care service, a fact weakens the Black community. Modern Black Codes.

Criminal Justice

Criminal justice as a mode of racial oppression is often referred to by those writing about American racism. However, it also constitutes a special form of racism in its dimension of physical punishment, as opposed to the civil racism that exists in other areas of American life, where individuals and groups exercise relative freedom of mobility. In another work, I theorized that, as the white majority controlled the state institutions, white nationalist politicians were able to foster a punishment regime targeted at Blacks through the promulgation of criminal justice legislation. David Crocker, in his discussion of retributive justice and reconciliation, cites Michael Nozick's view that retribution and revenge stem from the same motive, an attempt by persons or groups who consider themselves victims to attempt to exact justice by "getting even."[49] Nozick's view is that retribution and revenge leading to retaliation are undertaken to restore a sense of self-respect (one of the ingredients in nationalism). This may provide a rationale for the incarceration of Blacks, which has taken place out of all proportion to their commission of crimes, a fact that makes the regime that allows it immoral.

Blacks have been incarcerated more than whites for petty drug offenses, in what Human Rights Watch regards as "a national scandal," suggesting that "Black and white drug offenders get radically different treatment in the American justice system. This is not only profoundly unfair to blacks, it also corrodes the American ideal of equal justice for all."[50] Its 1996 study found that, although Blacks were 13 percent of the population, they comprised 62.7 percent of the drug offenders sent to prison, while whites were 36.7 percent.[51] Moreover, in states such as Illinois and Maryland, Blacks were 90 percent of those sent to prison, while they were 80 percent in Louisiana, New Jersey, North Carolina, South Carolina, and Virginia. The Justice Policy Institute fond that this was the result of a frenzy in the incarceration rate of Black males that began in the early 1980s, having grown fivefold by the year 2000 such that there were 791,600 Black men in jails and prisons, but 603,032 enrolled in colleges and universities.[52] The comparable figures in 1980 were 143,000 Black men in jails and prisons and 463,700 enrolled in colleges and universities.

In addition, America now incarcerates more people at a greater rate than in South Africa, formerly controlled by an acknowledged racist government. In the 1989–90 period, the U.S. incarceration rate was 455 per 100,000, the rate in South Africa 311 per 100,000. On any given day, one in four Black men in America between the ages of twenty and twenty-nine will have some relationship to the criminal justice system.[53] In addition, the death penalty is widely acknowledged to have been administered on a racist basis, and data from the Department of Justice reveals that as of December 31, 1990, Blacks, who are 13 percent of the population, comprised 40 percent of death row inmates, or 943 of 1,375 prisoners condemned to die.[54] A study by the University of Maryland of inmates in Maryland, a state with a tradition of high incarceration rate of Blacks, found that race plays a substantial role in decision to award the death penalty to Blacks for killing whites.[55]

The seventeen-member New York State Judicial Commission on Minorities issued a report based upon a three-year period that found that the court system itself was racist.[56] Moreover, racial discrimination does not stop with the court system, but occurs within the prisons. A survey by a New York City judge in 1992 found that preferential treatment went to white prisoners, and that Blacks faced systematic discrimination in housing, job assignments, and the application of discipline.[57] The fact that much of the above problem was a result of structural racism was confronted by the Supreme Court in 2002, which invalidated peremptory challenges made on the basis of race, a practice that was common in many states.[58]

Another structural feature of the law was selective arrest through racial profiling. In 1998, New Jersey troopers James Kennan and John Hogan stopped a van containing three Black males and one Hispanic male on a stretch of the turnpike and subsequently fired their weapons upon the van; the incident brought "racial profiling" to national attention. In 2000 the governor of New Jersey, Christy Todd Whitman, received a report stating that in fact, racial profiling had occurred in police practices in the state; however, it offered no restitution to the victims. Nevertheless, Attorney General John Ashcroft issued a report in 2001 stating that there was no racial or ethnic bias in federal death penalties, causing Hugh Price, head of the National Urban League, to challenge the federal government to deal forthrightly with racism in the criminal justice, from racial profiling to the death penalty.[59]

Consumer Discrimination

Consumer discrimination occurs frequently when Blacks of all classes attempt to purchase goods or access services because racial stereotyping suggests that Blacks are prone to theft and violence.[60] In 1991 a study appearing in the *Harvard Law Review* found frequent racial and gender discrimination in the purchase of automobiles. For example, Blacks were often quoted higher prices at more than twice the markup of white males, and Black women paid more than three times the markup.[61] An example of this is the settlement entered into by Nissan Motors in 2003, responding to a plaintiff who alleged that Nissan car dealers were more likely to mark up the interest rate for the sale of their products to Blacks and Hispanics than to whites.[62] This suit was settled by Nissan, including payments to those who brought the lawsuit and the establishment of programs of restitution. As a result of these and other complaints, testing programs were established by the NAACP in the 1990s that used Black and white individuals seeking the same service, resulting in legal action against such firms as Lord & Taylor, State Farm Insurance, Lucky Stores, Denny's, and Shoney's Big Boy restaurants.

News Coverage

Racial discrimination is also an underlying problem in the news coverage of Blacks. One example is that the Black middle class is largely missing from consistent coverage. Instead crime and violence are racial staples, which frequent the media and contribute to racial stereotypes.[63] On the other hand, more positive news coverage is available for whites, including more sensitive stories about white victimization.[64] The news media—and other purveyors of popular culture—propagate stereotypes about Blacks' role in crime and as drug dealers, rather than focusing on the largely white population of consumers, addicts, transporters, and financiers of the drug trade.[65] This, of course, is but a suggestion of the daily incidents of racism faced by Blacks of all classes and constitutes the factual basis for the demand that the civil rights regime be continued so as to protect—even imperfectly—the rights of Blacks in many areas of life.

Modern Lynching

In Brooklyn, New York, several incidents of arson and other acts of violence were perpetrated against Blacks moving into certain neighborhoods. In one incident, Reverend Donovan Leys's family automobile was set afire shortly after he moved into the Midwood section.[66] Similar acts of violence were also visited against Blacks moving into public housing projects in Vidor, Texas. In a town known for Ku Klux Klan activity, all Blacks were driven from the town.[67]

In 1992 two Black women were abducted by two white males in Montgomery County, Maryland, taken to a field, beaten, and set on fire. However, this was not an isolated event. Jermaine Ewell was beaten in New York City by a gang of white toughs for no apparent reason.[68] Then there was the killing of Yusef Hawkins in Brooklyn by white youths.[69] And in similar patterns in Columbus, Ohio, and other cities, a Black man in Tampa, Florida, was abducted and set on fire.[70] The Mississippi Coalition for Justice, a grassroots organization, found that in three years (1988–91), twenty-four Blacks died while in the custody of law enforcement officers in Mississippi.[71] On June 7, 1998, James Byrd, a Black man, was killed when he was dragged from the back of a pickup truck in Jasper, Texas, by three men, Shawn Berry, Lawrence Brewer, and John King, who had been known to participate in Ku Klux Klan activities.[72] Five days later, a similar incident in Illinois involved Byron Manning, a seventeen-year-old, who reported that he was dragged alongside a sports utility vehicle "by three white youths yelling racial slurs." On June 14, in Slidell, Louisiana, a man reported that he was also dragged alongside a car by three white man who also yelled racial slurs.[73] Then, in late July 2003, in Belle Glade, Florida, a small town of fifteen thousand, a Black man was found hanging from a tree under what the local NAACP regarded as suspicious circumstances, but the judge ruled the case a suicide.[74] Finally, in August 2004, a Black man was similarly found hanging from a tree in Tuskegee, Alabama, another case that law enforcement officials judged a suicide.[75]

Breaking the Cycle

This relatively static picture in the comparative position between Blacks and whites in American society states a fact and poses a question. The fact is that the goal of equality in the use of public accommodations, in the right to purchase housing and other consumer goods, in education, and in employment has not been achieved and perhaps cannot be achieved by the strategy of integration as such. This means that the quest for equality will be substantially incomplete if the goal of equalizing wealth is not achieved in order that equality in these and other areas might also be pursued and realized much more substantially through the efforts of Blacks themselves, based on the acquisition of their own private resources or those of their community.

Reparations pose the probability of changing the wealth equation in order for Black development to happen. Yet, unlike what occurred in South Africa, that slavery and postslavery racism are culpable in the Black condition is being fought as a plausible explanation, and the demand for reparations is being rejected. In initiating the "race dialogue" President Bill Clinton did not allow the commission to consider reparations. Moreover, in the tense debate over whether the United States should send representation to the United Nations Conference against Racism in Durban, South Africa, President George Bush authorized his spokesperson, Ari Fleischer, to say that he did not believe in reparations for slavery.[76] A key to the position of both presidents was the fact that most white Americans do not believe that companies that made profits from slavery should apologize to Blacks today, or should pay compensation to Blacks today or set up scholarship funds, or that the government should make cash payments to Blacks who are descendants of slaves, or apologize to Blacks for slavery.[77] In one poll, the highest negative response from the public came on the questions relative to cash payments.

The irony is that, according to a 1997 Gallup Poll on race, most Americans also oppose affirmative action and yet understand that racism is still a fact of American life.[78] But just as ironically, President George Bush stated on his trip to Africa at the slave castle on Goree Island that "one of the largest migrations of history was also one of the greatest crimes of history."[79] Bush also recognized that slavery was the continuing source of problems that African Americans face today. While I would register strong disagreement with the characterization of slavery—essentially a forced movement—as a migration, nevertheless, his sentiment was correct. It was also strange, inasmuch as one of the reasons that Bush did not allow appropriate American representation at the Durban conference was fear, despite to his own characterization of slavery as a "crime," that slavery would be condemned at the conference as a crime against humanity. The report that emerged from the conference indeed acknowledges

> that slavery and the slave trade are a crime against humanity and should always have been so, especially the transatlantic slave trade, and are among the major sources and manifestations of racism, racial discrimination, xenophobia and related intolerance, and that Africans and people of African descent,

Asians and people of Asian descent and indigenous peoples were victims of these acts and continue to be victims of their consequences.[80]

The U.S. government might have been reluctant to sign on to an international convention ostensibly superceding American law that had no limitation on the longevity of the damage done by the crime of slavery on the descendants of slaves. Thus the fear could have been that the legitimization of this characterization by an official U.S. delegation could be used in American courts to challenge the opinion of some judges that the injury of slavery cannot be adjudicated because it has outrun the statute of limitations. Congress has not acted on the reparations bill presented in the House of Representatives by Rep. John Conyers, who has not been successful in attracting the full support of his African American colleagues, so deep is their belief that it will not be considered at any time, in any form. In any case, the rejection of the demand for reparations at the highest levels of government has been palpably clear.

Perhaps the ultimate reason why policy is an anemic vehicle is the scope of the wrong, which conjures up more than policy as a corrective but instead requires a convergence of truth and will that tests the very mettle of the democratic idea. It has been more half a century since the civil rights movement, and the current Supreme Court has thrown a generation of legal precedent to the wind and instituted a conservative ideological screen in its decision making. It has weakened the infrastructure of civil rights and social justice for African Americans, rejecting the use of race in political redistricting, in minority contracting, and in higher education. The fiction that undergirds the white consensus on race, which has driven the political system to reject further advances in civil rights, is that Blacks are not oppressed—an erroneous and ultimately dangerous misjudgment. Without presenting here a legal analysis of affirmative action, it can be said to have fulfilled three functions.

1. It is a historical corrective measure that has provided a method for disadvantaged groups and individuals to receive compensation for past subjugation that has prevented them from exercising their own human initiative equally with other citizens, mandating that institutions include them in consideration for participation in enterprises both public and private.

2. It has been complementary to the self-determination of individuals and their groups because of the presumption of human equality, which is at its heart, or the notion that if only opportunity and access are made available on a fair basis, Blacks and other disadvantaged people are able to compete with others and earn their just place in society. In making this presumption, it strikes directly at the heart of the doctrine and the practice of white supremacy.

3. The development of an affirmative action program is a symbolic reference that a regime intends to pursue a democratic form of government and society. In fact, one could say that it is a sine qua non of the character of such a society, given that in every society individuals are oppressed on some basis and there is a necessity to have strategies to promote national integration through the dignified inclusion of peoples. The distinction between government and society made above is deliberate, since the West has offered forms of political democracy based on the fair participation of groups. However, such regressive features of the state as the tendency toward cultural homogeneity, the negative class features of capitalism, the practice of white supremacy in multiracial systems, and the appropriation of the use of technology and information, have all made necessary the existence of mechanisms of social amelioration beyond the political definition of citizenship that extend to the fair distribution of resources.

Conclusion: Renegotiating the Racial Contract

Reparations are not about achieving equality in wages but equality in wealth, because wealth-based equality is the key to achieving individual, family, and group self-determination on a par with whites. In short, the inverse of the argument must be made: that the civil rights movement was designed to foster wage-based equality, but even if this goal were to be achieved, Blacks will never be equal in an American racist and capitalist society. Racism in the labor force will likely prevent wage equality for a long time to come. The 2000 census data reported that in 1999, the median family income of Blacks was \$31,778, or 62 percent of whites' income.[81] However, in 1984, the median monthly income of Black households as a percentage of white household was also 62 percent.[82] Nevertheless, the Gini coefficient in 1980 between Blacks and whites was 64 and by 1999 it was 18, which means that at some time in the future, theoretically, monthly household income could be equal.

In 1984, per capita wealth for Blacks was $6,837, compared with $32,667 for whites. Black householders had a median net worth of $3,397 and white householders $39,135, so for every dollar of wealth in the median white household, the median Black household had mere a nine cents.[83]

Let us envision for a moment that equal monthly family income is achieved at some time in the next decade. Blacks would still not be "equal" economically because they would still lack the scale of wealth to achieve equality with whites. Thus, the wealth of whites would still afford them a level of self-determination superior to Blacks because the disparity in total household wealth between Blacks and whites is greater than the monthly income gap. This means that Blacks must decide whether they wish to remain a wage-based class that is clearly subordinate to whites or find the means to achieve the kind of wealth that will enable them to be truly equal.

If a national consensus is to be regained, it will have to take into consideration the fact that racism not only still exists, but in many ways is growing more virulent and destructive, as the modern Black Codes suggest. Thus, ameliorative acts should not be conceived of as a zero-sum game, but in the interests of the whole nation. That is to say, whereas the moral strength of the case that Black people presented to the nation gave rise to the civil rights movement as a just claim for amelioration in the 1960s, today the moral basis for the continued attempt to rectify past oppression rests not only on the foundation of Blacks alone, but on the survival of the democratic idea. In the next chapter, I will make the case that, for these reasons, reparations are the current phase of the demand and that it should be taken seriously.

CHAPTER SEVEN

༭

Barriers to Truth and Reconciliation in America

R EVEALING SOME OF THE ISSUES INVOLVED as a prelude to the discussion of reparations, the South African case cautions us that race reconciliation is not simply a problem of deriving an exact value of past oppressive events and circumstances. In fact, it is a process that signals a desire for making restitution that is recognized as a tender, or sincere gesture toward reconciliation. Whether or not reconciliation occurs depends upon the impact of that gesture in the interaction between the group extending the gesture and group to which it is directed. Once the gesture is made, exceedingly complex problems remain to be solved. As previously discussed, some of those that were addressed in the South Africa symposia that led to the formation of the Truth and Reconciliation Commission included the character of the state, victimization and dependency, the resulting invisibility of the Black voice, the continuing presence of pain and its psychological effect, and the extent to which justice is served by reparations. Here, I will discuss these issues in the American context in an effort to show how tenuous the quest for racial reconciliation may be because of the complexity of the response that oppression has created in the dynamics of race relations in this country.

The American State Context

Whether Black Americans receive reparations for slavery and postslavery racism or not is largely a matter of the strength of the demand that they put forth and the response of the state based on its acceptance of the cause as just. In the South African instance, the reparations had to await the political change to Black majority rule as the most legitimate context in which the measure could be considered. Even in the period of liberalization after the coming to power of the De Klerk government, the matter would still not have allowed to arise.

Bringing that fact to bear on the United States, one asks what kind of change would be necessary to effect reparations. At the outset, it would mean that as long as the current conservative, white nationalist government is in place—which not only rejects reparations, but promulgates public policies that are destructive to Blacks—there is no chance that the state will seriously consider payment for past injustices.

In light of the fact that reconciliation entails a response to a demand, and that the present government is stubbornly hostile, Blacks would require a monumental demand for the government to consider it. A rough parallel would be the Anti-Apartheid Act of 1986, which was vetoed by President Ronald Reagan, but subsequently passed by Congress over his objection. This occurred because opposing Apartheid had become a popular matter among people of all races, which suggests that ultimately reparations will have to take on the character of the civil rights movement, with whites coming to see the moral claim of reparations as legitimate and pressuring their congressional representatives or taking other forms of civil action. Therefore, part of the political agenda of the Black community should include reparations, in the event that a government evolves that includes a sufficient coalition of those sympathetic to H.R. 40, the issue sponsored by Rep. John Conyers, and to positive recommendations that might emerge from it.

At the moment, the state's attitude toward reparations is determined by its belief that Black people are free: that there are no victims of slavery or racist oppression, that Blacks can voice their demands and participate with other citizens in the public square, and that the state has no further responsibility to redress past harms. This attitude has permeated the political culture, carried along by its advocates in Congress, the White House, and the Supreme Court. From those posts, they reject the demand for reparations as illegitimate at best and at worst a divisive impetus toward intramajority conflict. Most especially, their view is that the efforts of the past prove that the white majority has made a good-faith gesture for reconciliation and the rest should now become a matter of personal responsibility. Such a view is both shortsighted and ahistorical, causing those who hold power to undervalue Blacks and their demands for redress, not only on the basis of their suffering, but equally on the basis of their contributions to the making of America. Having elaborated these points in what follows, I will address aspects of this dominant perspective that pose barriers to the fulfillment of racial reconciliation.

The Rise of White Nationalism

Within the American state a powerful conservative movement has arisen. It began as a counter to the civil rights movement of the 1960s, but in the following decades it has become positioned to pose a formidable barrier to the reparations movement. In the political culture a powerful movement has gained ascendancy that, rather than vigorously pursue integration as public policy, rejects that goal, as I described in *White Nationalism, Black Interests.*[1] The political system has been retreating from the goal of equality since the Reagan presidency and has influenced even Democratic administrations to follow its lead, the surest sign that there is a conservative consensus among whites about the best course for politics.

In *The Negro in Politics* (1886), T. Thomas Fortune, a Black author and editor living in New York City, described as a "revolution gone backwards" the events beginning with the 1877 bargain that found Democrats ceding the presidency to Rutherford B. Hayes in exchange for removing Union soldiers from the South.[2] In words that might be appropriately applied to the Democratic Party today, he noted that the Republican Party had sacrificed principle to maintain its control over federal power and patronage.[3] During Reconstruction the Republican Party represented Black hopes for inclusion in American society, but it retreated from that goal in order to make common cause with southern whites in a larger project that would bind up the nation—and in that project reinvest white control over it, in both the North and the South.

Today, that Republican Party has become the leader of the conservative movement, once again reestablishing white power and control over the distribution of public goods, by enacting conservative public policies and viciously challenging any residue of liberalism. The Democratic Party, widely perceived to advance liberal causes, even to be dominated by them, has been attacked and subdued by the conservative establishment. Bill Clinton, the only Democratic president in the conservative interregnum, was impeached by the Republicans.

On December 12, 1998, during the impeachment hearings, John Conyers, ranking member of the Democratic minority on the House Judiciary Committee, stated that impeachment bordered on a coup d'état against a president who had won two elections and who had the overwhelming mandate of the people to remain in office. A Republican member of the committee rejected Conyers's formulation, saying that there were no troops in the streets, and that a constitutional process was working during the procedures of the committee in voting through each of the impeachment resolutions.

Perhaps the impeachment reflected the toxic conservatism of the post-election period that led President Clinton in June of 1997, to offer a relatively mild mandate to begin the discussion about the impact of race in America. His emphasis on looking forward toward the future development of the United States as a multiracial country eliminated past racial oppression as the reason such a discussion was necessary, making the race initiative a hollow instrument for racial reconciliation and confirming the attempt to blot out historical memory and move on without addressing its damage. We have discussed Clinton's initiative in chapter 6, but what is important to point out here is its fierce rejection by conservatives and liberals alike. To strengthen his effort, Clinton visited Africa in the spring of 1998, and while in Uganda, he made a modest apology for the American participation in slavery:

> "Going back to the time before we were even a nation, Euro-pean-Americans received the fruits of the slave trade. And we were wrong in that. It is as well not to dwell too much on the past, but I think it is worth pointing out that the United States has not always done the right thing by Africa." Then, he continued with a striking observation about members of his delegation: "Most of my African-American friends and advisers don't believe that we should get into what was essentially a press story about whether there should be an apology for slavery in America. They think that that's what the 13th, 14th and 15th Amendment was, they think that's what the Civil Rights Amendment was and they think we need to be looking toward the future."[4]

This may have been a tactical ploy by Clinton's African American advisers, geared to lessen the possibility that the trip would be over-shadowed by a resolution submitted in the House of Representatives by

Congressman Tony P. Hall of Ohio, which included both an apology for slavery and the creation of a commission to study its legacy. In any case, Clinton's remarks were immediately rebuked by Tom DeLay, Republican majority whip, who referred to President Clinton as a "flower child with gray hair doing exactly what he did back in the sixties. He is apologizing for the actions of the United States."[5] DeLay's remarks were criticized by Rep. Sheila Jackson-Lee, a member of the Texas delegation, and Rep. John Lewis of Georgia, venerable former civil rights leader. So ended Clinton's mentions of slavery while he was in Africa, but many Blacks believed that this was not enough. Blacks interviewed by the press were thankful that Clinton went to Africa, but one said: "[I]f he went all the way to Africa to apologize, that makes no sense. The former slaves are here, not back in Africa." Another unemployed person said: "African Americans are still enslaved, but in a different form now. There are a lot of black young men locked up in jails. And, for what? A Black man has a hard way to go, that's for sure. And if they see you moving forward, they try to knock you down again."[6]

Victimization

Injustice: The Basis of Modern Victimization

The grand narrative of oppression suggests that the agenda of the state should include reparations not only because of the unrequited era of slavery, as described in the preceding chapter, but because of contemporary racism. Racism can assume many aspects and degrees. There may be, for example, what J. Angelo Corlett refers to as "personal racism," in which two individuals of different races are predisposed to dislike each other on that ground alone. This is what sociologists used to call race "prejudice."[7] This form of racism, however, which rests upon attitudes, is far less powerful than a racism that provokes offensive, even violent, acts. Again, prejudicial attitudes of an individual may be shared by many individuals who constitute a group, and group attitudes may lead to destructive social practices and unfair institutions.[8] Corlett believes that control over such harms, which belongs to the state, creates the moral responsibility of the perpetrator to satisfy the consequences of racist acts perpetrated by the authoritative institutions such as a government or as authorized by such institutions.

The Absence of American Victims

The white nationalist philosophers have sought to cloud the state's responsibility for the past and present by invoking a rhetoric of "personal responsibility," demanding that Blacks take responsibility for problems created by their own oppression. In short, the nationalists' view is that victimhood is an option one chooses, not the result of actual historical events. But one of the reasons why victimhood and oppression have surfaced as political issues is that they are resident in the personality of the state, in the personality of those who have suffered at the hands of the state as special memories that will not die. The truth in these memories is historical in the sense that what is remembered actually happened.[9]

Nevertheless, these memories and thus the history that comprises them are special and powerful because they are the remembrances of highly traumatic events, and such remembrances, experts conclude, are "different from other memories."[10] This is why, as Angelyn Mitchell avers, slavery is a particularly emotional site of memory, as perhaps "America's greatest traumatic experience."[11] War is a another traumatic event, and therefore what happens in the space of two months or five years may be burned into the memory. The racist enslavement of African people and the racist citizenship that has followed consist of millions of traumatic acts, many of which are still alive in memory because they were never accepted as morally right by the criteria of those against whom they were perpetrated. They create a kind of "rememory," that is, the process of remembering not only what one has forgotten but also what one wants to forget and cannot."[12]

The deep trauma of rememory is the central reason why, despite social progress, Blacks are unable to accord a mass forgiveness to whites for the pain of the past. The forgiveness sought by Tutu has not worked on a mass basis in South Africa because of the connection of memory to the present condition of Black people in that country. In short, they have not recovered enough materially to have the resources to cultivate the generosity of the spirit, except in some unusual circumstances, to absolve the white minority regime of its historical crimes. Similarly, Black people are the most churched segment of American society—and many would say a forgiving community—yet the seeming permanence of their debased socioeconomic status provides a link between the past and the present, reminding them of the sources of their daily travail.

Moreover, unlike Black South Africans, they are not the majority population and cannot look forward to the acquisition of political power as a substitute for economic power to use as a resource to cultivate the generosity of the spirit that leads to mass forgiveness.

As in South Africa, so in America: ignoring the victim and the history of his circumstances cloaks with invisibility those who suffered oppression. None of the speakers at the series of conferences that set up the Truth and Reconciliation Commission were African Americans, although speakers who reflected the Jewish experience of Nazi German oppression were participants. Thus the Nuremberg model of restitution was debated, and Bishop Tutu took the strongest position rejecting it. Could the Nuremberg model be used to assess American culpability for slavery and racism? No, not as long as the sons and daughters of slave owners and those who stole Black land and those who perpetrate racism are a functional and decisive part of the civic culture. However, it is also true that a Nuremberg model would be rejected by Black people in America for many of the same reasons it was rejected by the TRC in South Africa. In a society that requires a relatively harmonious social interdependence, there would be wide latitude for past crimes. Thus Tutu's notion of forgiveness, whether or not codified in a process as rigorous as the TRC, would be obtained at some level.

Although Black Americans are recognized worldwide as victims of historical oppression, the relative absence of Black voices in the United States may reflect the way that oppression is viewed today. America is widely regarded as not only a country where one can dream of material wealth, but also as a land of civil rights and social justice where individual dignity is respected. Some find it difficult to conceive of America in the same category with El Salvador, Argentina, Chile, Bosnia, or other countries that have recently perpetrated torture, mass killings, or other forms of raw subordination. Such observers may conclude that the subordinate Black population in America is not in need of reparations.

Nevertheless, though the status of Black people in America has changed in absolute terms, comparison with whites reveals the structure of deep inequality. In any case, it is for the victim to determine how deeply felt is the harm, how much the victimizing acts have damaged the spirit, and how a complete sense of humanity is best reclaimed. This victim-centered assessment, as we observe in the discussion of the politics of voice, has been usurped by the oppressor, making victimhood of Blacks invisible and unspoken.

Ultimately there can be no real restitution without an acknowledgment that there are victims in society as a result of actions taken against them. However, not only is the victim denied a visible status today, the act that resulted in victimhood is also rejected as a corporate act that involved legitimate permission and cultural sanction by real people. The result is that African Americans exist in a moral suspension with respect to their victim status in the twenty-first century and the source of that status. I will attempt below to make the sources of modern oppression, dependency, and victimhood more visible through a discussion of the Black voice.

The Black Voice

Where a group has been the subject of oppression over time, it develops a grand narrative of its oppression. The "memory traces" that constitute the individual memories of the history of that oppression create the grand consensus of the group about its experiences. What experts do not sufficiently acknowledge is the extent to which those "memory traces" are inherited, the extent to which they affect the perceptions and actions in the life experiences of each generation.[13] The narrative of the Black voice is a powerful record of the shared experiences of Black people down through the generations, of the extent to which the shared harms are real, and of the extent to which they have constituted in each age the basis for restitution. Nevertheless, that voice has been suppressed, and in its place the notion of false memory has been created, suggesting that the oppression suffered was not as great as alleged, and was jointly perpetrated by both Blacks and whites, thus neutralizing white responsibility.

Who speaks for Black people is critical. It has been critical to their liberation, since many plans have been devised in their name, and have failed—only to have Black people themselves blamed for the failure to pursue plans that were ill-conceived since they did not contain their intelligence. Indeed, the Black historian Carter Woodson said, "History does not furnish a case of the elevation of a people by ignoring the thought and aspirations of the people thus served."[14] In this sense, while Blacks have wanted to acquire an authentic public voice as a counter to those who meant them harm, they have also wanted to cultivate an independent voice separate even from those who have been their friends and who have often sought to speak for them.

For example, while it is well known that Frederick Douglass began publication of the *North Star* newspaper in Rochester, New York, to further the antislavery cause and popularize the views of William Lloyd Garrison, it is also true that he wanted to develop a voice separate from Garrison's. For this reason, Garrison was not charitable to the initiation of Douglass's newspaper and subtly opposed it, as well as a newspaper begun in Garrison's city of Boston by a Black activist, Benjamin Roberts. Like Douglass, Roberts published a paper in which the "Black community's voice was not muffled, interpreted and inflected by a white abolitionist perspective."[15]

The Suppression of Voice

What was the important legacy of slavery and postslavery racial oppression for the social status of Blacks? Part of the oppression was a deliberate and successful effort to prevent Blacks from having a legitimate presence in the social center of the country that would enable them to participate in its affairs, and, thus, be able to voice their demands upon the national resources and influence national behavior in the direction of their wishes and desires. I mean by "voice" the perspective of Blacks in both the description of their socioeconomic position as well as the interests of Blacks in resolving problems attendant to that position, as publicly expressed by their legitimate representatives, such as the heads of mainstream organizations and elected officials. Therefore, public "voice" assures a group or an individual access to the potential for public recognition of their person and their claims. Moreover, they are able to participate in the democratic process, and thus the suppression of the Black voice marks their exclusion from the public square and devalues the claim of America as a nationally democratic state. In fact, it perpetuates some of the features of the "Herrenvolk democracy" referred to in chapter 3, where the privileges and rights are enjoyed by a power segment of society rather than by the whole.

In the South African symposia, it was striking to hear discussions from the Latin American participants who said that with the suppression of voice, dissident groups in society were effectively "disappeared" from the public in a manner that defined the very antidemocratic nature of the methods and goals of the powerful. So one of the objectives of the subordinate groups was to regain their voice and their legitimate authority to make their case, through access to the media or representation in forums that mattered. In this, one confronts the fight for legitimacy as a question of moral entitlement or rights. In discussing the moral context of the way in which memory is legitimized, Avishai Margalit asks,

> [I]sn't the victim morally entitled to impose—if he only could— his memory of what happened to him on his tormentors?
> . . . [A]re not the Korean "comfort women" morally entitled to impose on the Japanese people their memory of horrific violations at the hands of Japanese soldiers during World War II? Are not the Jews morally entitled to impose the memory of their destruction not only on their German tormentors but also on those that knew and yet did nothing to help?[16]

By this logic, it is also pertinent to ask whether Blacks who suffered from slavery and postslavery racism are entitled to impose the memory of their oppression not only on their American tormentors, but also on those who have benefited from it in each age of American history?

The point that I attempted to make in my book on white nationalism was that a major consequence of the emergence of the conservative movement in the national political culture was that it further depressed the voice of Blacks, first in denying that there was, in fact a coherent voice that expressed Black interests, and second elevating the voices of whites in the determination of what would be done to address the Black condition in the council of decision-making. With the rise of the white nationalist movement and its control of the political system, the Black voice has been depressed to the extent that additional amelioration of their wrongs has been strongly contested to the point of dismissal. The culture of this movement has contested the legitimacy of the Black voice by various means; the most frequent is to position oppositional views in powerful places in the media, by either white or Black spokespersons representing the establishment interests. Most important, it legitimized attitudes toward reparations that were designed to shield whites from responsibility for the past. Molly Secours discusses some of these well-known denials of responsibility: "My family didn't own slaves." "I'm not a racist." "Reparations are only going to divide us more." "Blacks receive preferential treatment. What about me?" "Slavery is over. Let's move on and forget about the past."[17]

Finally, I noted that, insofar as the voice of whites was that which was used to shape measures, they constituted a form of oppression consistent with the objective of social control of Blacks as a subordinate group. This displacement has made the authority of the Black voice consistent with or parallel to a subordinate condition in society; it might be regarded as the "normalization" of the Black voice in a suspiciously weakened condition. It cannot be the voice of those in the Black community who want to challenge America to change the worst features of the Black condition.

Concrete Issues in a Black Agenda

To deepen the discussion of "voice" somewhat: agenda-setting theory takes into consideration the *authoritative voice* that shapes public policy. As the medium through which such a voice reaches the public, the national media are inordinately influential in shaping of attitudes toward public issues. In that process, the Black voice is restricted from regular access to the public, filtered by editors and producers who determine what is culturally and commercially acceptable or desirable for a majority white public to consume. Although there is a marginalized Black press, and a few Black voices heard at the level of the national media, these exceptions prove the rule.

The concept of "voice," however, does not refer only to actual voices, but is also a symbol for participation and thus representation in various areas of life. An example of the suppression of the Black voice in public policy comes from the high-profile case of the Supreme Court challenge to the use of affirmative action by the University of Michigan in 2003. The defendant in the case was the University as an institution. However, African American students had a vital interest in presenting their case before the Court because the University had exercised racial exclusion in the past and affirmative action had been an effective, but relatively moderate, instrument for correcting past discrimination. The Supreme Court itself denied argument time to the NAACP Legal Defense Fund, which represented the Black students. Ted Shaw, counsel for the NAACP, said that if the Court had allowed such time for argument, his organization's presentation would have focused on the historical origins of affirmative action at the university.

What's really at stake here is higher education opportunities for African Americans and Latino students. I think it's a tragedy that those students were not allowed to have their voices heard in this case.[18]

This is yet another example of an institution fashioning a policy related to the resolution of a racial issue, yet rejecting the voice of those most seriously affected, in a manner that conforms to the point we have raised about the uses of both race and power in America by the majority.

The enabling factor used to suppress the Black voice is surely the power of the majority. Insofar as that power reflects the supremacy of whites, it also emanates from a philosophical view of white supremacy and its attitude toward Black powerlessness. An example of that view is exposed in a discussion by Judith Roof and Robyn Wiegman about the legitimacy of the subaltern's right to a voice in public affairs.[19] They point to the disagreement between Hannah Arendt and Ralph Ellison in the 1950s over African American priorities. In "Reflections on Little Rock" (the momentous event when Blacks integrated Central High School in the capital of Arkansas) Arendt expressed the view that miscegenation laws were most offensive to her and that inasmuch as Blacks were more concerned with discrimination in employment, housing, and education, "this is understandable. Oppressed minorities were never the best judges of the order of priorities on such matters. They preferred to fight for social opportunities rather than for basic human or political rights."[20]

Although Arendt expressed sympathy with the civil rights movement led by Blacks, she nevertheless also said that as a European Jew she was unfamiliar with the intimacies of Black thinking on these issues. She also spoke as a member of the American elite, in the context of such attitudes about the underclass in general.

Leaders of the Black community strongly objected to such sentiments. Ralph Ellison, for instance, said that Arendt, writing from an "olympian position," did not understand the issues involved in Blacks fighting for open education in Little Rock for Black families and the future of their children.[21] But Roof and Wiegman ask whether Ellison should be given the last word on this subject. They say that Arendt's view parallels Gayatri Chakravorty Spivak's, that the subaltern cannot speak. Spivak's view is that "we cannot merely drop our common prejudices, take our sympathies for granted, and permit the underclass to speak; that they are an underclass is precisely what constitutes their silence. It is a function of the elite—and what makes them elite—to indicate and instantiate this silence."[22] The authors conclude that the force of Arendt's position, therefore, was that ideas that flowed from the cultural, political, and social blackness of African Americans were tagged with their underclass status, and in the political market place of ideas were devalued precisely because of that sign.[23]

To support this theory, consider the explanation of a subject like Black poverty. Blacks and whites view the reasons for it differently, according to a study by Matthew Hunt. While Blacks and Latinos attribute poverty to the social and economic structure, they also view individual inability to compete as caused by poverty. Given that whites favor individualist rationales for poverty more consistently and hold political power, their analysis of poverty shapes public policy, which Black opinion is peripheral. Hunt confirms that "the voices subscribing most strongly to the alternative to the dominant ideology are the politically weakest voices in the crowd."[24]

Public interest in certain issues rises and falls with the pressure applied to keep them in the public eye and make them important considerations for policymakers. The Black voice has driven and followed such cycles: historical movements to redress the Black condition, including the most recent civil rights movement, required the elevation of the Black voice, specifically the quality of its authority. The civil rights movement, for example, stressed the moral authority of the demand for change. The content of this authority was vested in the success of the movement's tactics and methods of dramatically illustrating the condition of Blacks to the nation and thereby mobilizing pressure on the political system to affect legislation to address discrimination.

The moral aspect that contributed to the public authority of the voice of the civil rights movement, however, was based upon illustrations of the profound subordination of Blacks. Thus, the task of the movement was not only to hold up the banner of pain caused by that subordination, but to simultaneously hold up the mirror of democracy to let all see the contradiction between the treatment of Blacks and the ideals Americans espoused. In the process, advocates of civil rights posed the question of which voice would tell the story, which would be perceived to have the most correct version of the story. The decision, ratified repeatedly by legislation passed in the 1960s, was that the vision Blacks had put before the nation was just, both because it was accurate and, most importantly, because it came from the authentic voice of the oppressed.

In the current attempt to "normalize" the Black voice, decision-makers and the general public have lost sight of the fact that, although they have the power to depress the authoritative voices of Blacks, their condition still deserves public attention. In other words, just because the Black agenda is driven out of sight and out of mind, it is no less urgent and painful, and ignoring it is no less poisonous to the project of democracy. Black concerns are allowed to fester, to become periodic disruptions in the social order, a drain on the life chances of those who are challenged to believe in the American dream, a continuing stain on the dream itself. This is one mistake.

Another mistake is made by Blacks who believe that the normalization of the Black voice is unproblematic, since their agenda is now actionable through channels of redress available to all citizens. This false assumption is, first, the root of the increasing cynicism of Blacks about the direction of the nation and, second, part of the reason why the demand for reparations arises at this time.

As for the first of these points, Blacks and whites have maintained in recent years a considerable difference of opinion on the direction of the nation. For example, conservative researchers and many others have sought to dilute the moral claim of Blacks, asserting that Blacks are sufficiently advantaged by government programs to make the taxes whites pay unfair; that despite attempts to assist Blacks with special programs, they have not achieved equality, so additional support is futile; that whites are now "discriminated against" by affirmative action programs; and that discrimination against Blacks is a logical consequence of their failure to perform as equals in many type of behaviors. In addition, there is an unarticulated, but nonetheless visible racial animus against Blacks that motivates policy and drives the more civil conservative arguments in the public sphere. This is a dispiriting concept not only because it is largely false even though strongly felt, but also because it has dangerously found its way into government to affect policies in which Black interests are at stake.

Corrective public policy addressed toward Blacks requires the strong inclusion of the Black voice. However, introduction of the Black voice is often regarded as a negative, as a "race card," "political correctness," or some other pejorative—according to a strange idea that race should blocked from consideration even where race is patently the underlying cause or cure. While whites may live in an atmosphere where racial damage is not immediately visible, one of the great illusions of majoritarian culture is that it is not relevant to their daily lives. This desire to avoid looking at the effects of race is so strong that the introduction of racial perspectives is often alienating, driving the majority to suppress the Black voice even further.

Therefore, in a world where the Black voice has been marginalized, the instruments of marginalization have included exclusion, but also distortion by the weapon of ideology. For example, some white conservatives object to the presentation of academic information to students that suggests that whites are "oppressors."[25] But the question is whether they object on the basis of the truth of the matter or on their interpretation of the truth. In America Blacks were oppressed, but to name the oppressor as such violates the etiquette of race relations, leaving open the question of culpability as, oddly, a debatable proposition. One could then easily acquire the notion that oppression happened by accident or that Blacks themselves were involved in the perpetration, taking the moral stigma of culpability away from the major perpetrator. That whites have perpetrated crimes against Blacks should not be considered an ambiguous proposition, subject to distortion or the kind of reinterpretation that substitutes oppressors for heroes. Dinesh D'Souza pointedly criticizes what he calls "oppression theory," and raises the fact that Blacks owned slaves as a generally common occurrence. He then praises America for ending slavery in a manner that seems to suggest a moral superiority that trumps the hundreds of years slavery was practiced by whites.[26] This example of the demand by conservatives to reempower alienated whites and their allies of color skews the truth of history and makes it a casualty of the conservative movement.

The importance of this is that if, in contradistinction to the Truth and Reconciliation Commission's process, there can be no agreement on the truth, then there can be no process established for restitution, and there can ultimately be no reconciliation. In that case, we repair to the fiction that events shaped the Black community in its current powerless state, but there are no victims to witness what occurred and no perpetrators who committed the acts that oppressed them.

Mass Pain

A major consequence of suppression of the Black voice is that the pain that has accompanied the subordination of Black people is unheard. This pain is an unspoken and often unacknowledged ingredient in the conflict and tension between Blacks and whites, which reparations have the potential to lessen.

The Pain of White People

If conservative voices can perpetuate the fiction that Black people have attained equality with whites, then they have created an intellectual barrier to considering Black pain. Part of their motivation is to shield whites from the pain, the anguish and embarrassment, of having slavery and racial subordination raised to public consciousness.

As indicated in chapter 4, lynchings of Blacks raise thunderous questions about the moral character of the whites who performed them, and those who were spectators. Perpetrators and their apologists justified this mass behavior as have many others who committed atrocities against people they considered inhuman, or the enemy, or whom they feared or envied. Philip Dray asks in his study of lynching, *At the Hands of Persons Unknown*, what type of person was involved. He points out that those who carried out the punishment of Blacks were "pointedly anonymous" and that coroners' reports most often noted "death at the hands of persons unknown."[27] This phenomenon demonstrates the power of a group consensus to authorize attacks on those presumed to threaten the interests of the group, even if the consensus is pointedly immoral.

Today the pain of whites is evident in the guilt and confusion behind their tortuous questioning of the justness of reparations, of why they should pay since their families did not own slaves (though their families may have sanctioned slavery, participated in its culture, or benefited economically) or immigrated to the United States only recently. Or they simply say that these things happened too long ago. The pain is that the treatment of Blacks contradicts the myth of American exceptionalism: the unique qualities of American democracy and the near-saintliness of the founding fathers.

But the pain is also evident in subtle ways in white people who remain committed to the project of social justice for all. An example is Lewis M. Steel, profiled as a "longtime civil rights worker" by *New York Times* journalist Lynda Richardson, who asked him about the status of civil rights. Steel answered:

> The problem is more than statistics; it's attitude. It's the same thing that has so limited progress for African-Americans and Hispanics since the 1960s, when some progress was made and overt forms of apartheid were broken down.[28]

He continued,

> Somehow people in leadership positions are either completely indifferent to racial progress, or worse, deep down, they have some sense, really, that people of color are not up to it in the same way that whites are. You don't just wave a magic wand and say it's over.[29]

Probing into the depths of the reasons for his commitment to civil rights in such difficult times, Steel, a step-grandson of Albert Warner of the Warner Brothers movie empire, related the story of his relationship as a youth with the family's Black caretaker, William Rutherford, who had been dead for thirty-five years when Steel was interviewed: "So, really, the pain is that I lost him on the one hand, and the pain is on the other hand that I saw what we white people had done to him."[30] As a person who basically lives in a white world, he stated that his "purpose . . . is to try and help white people understand the reality of racism and how it adversely affects all of us, how destructive it is to our society, our community, our ideals."[31]

So, while some whites work at eliminating racism as a response to the pain that oppression caused, others reject reparations because of the pain and fear about disclosing their role or that of their ancestors. This latter response exhibits an illogical proposition, which suggests that a country as large and complex as America does not consistently tend to the ancient past as a resource to inform present and future actions. A veritable government industry helps Americans refresh and enrich their linkages to the past in the form of a stream of monuments, archival sources that contain genealogical information, and other information about past government actions, all helpful to individual citizens as well as to the functioning of government itself. The primary exception appears to be monuments to slavery and Black subordination.

The Pain of Black People

The concept of mass pain as a consequence of Black subordination may be too serious, too outlandish to be considered, or even rejected altogether by Black people. Nevertheless, there are vital signs of its existence. The problem is that we may have become socialized to it in such a way that it now constitutes a condition, rather than a special feature of the Black personality.

Therefore, one of the most difficult problems faced by the reparations movement is to appeal to the American people to recognize a just cause based not on mere "inequality" but upon the suffering that oppression has caused. Thus far the movement has been unable to derive from that injustice the moral capital requisite to the general acceptance of the injustice as demanding restitution. Central to the issue of movement is that of "drama," or the creation of a sense of deep-seated alienation, which shapes the public cause and thus puts forth the demand for justice.

In many movements, public presentation of the cause is the result of mobilizations. Although there is no guarantee that the public will accept the cause as just, the drama of the mobilization is an effective way to present the issues involved. The reparations movement has been based on an intellectual rendering of an indisputable fact of slavery in American history and in the attendant racial subordination of Black people that has existed until this very day. Always—always—in the past, movements for the liberation of Black people have been accompanied by a mobilization that has included a public presentation.

The pictorial images of slavery that appeared in the newspapers focused on the commercial aspects of buying, selling, and recovery of Blacks and on the occasional insurrection, but not on the pain that is so vividly recorded in slave narratives. Even the classic picture of slaves packed into the hold of ships does not have the public exposure necessary to evoke the emotional content of the human experiences of slaves. It is omitted from the most esteemed American history texts and does not have the aura that should accompany such a dehumanizing process. In fact, one could say the same about the slave castles on the coast of

West Africa, the ships, and the the "seasoning ports" in the West Indies, through which Africans were often made into "slaves." These images do not have a frequent role in the presentation of American history, but are restricted to specific studies of slavery tended to by highly specialized scholars.

The Civil War was a dramatic presentation that tendered slavery as a fact that no person in the country could erase from consciousness. Yet although modern presentations of the Civil War are numerous, they focus on its political aspect and do not present the pain endured by Black slaves and the deficits that resulted from it.

The American civil rights movement created dramatic images for presentation in the living rooms of Americans, pictures of Blacks being beaten, showered with water, and bitten by dogs. Americans experienced the dramatic demonstrations at the Lincoln Monument by activists, whose presence as representatives of all sectors of American society made visible the wide public support for erasing the injustice of segregation and racism.

Similarly, the movement against U.S. relations with the Apartheid regime in South Africa in the 1980s, which occurred during one of the most conservative presidencies in the twentieth century, was successful because it created a globally dramatic presentation that made Americans sensitive to their complicity with a racist regime. The presidential campaign of Reverend Jesse Jackson carried the issue into the presidential debates, and large-scale demonstrations were initiated by TransAfrica. TransAfrica and its allies made visible American complicity in the crime of Apartheid, imaging the damage to human life that was at stake.

In the current attempt to mobilize support for reparations, there has been no comparable public drama. No photographs, no videos, for example, have educated the public about the problem, the cause, and the remedy. In any case, the lack of a presentation of the cause, other than in newspaper stories, symposia, and lawsuits—which, while important, do not have a mass appeal—is debilitating. The absence of the dramatic dimension means that Americans do not have the opportunity to share the pain of subordination.

Susan Sontag's *The Pain of Others* examines photographs of scenes from the Nazi Holocaust against Jews.[32] She remarks that previously she believed that people could become inured to war by repeated exposure to images capturing the suffering of civilians, but she revisits this theme to celebrate the enduring power of such images. In her attempt to understand human suffering through the images captured on film, she makes trenchant comments about the function of collective memory.

> What is called collective memory is not a remembering but a stipulating: that this is important, and this is the story about how it happened, with the pictures that lock the story in our minds. Ideologies create substantiating archives of images, representative images, which encapsulate common ideas of significance and trigger predictable thoughts, feelings.[33]

Sontag notes that European Jewry institutionalized collective memories in the Holocaust Memorial Museum in Washington, DC, to perpetuate memories of "death, failure and victimization" and to "invoke the miracle of survival."[34] Many victims want a "memory museum"; why, she asks, is there not already in the nation's capital a museum of the history of slavery, "the whole story, starting with the slave trade in Africa itself, not just selected parts, such as the Underground Railroad"?[35] She answers her own question by noting that the Holocaust didn't happen in America, such that it "doesn't risk arousing an embittered domestic population against authority. To have a museum chronicling the great crime that was African slavery in the United States of America would be to acknowledge that the evil was here. Americans prefer to picture the evil that was there and from which the United States—a unique nation, one without any certifiably wicked leaders throughout its entire history—is exempt."[36]

Thus, while it is easy to conclude that the rejection of Black issues constitutes yet another aspect of racism, those who support the reparations movement cannot rest with that conclusion. It does not relieve them from the attempt to develop an effective case that has the power of the Holocaust, based not just on the intellectual persuasiveness that is now the most salient feature, but on its dramatic visibility.

Spiritual Damage

Many African Americans have adjusted to the pain of their role in society in ways that narcotize its effect, just as many Black South Africans adjusted to Apartheid and its pain as inevitable features of daily life. In both societies, values assembled from the raw sewage of oppression become a pursuit: elevated position, petty advantage, jealousy and envy, extreme risk-taking, extreme risk-aversion, exaggerated stylistic invention, the use of delusional drugs and alcohol, macho proving acts, and so on. One result is that harmful values and behaviors are visited internally, upon others within the oppressed group. This is another cost of slavery and postslavery racism, largely unacknowledged by both Blacks and whites.

This is one fundamental reason for the pervasiveness of the deep and abiding corrective of Black religious experience, the major antidote to the pain of both the past and the present. It is an attempt to cope with the pressures of circumstances, which one can hear and feel in the songs and ritual of religious worship: the wailing from the bowels of pain, the expressions of power and mystery, the exhilaration of understanding life through the Scriptures and by other aspects, the tremendous collective vessel that the church provides as a healing force and as an instrument of hope.

In fact, writers on the early Black religious experience have referred to its content as "otherworldly" because Jesus Christ was regarded by the slave and freed Black alike as a deliverer from the abominations they faced in daily work and life on plantations and in the cities. African religions were prohibited by slavery's institutions, clearing the way for the adaptation of a new basis for coherence and a new orientation toward existence.[37] The parables of the life of Jesus represented the hope the enslaved African too might eventually be free. At the very least, his miracles provided access to a supernatural plane above the physical experiences of oppression and an ethic of justice that was also above white supremacy: When Frederick Douglass was faced with the Dred Scott decision by the Supreme Court, he denied the Court's supremacy, saying there was a "higher power."[38]

A sense of redemption and delivery from the pain of the often invisible forces that oppress Black people can be witnessed in Black working churches, which lack pretense and which beckon forth raw emotions for resolution. But the congregation is also majority female and elderly. Through the church Black women deal with raising children alone, children who are out of control; with providing their families shelter and food out of insufficient financial resources; and with relationships with men who are abusive or in prison. The elderly have been the church stewards, keepers of the institution's history, ritual, and stability. They are involved in the mysteries of religious concepts and teachings that have rationalized for them the gross contradiction between the depths of their oppression and the promises of peace and justice and eternal life by a God who is also all-forgiving and all-knowing. For them, the church culture—choirs and other musical roles; missionary programs; attention to individuals who are in need, or sick, or shut-in; a sense of order; and other aspects of Black religious life—has attended to their suffering and strengthened them to meet the challenges they know lie ahead.

While Black people live in a human culture that comprises the full dimension of the positive traits of joy and happiness, it is also true that there exists a substantial aspect of the culture that is described in the Black art form as "the Blues." Emanating in the Black Belt South, in the middle of the cotton culture, the creators of the art form told many stories that described in their totality a life of oppression that yielded the contradictions of Black existence, distortions of human relations and personalities, the lack of material and psychological resources, that evoked feelings of inferiority, pain and misery. The Blues told a truth about the Black existence that resonated with those who consumed the music whether one enjoyed or preferred it or not, and the music exists as one of the strongest bodies of evidence of how Blacks felt about their condition.

The Blues are not just an art form. They derive from experiences that have driven many Black people to the depths of despair and colored the character of their personal spirit, that of their family and their community relationships. Blacks are not unique in this respect, since oppressed people all over the world create and pass on folk songs that express their condition. However, Black expression of it, in the context of oppressive work, race relations, and philosophical vision of Blacks' possibilities as a people, have made the Blues unique in this country.

The hard reality is that Black communities exhibit the scars of substantive suffering. Ride down any inner-city neighborhood street and you will be impressed by two phenomena: the sheer number of liquor stores and the sheer number of churches, one or the other on almost every corner. Both play a role in anesthetizing the pain that Black people suffer, but the conservative ideology of our time, such as the "war on drugs," marks this effort to dull the pain as proof of immorality, rather than proof of suffering. Crimes that some Black people commit are oftentimes not comprehended as acts of survival, even sometimes as acts of war, but as criminal in the purest sense. Surely they are committed out of a desperate sense that one's life or one's family or community is at stake. As a result, the Blues are a leaven in the content of Black culture: they are the indescribable element in who we are, and they color everything we do.

Body Damage: Racism Kills

In the South African symposia the idea was expressed that the historical process of subordination had dealt Black people a mass psychological trauma, akin to the experience of war. The antidote or cure is to undergo some form of mass decompression and treatment. In fact, body memories are important indicators of the pain suffered in an oppressive state, because "the body has no intellectual defenses and therefore cannot screen out memory imprints. . . . [A] 'survivor,' who may have no abuse memories, will retrieve colors, hear sounds, or experience smells, odors, and taste sensations and her body may react in pain reflecting the purported abuse as the memory is retrieved. The body memory can even be an actual physical representation of an event."[39]

One psychologist, Jeff Gardere, suggests that Blacks have little awareness of the psychological toll that slavery and racism has taken upon their bodies and minds.[40] In fact, the damage done in the social conflict between Blacks and whites resembles that of the traumatic experiences in war; Gardere calls it "post traumatic slavery disorder." In his way of thinking, the mass stress that Blacks have experienced historically and daily emanates from their lives as an oppressed people and is often at the root of their dysfunctional behavior. It is manifested by symptoms of anger, distrust, low or nonexistent self-esteem, and chronic flashbacks of incidences of racism.

Gardere's view has long been supported by psychology professor Na'im Akbar, whose has concluded that slavery left psychological scars clearly manifested in the modern life of Black people, for example, in a negative orientation to menial forms of work, destruction of the "master's" property, the tendency to clown or "play the fool," personal inferiority or lack of confidence in one's ability, social disorganization, and distorted family life and color discrimination.[41]

Gardere's view is supported by some of the best scientific studies by medical researchers. For example, one study found that the socioeconomic status of the neighborhood affects an individual's health.

Neighborhoods affect individuals' physical health, in part because communities vary in the prevalence and intensity of stressors and resources. Environmental stressors such as noise, overcrowding, and violence, or economic stressors such as chronic poverty, may abound in inner-city neighborhoods, which may in turn influence essential hypertension . . . and related health outcomes in children and youth.[42]

The authors cite a study by B. R. Gump and others, which found that Black youth who lived in lower socioeconomic status neighborhoods showed greater blood pressure reaction to stressors than did white youth. A study by Jackson and colleagues found that Black youth in higher socioeconomic status neighborhoods manifested even higher blood pressure reactions than Blacks in lower socioeconomic neighborhoods.[43]

Katherine Light and others found that work-related stress in Blacks ocurred in high-status jobs that boosted the risks of hypertension and severe cardiovascular problems.[44] The term they coined for this phenomenon is "John Henryism," for the Black folk hero who refused to quit in a contest with a machine. The concept was used to examine "high-effort coping": that is, Blacks and women tend to exhibit strong effort in a context where "a smaller proportion of women and Black men hold high status jobs, and there is a perception that greater effort and perseverance are required to achieve and retain such jobs."[45] Among adults with low levels of education, the level of John Henryism observed was three times as great in Black as in whites.

Finally, Blacks' perceptions of racism also harm their health in the form of hypertension and cardiovascular problems. A 2003 study by Andrew Sherwood and colleagues monitored blood pressure of sixty-nine African American men and women over a twenty-four-month period. The researchers asked the respondents how frequently they experienced racism; nearly 80 percent reported that they experienced racism several times a month (33 percent), several times a week (17 percent), or several times a day (33 percent). The news report of the study noted, "Experiencing racism in everyday life contributes around the clock to high blood pressure in African Americans, say Duke University Medical Center researchers."[46] Blacks perceiving racism "tended to internalize their anger rather than express it openly"—a tendency that must have had even more pernicious effects during the era of slavery.

Thus, the medical evidence supports the view that a strong and debilitating source of health risk among Blacks has been the internalization of the anger they have felt as a result of the abuse of slavery and post-slavery racial oppression but have not expressed.

Therefore, the process of restitution must entail resources to enable Blacks to recover a sense of legitimacy through a confrontation with what has happened to them: who and what was responsible and what was the cost. Only then is it possible to design correctives for personal and collective healing.

Sharing the Pain: The "Never Again" Symbol

The significance of Black pain has not been presented as effectively as that of the Jewish American experience with the Holocaust. A superior class position in American society has enabled them to pursue public presentations of the Holocaust in ways that have made it a standard feature of American culture in art, drama, cinema, and a national museum. As a result, the Holocaust is widely known and comprehended as a unique horror, and its victims are widely sympathized with. In other words, there is no "Black History Month" approach to the Holocaust, in which the rest of the year yields images of Blacks largely employed contradictorily as objects of humor.

The Holocaust is the best-known and most popularly acknowledged of the human tragedies that have befallen specific groups, and its visibility in the United States as a specific memory of the collective oppression and the continued suffering of a people is well acknowledged. It is registered in popular culture in a manner unlike African slavery and has a level of public memory and popular recognition unmatched by any other event of World War II.

There is a popular saying among those (not just Jews) who have understood that the Holocaust represented the depths of human barbarity: we must insure that such a thing happens "never again." This is an altogether logical and necessary denunciation of what the Jewish people have experienced and is a symbolic response to inhumanity in general.

It is surprising, therefore, that this deep knowledge of suffering and oppression does not extend to Blacks, and that some prominent Jewish spokesmen have rejected the idea of reparations in the United States.

Where is the equally fervent denunciation by Jews of what happened during the course of slavery and its aftermath? Are Jews, like other whites, intimidated as individual perpetrators of crimes against Blacks? It may be the case that Jews are made sensitive by charges that they "financed African slavery."

The modern conflict between Blacks and Jews over affirmative action may have also have played a role in preventing Jews from validating the claim of Blacks to reparations. As many Jews have become "white," they have also assumed many of the negative attitudes toward Blacks resident in the culture, and some play a leading role as governmental officials and in the neoconservative movement. Therefore, have played a role in the new suppression of the Black voice by the radical conservative movement.

The symbolic phrase "Never again!" has been uttered by top officials of the American government to give voice and memory to the Holocaust. For example, Richard Armitage, deputy secretary of state, said, in a speech to the Holocaust Task Force, which was seeking reparations from American institutions:

> Never again the totalitarian brutality that consumed Europe[an] Jews and millions of others. Never again the genocide that was planned and executed with scientific malice and mechanical efficiency. Never again the sweeping oppression that suborned whole societies on behalf of hatred and on behalf of death. But you have also helped us teach our people that when we say "never again," we are speaking not just of historical forces but directly to the faces and the names of those who perished and to those who survived the Holocaust. And it is to them that we make our pledge.[47]

This was an exceedingly strong commitment of the U.S. government to the Jewish people and their experience with the Holocaust, and Armitage suggests that it was confirmed by the highest official in the State Department, Secretary of State Colin Powell, who said on the occasion of the National Day of Remembrance, "The millions of men, women and children who were killed in the Holocaust once had dreams for the future, each and every one of them, dreams denied. We, the living, have the power to create hope, defend freedom and build peace."[48]

Powell is also an African American who agreed with his president that the United States should not send a high-level delegation to the United Nations Conference against Racism in Durban. Part of the reason was that African slavery might be declared a "crime against humanity," a concept that would strengthen the demand for reparations.

At all ends, there is a contradiction in this for those Jews whose pain has brought them to memorialize the specificity of their experience, which at the same time prevents them, because of the depths of that specificity, from sharing the experience with other people. The nature of the antihuman acts perpetrated against Jews would seem to induce a universal "never again" code of conscience that would make them first in line to support the demand for restitution to those who have been harmed. During the attempt by the United Nations to stop the "ethnic cleansing" in Bosnia, Roy Gutman, a journalist much celebrated for his coverage of that war, was quoted as saying:

> Well, I'm Jewish, and yes, the Holocaust is something I believe must never happen again. Somewhere, back in my first thoughts about going into journalism, I considered that maybe if reporters had been out there to issue warnings at the time, they could have stopped it—But I never expected I would be the warning system for some other group.[49]

Many Jews have honored that responsibility, since African peoples have had, and continue to have, Jewish allies in many venues of social struggle. In fact, one wishes that members of the Black middle class would populate nonprofit organizations—foundations, think tanks, community organizations, and so on—as frequently as Jews, who are still disproportionately engaged as progressives in making a better world. The Tikkun symbol of progressive Jewish thought and activism, however, is also a minority power within the Jewish community and pales against those who have joined the conservative movement— including some outright leaders of the antireparations movement, such as Richard Horowitz. They have not elevated the particularism of the Holocaust to the universal plane, or, if they do accomplish this, they do not imbue this universalism with the fundamental nonracialism that befits a commitment to the memory of the Holocaust and rehabilitates other victims of oppression.

Accusation and Guilt

One of the powerful reasons why many whites reject reparations is not the facts of history, but because they feel they are being accused of a crime and, therefore, that guilt is personalized. Although activists and scholars have suggested that individual culpability is not relevant in the project of restitution and that the primary culpability is with the state and private corporations, the feeling of personal accusation remains. However, the accusation of the historical and continuing oppression of Blacks is being made against America, not individuals. Individuals do not have the power to make restitution; in fact, the only effective way that they can participate is to sanction restitution by government and by the financial and business institutions in which they participate.

Yet reparations as a restorative measure are rejected by a political culture that has grown more conservative. There is an uneasiness between nationalism and guilt. In one sense, nationalism may be a powerful factor in the formation of movements to repress guilt, as in the Tutsi-Hutu wars in Rwanda. And a nationalist movement that asserts the superiority and interests of the group that mobilizes it clashes with those of the oppressed classes, as a natural conflict of group interests.

In addition, the powerful always blanch at the thought of having their own motives of domination, and the culture of domination, interrogated, as a threat to their power. Thus, it is a natural reaction of the powerful to resist demands of the oppressed and even to distort the situation of the oppressed in order to reaffirm their position in the social order, as I have described in *White Nationalism, Black Interests.* Nevertheless, the oppressed continue to make demands because of the shared knowledge by both groups: that with power comes responsibility. As powerful as the British were in the heyday of their empire, they adopted a colonial policy that was at least theoretically sensitive to the care of the so-called native populations. Likewise, in the United States various regimes have been sensitive to this policy, but they have either not understood or have rejected the gravity of the demands by Blacks and the urgency of the situation that the Black community faced. Nevertheless, in some eras the powerful have been pushed toward measures of amelioration, but have always encountered severe limitations to the initiative, whether it be Roosevelt's New Deal or civil rights legislation in the 1960s.

Opponents of reparations have been successfully made guilt the

basis of the general American response. However, the response to reparations must go beyond personal guilt, to understand that, as always, the
condition of Black people, the most oppressed, has defined the character of American democracy itself. The existence of Black lynching was
brought to the attention of the U.S. government by countries abroad
even before World War II; surely after the war, such criticism undercut
American pretensions to be the most democratic nation in the world.
Today American leaders have invaded and badly damaged Iraq, then
assumed a responsibility for its reconstruction, placing hundreds of billions of dollars paid by Black taxpayers at risk. Yet the communities in
which many Blacks live rival those in Iraq in their level of underdevelopment—confirming the sense of Dr. Martin Luther King's observation about the Vietnam War, that the bombs dropped there blew up in
the ghettoes of America.[50]

In a context where the voice and visibility of white privilege and
power are determinative, the demand for reparations makes a simple
charge: With power comes the responsibility to correct the historical
mistakes of slavery and modern racism. The great power at the command of the white majority cannot be used to put a fig leaf over a petu-
lance about guilt; it should instead help build a democratic edifice that
is truly a model for global humanity. Indeed, Eric Yamamoto refers to
a sentiment expressed by a South African reporter: "Precisely because
reconciliation has not been earned, it functions as nothing more than a
bandage that splits as soon as there is any pressure applied to it."[51]
America has not yet "earned reconciliation" by adopting realistic measures that address the national question, and for that reason social
. events split the bandage over race relations every time pressure is
applied.

In Paula Rothenberg's volume on white privilege, several of the
contributors are concerned with making white privilege visible to
whites. For while it is highly visible to Blacks and other nonwhites, very
often whites rely on it unconsciously, meanwhile imagining that they
operate in a mythical individualistic field of social relations. Stephanie
Wildman and Adrienne Davis believe that

> the invisibility of privilege strengthens the power it creates and
> maintains. The invisible cannot be combated, and as a result
> privilege is allowed to perpetuate, regenerate, and re-create
> itself. Privilege is systemic, not an occasional occurrence. Priv-

ilege is invisible only until looked for, but silence in the face of privilege sustains its invisibility.[52]

This misrecognition is not accidental; Peggy McIntosh, for example, believes that "whites are carefully taught not to recognize White privilege, males are taught not to recognize male privilege."[53] Tim Wise makes a number of useful observations, the first of which is that this "virtual invisibility" behaves like "psychological money in the bank, the proceeds of which we cash in every day while others are in a state of perpetual overdraft."[54] Given the power and invisibility of white privilege, Wise asks, why would one want to end it? He answers that the price of white privilege is too high. The social structure must maintain a pool of cheap Black labor that drives down all wages, a poverty-stricken educational system for people of color who are critical to the viability of whites, and a prison-industrial complex for confinement of Blacks that eats up social resources.[55] Making white privilege visible is key to illuminating the present and historical damage it has done to Blacks.

Conclusion

The attitudes and practices that were a part of formal slavery created the paradigm for the continued oppression of Blacks in the periods of informal slavery and discrimination. They are a legacy of American indebtedness to Blacks, as measures and attitudes that have brought harm and death to the Black population. However, where reparations are concerned, it is the expropriation of Black resources that is crucial, for these stolen resources both impoverished Blacks and enriched those who oppressed them. Those resources enabled many whites to maintain and improve their condition as small farmers and businesspeople, but the massive expropriation also made possible the industrial development and agricultural viability of the country, as a substantial pool of capital that cost nothing. It was an invisible grant to the nation, a foundation of its institutions and ultimately of its ability to become a powerful nation.

The victims are not invisible. The original slave population produced heirs, now tenfold the size of that group, who still lag behind the rest of the nation, not only the progeny of the original white settlers but even people of color who have freely emigrated to this country and have been able to take advantage of its institutions, its resources, and share in the myth and reality of its international power. Thus, ironically, Black people have given an unacknowledged gift to the nation and continue to give it, all the while experiencing discrimination. This irony is one of the social and historical dynamics that keep Black-white racial tensions alive and will do so until it is resolved and Blacks and whites become reconciled through a sufficient program of restitution.

We have addressed some of the central questions in the proposal to provide restitution to African descendants in America, through considering the South African model of restitution. This model confirms the simple but powerful proposition that the conditions suffered by Blacks in America today are a result of their experiences during and after slavery, which are the central cause of the racial problem in America today.

CHAPTER EIGHT

The Reparations Movement:
A Liberatory Narrative

THE RIGHT WING IN AMERICAN POLITICS has labored mightily to promote the notion that liberal policies have been a major cause of Black inequality—encouraging Black people to fail, as it were. However, conservative policies have pushed the Black community backward further than liberal policies. A reasonable person must conclude that policy paradigms matter, and that the paradigms applied so far have been implicated in the failure to achieve equality.

The reparations movement is different paradigm, one with a "liberatory narrative" that builds a path toward eventual Black freedom. Angelyn Mitchell explains that liberatory narratives

> are concerned with more than a state of being; their primary function indeed is in describing how to achieve freedom. In doing so, the liberatory narrative seeks to eclipse the deterministic conditions of racial enslavement. This move is important because it cannot proffer or embrace paradigms of freedom if one is still chained to the old paradigm with its language of bondage.[1]

The language of liberation should be grounded in action directed toward the goal of liberation. The reparations movement is a concrete example of such action, which tests the motivations of the state toward African peoples.

Our examination of the reparations movement from this perspective will take into consideration the responsibility of the state to take measures to pursue meaningful democracy, and what the movement should reclaim from American society and how. There are also issues of the importance of the self and self-determination of Black people, the price of racial reconciliation, and the status of mobilizing Black leaders toward these ends.

Liberation toward What Goal?

Elsewhere in this work, I have argued that the objectives embedded in the "race relations" improvement model have not been reached, largely because they have been circumvented by the radical conservative movement. The objective of "equality" that emanated from the race-relations model is different from that offered by the reparations model. The latter, which includes both internal Black rehabilitation and external payment of the debt owed the Black community by the state and private interests, leads toward self-determination, an objective far more pertinent to Black interests than equality and more effective in achieving equality.

Put another way, in order for the project of equality to be effective, it must encompass the equalization of the resources of the Black community with the rest of society, not just equal access to opportunities. An "access only" paradigm ignores the theft of resources during slavery and thus the head start that other groups have enjoyed in the accumulation of economic resources. It ignores the cultural damage done to the Black community that inhibits the trust necessary to pool their resources for economic and social development; it ignores the social pressure on the Black community, which is different from that experienced by other groups. And it feeds into the view that Blacks will accept a place in America that is inferior to that of other groups.

The liberatory narrative is the antidote to the "grand narrative of oppression" and thus, the antidote must be administered using two types of action. First, reparations are a concrete act that can be taken by the state and by private interests to assist in eventual racial reconciliation. This is so because in the history of the United States, reparations, in the form of government and private support, were given to white citizens not only as a salve to group pain and damage, but also to assist them to develop and maintain a positive frame of reference toward the state in fulfilling national objectives.

Thus, it matters in which context the state is operating. In the case of South Africa, the transition from white oppression to Black state control meant reparations to be considered as a legitimate corrective by the state. In the United States, however, the white majority has been in power since the founding of the nation and, despite the active program of racial subordination it effected, considers reparations to be an unsupportable grant of power to African descendants at whites' expense. Indeed, J. Angelo Corlett believes that the refusal of the state to grant the power inherent in sufficient reparations only deepens the immorality from generation to generation.

> reparations seem to be the moral cost of the United States to attempt to redeem itself from the dredges of immorality in which it alone has placed itself, generation after generation, by simply refusing to pay what it owes to those whom it has murdered, enslaved, and otherwise oppressed.[2]

The state could alter the context of white power by a series of meaningful steps. It could play a role in influencing private interests to consider their role in the historical process of oppression and lend, as was done in the case of Holocaust victims, official support for claims for compensation. Then, the state could consider the size of the demand as a legitimate point of reference for negotiations (given what credible analyses estimate as the amount of the damage) given the oppression the Blacks have faced and still face today.[3]

Both the state and Blacks who are potentially engaged in the negotiations for reparations should take a lesson from Jewish tactics of negotiation. First, the Jewish case is important since before 1952, there was no precedent for a nation-state assuming responsibility for crimes in the past that it had committed against a minority in its country and thus, no precedent existed for legitimizing claims of this nature.[4] Second, uncertainty about the amount of reparations should not be allowed to sabotage consideration of whether to pay them at all. When Stuart Eizenstat, American ambassador to the European Union, met with the Swiss bankers on behalf of Jewish Holocaust victims, the offer of $32 million was considered insulting by Edgar Bronfman, millionaire New Yorker and vigorous advocate for Jewish Holocaust claims.[5] This led the Swiss to reconsider and offer $300 million, whereupon Bronfman demanded $3 billion, which led to a mutually agreeable figure of $1.25 billion. Similarly, lawyers first believed that the German government would pay $30 billion in Holocaust claims, but negotiations led to the Luxemburg agreement in 1952, which amounted to $60 billion to 500,000 survivors.[6] So the amount of African-descendant reparations, a bone of contention and disbelief among opponents because of the magnitude of plausible figures, must not be the basis for the refusal to consider reparations, given that all numbers are subject to negotiation and none equals the actual damage that has been sustained.

Rehabilitation of the Self

The liberatory narrative, although it may be directed toward the actions of others, begins with the requirement for acts of personal and group responsibility. Such responsibility is not that kind which comes from outside imposition or blames the victim, but that which consists of elective acts of individuals who have been oppressed, who volunteer to join a cause that may lead to the enhancement of their power and foster programs that rehabilitate the Black community from within. This means that the demand for reparations must achieve a consensus within the Black community that makes the demand undeniable to those who receive it.

The liberatory narrative also means that if a sense of group responsibility is not achieved, in which Blacks sense possible victory over the impediments to their achievements, through the use of more adequate material resources directed by fresh strategies, then the mere grant of money will fall into old channels of cultural confusion, mimicry of the mainstream, waste, and finally failure. That is why social movements are not only politically necessary, but, as Frantz Fanon suggested in *The Wretched of the Earth*, promote a psychological cleansing that centers the acts that lead to justice, empowering the group itself which claims the victory in subjective terms.

Evidence of Blacks' acknowledgment of the necessity of self-direction is expressed in public opinion polls: they believe that the responsibility for their advancement resides primarily with themselves, and that they have not done enough to foster a positive sense of self-determination.[7] Randall Robinson, in a discussion with the Reparations Coordinating Committee, commented that the project of reparations, largely defined by those who have assumed leadership, must provide an opportunity for the masses to heal themselves.[8] This observation acknowledges the side benefits of a social movement that can focus the Black community on addressing the pathologies derived from oppression. As I have said previously, these are manifest attempts to ward off the pain, confusion, and constriction of human possibilities that are part of Blacks' circumscribed status. This point does not negate the understanding that the most powerful factor in shaping positive behavior is in positive institutional change toward that objective, since institutions have the opportunity to affect human behavior over time through their use of substantial resources.

So the reparations movement can become a process that encompasses a subliminal process of healing. This component of social movements often goes unrecognized, in that political objectives are the most public manifestation of the goals espoused. Nonetheless, the movement itself offers possibilities for self-renewal and rehabilitation. Perhaps correctives always require that the people take responsibility, in an inward dynamic parallel to whatever outward, public project is initiated.

Reparations as a Demand for Justice

Demanding Human Rights

One of the ends of the liberatory narrative is to enable Blacks to pursue their goals to the maximum of their desires and needs, in the context of their own conceptions of what a democratic state offers. The simple fact is that slavery and its aftermath robbed Blacks of the ability to achieve their self-determined objectives on a par with others. However, this fact cannot be reversed by a state-sponsored liberation paradigm; that alone will never resolve what Gunnar Myrdal long ago posed as "an American dilemma." As we saw in chapter 5, strategies of ameliorization have been devised without the insights or guidance of the African American community—and thus have failed to produce "equality." Equality of opportunity, the goal established by the civil rights movement, was modest enough, but it will never be achieved so long as the paradigm of self-determination is weak.

A democratic state does not bludgeon citizens into the pursuit of authoritarian ends, but allows them to full citizenship on their own terms. In the United States, that would mean enlarging the definition of Americanness to include Blacks and other groups who have been excluded. This is important because the ability of Blacks to claim their Americanness has been restricted because "the American way" has been the race-privileged definition of the white majority. This was certainly the case in the nationalist era of the early part of the twentieth century:

> So it was that the most avid foes of labor unions underwrote a campaign to equate the open shop with "Americanism." So it was that those who distrusted Negroes or Catholics or Jews now did so in the name of Americanism. It was a word that the opponents of women's suffrage used, a word used also by the advocates of a literacy test for immigrants.[9]

This restrictive definition of who was an American and belonged to the nation has not vanished and racism has always left those who were defined out of the nation with a question-mark identity. For this reason, reparations are a relevant corrective, since they begin with the politics of memory, developing an objective to honor the dignity and contribution of those who have contributed so much to allow others to enjoy American democracy, which they could not enjoy themselves because of their subjugation. This leads to a conditional observation on the possibility of the full and complete enjoyment by Black people of American democracy: if reparations (or something equivalent) are not given, Blacks will remain largely dependent within American society, a posture that entails an ongoing demand upon the state for ameliorative public policies that will produce only incremental steps toward the goal of freedom. Democratic rights alone are simply insufficient to lead to true equality in a capitalist society where those rights can be enjoyed only if one possesses the means to mobilize them. Thus, reparations are a politics of democracy.

Demanding Dignity

One reason others do not commit themselves to restitution is that Blacks themselves are not publicly committed. Where is the Black commitment to a slogan equivalent to "Never again," pledging them to action? For Blacks in America, forgetting is suicidal, because so much of who they are is contained in the memory who they were and what has transpired to bring them to this moment in history. The former slaves very often did not want to talk about their past because the memories were painful, but even they did not forget. Imagine the awful anguish and lament in the voice of John Crawford as he told interviewers in October 1937 about his life as a slave in Austin, Texas, and about his expectation that restitution would be made for what had happened to him.

> It's a fact dat after freedom we was told dat we was to get 40 acres, and a mule. Dis was de talk in de country at dat time, but we never did git dat mule and forty acres. I never did hear no talk about dividin' up our master's land.[10]

To fail to even attempt to redeem the memory and expectation of John Crawford is to confirm that writing off the debt owed to him and millions of others is right and just. But it is not right and just, and thus the restoration of his memory is the route to justice, and restitution is its satisfaction.

In order to envision the possibility that Blacks might reacquire the wholeness of their personality in the American national context, it is necessary, in the words of Charles Ogletree, to make an assessment of what was lost, through the oppressive mechanisms of slavery and racial discrimination, in comparative terms with the rest of society. Often, in such an assessment, one begins with the material dimension; however, if we argue that reparations can help make possible rehabilitation of the Black personality, then they must be mobilized in the service of rehabilitating what Avishai Margalit has called "negative moral emotions," such as the humiliation that accompanied slavery.[11] It was the pain of humiliation that sets up the craving for justice and launches the politics of dignity. Margalit says: "Dignity, unlike social honor, is not a positional good. It is supposed to be accorded to everybody, even to the one who is nobody, by virtue of the most universal common denominator of being human."[12]

A logical inference from this idea is that the politics of recognition is part of the restorative element in achieving dignity, for the absence of recognition is the absence of civil rights, the confirmation of dehumanization, and the debasement of the human personality. For who decides that it is just for Japanese "comfort women," or Jews, or Native Americans, who suffered from the indignity of their experience, to demand restitution, but that this same right does not extend to Blacks? It is for the oppressed to decide and through their demand for restitution begin to reclaim the dignity that they lost. Reparations are, therefore, a politics of dignity.

Demanding Resources

Another resource lost through oppression is a comprehensive infrastructure of Black financial institutions, the bedrock out of which emerge strong social and political institutions and activities, which would have enabled Blacks to financially independent, self-supporting, socially self-determining. Self-determination requires the possession of power in society, not only that which comes as a result of citizenship, but that which is created by the ability to build wealth.

Fundamentally, the experience of slavery meant that Blacks who came to America lost the power to determine their destiny, lost control over themselves, their environment, and their ability to determine outcomes for their families. Postslavery racism has had the same dramatic impact, robbing Black people of not only something known as "citizenship rights" but also human rights. Black oppression means relative loss of the ability to determine one's destiny, one's own life, to control one's environment, to seize opportunities open to other Americans. One says "relative" because although whites have more control than Blacks, there are zones where Blacks are able to exercise more control than in others, such as in religion, sports, or entertainment.

The possession of social power means that whites have not had to live in a society where others determine their destiny. But Blacks have had their entire life circumstance shaped by their relative powerlessness and others' dominance over the institutions that educate them, the information they consume, the employment they can acquire, the locations in which they live and the houses they are able to afford, the treatment they receive in public places, the people who are viewed as their legitimate representatives, the quality of their artistic aesthetic, the nature of their value system and psychological predilections, even their value as human beings.

At all ends, America must come to terms with the poison of racism and the fact that there are no substitutions that Black people will accept for a respectful place in society on the basis of an open opportunity structure. That is the primary nature of the struggle for "civil rights" and social justice in America. Nevertheless, it is important to understand that a struggle based on the achievement of civil rights, or the achievement of equality, or the elimination of racism, will only legitimize the status quo. These goals are interrelated and positive, but they won't be reached unless self-determination is achieved, and this route may take another hundred years or more.

In this sense, "Black Power" and "integration" were limited visions of the goals that Blacks would have to obtain in America to achieve true equality. Both assumed that the promulgation of public policies in the realm of education, civil rights, housing, public accommodations, voting, and employment would be sufficient to achieve equality. However, neither the civil rights nor the Black Power movement comprehended the demand for financial restitution, except for a moment in history. Thus, reparations are a politics of empowerment.

The struggle for reparations constitutes another level in the struggle for power, for the real power to determine the future, not merely to be a dignified, though still subordinate, part of it. The struggle to determine the destiny of a people as individuals or a group ("self-determination"), then, may be conceived as a series of rising steps, where one level was the struggle for civil rights, another, the struggle for human rights, and the final step, the struggle for the means of controlling Black destiny.

Renegotiating the Racial Contract

Dr. Manning Marable once voiced the view in a conversation with the author that at the heart of the debate over reparations was the idea of "renegotiation" of the contract between Blacks and the rest of the American nation. As argued here, the essence of the politics of memory has been the conflict generated by the existence of two different "memories" that have served as symbols for two different realities based two different conceptions of what America should be. There was no negotiation that led to freeing Blacks from slavery and the adoption of the Thirteenth, Fourteenth, and Fifteenth Amendments to the Constitution, ostensibly legitimizing the Black place in the American sociopolitical order. Under the guise of an imperfect contract, the demand of the white majority for forgetting and for the merger of the two realities into one—on the basis of the white view of reality—is not only unrealistic, but constitutes yet another form of oppression. And again, as is our thesis, it temporarily patches up the memory, but since the wound is not healed, the pain of subordination reemerges in different forms to remind all that racial conflict is still a dominant characteristic of the current version of American democracy. What is there to renegotiate?

Reparations give us the opportunity and the platform to entertain certain theories that have often placed Blacks on the wrong road. These concepts are put into raw perspective in the demand for reparations and ultimately must be challenged and changed:

Acknowledge the attack on Black opportunity by the radical conservative movement and its results, rolling back the civil rights regime and its legal structure.

Assert that the requirements for participation in American society go far beyond affirmative action and other civil rights laws, to participation in the economic structure of the country on the basis of equality.

Reject the assumption that, given political rights, Blacks could obtain economic rights, on the grounds that the logical consequence of political participation is not control over substantial economic resources.

Repudiate as a method of economic growth the philosophy of "bootstrapism," which ignores the fact that Blacks entered the capitalist system at its maturity, when everything had a price, and when Blacks were used as resources for capitalists to achieve outlandish profits.

Recognize that because slavery created the economic gulf between Black and white wealth and because mature capitalism maintains it, Blacks have limited capacity to make a substantial difference in their economic lives and the life of their community. Therefore, it is necessary to marry economic resources to law in order to make economic equality possible, so that the democratic promise of America becomes a reality for Blacks.

The Paradigm of Reconciliation

The racial paradigm of historical oppression and the modern attempt at racial renegotiation has similarities in the colonial system throughout the world and therefore in the requirements for undoing the modern residue of oppression. What is required at a minimum, derived from the models discussed from the United States and South Africa, is described in the following sections.

Context

America must come to terms with the fact that there are no good substitutes for the elimination of a negative racial past and present, that Black people will not accept a substitute. That is the primary nature of the struggle for civil rights and social justice in America, and if the signals now being sent by every major political institution in America are interpreted to mean that a line is being drawn in the sand, the decision that faces Black America is not whether, but when and how, to cross it.

When one says that "America" must do this or that, one recognizes that the country is comprised of sectors that have significant responsibilities to engage the public in the task of making it whole. And here, it must be remembered that most of the cases of reparations were not won in court by other aggrieved groups in American society. They were responsibilities taken up by the government itself, except for Jewish reparations. There, private companies were shamed into considering their World War II role and in making recompense to American Jews and others if they were to continue to profit from the global postwar economy.

But in remembering the case of other communities that have pursued the demand for reparations, context must also include the fact that they also differed in the ends for which the reparations would be used. It is reported that since Jewish Holocaust survivors have not reached a consensus about how funds obtained from German and Swiss companies should be spent, there have been "rancorous arguments" among them.[13] Some survivors complain that too much is being spent for "charitable institutions for Holocaust education and commemoration rather than being spent for the direct care of sick and aging people." This school of thought is that "survivors should come first" since many are aged and infirm and that since the funds obtained will not last indefinitely, they should be directed toward home-based medical care and other immediate needs.

Recognition

I believe that the South African model of the TRC as a government policy works least in the United States as a judicial process and best as a legislative process by which the issues of restitution are vetted and settled. This confirms the view of Robert Westley that the courts are an inappropriate venue before which to submit a claim of reparations, considering the precedents of the all of the previous reparations cases involving other groups both in the United States and elsewhere.[14] However, the application of the TRC model is problematic in America since the question of who are the victims is less specific and thus, more subject to the categorical treatment that is the methodology inherent in public policy-making. Nevertheless, a number of lawsuits have been launched to clarify this issue.

Using government records to develop a database of companies involved in the slave trade that are still in business, Deadria Farmer-Paellmann filed suit in 2002 against Aetna Insurance, alleging that the company profited from insuring slaves for their masters. Lawsuits have been also been filed against the government in San Francisco by direct descendants of slaves, by two hundred descendants of former slaves from Louisiana, and for families in Texas, Illinois, and New York. These lawsuits have touched off a national debate over whether or not reparations should be granted to Black Americans and under what conditions. They have also illuminated the efforts of Congressman John Conyers, who since the mid-1980s has proposed legislation in the House of Representatives to study the feasibility of reparations, receiving no support from his white colleagues and little from Black colleagues, at least until the cause became popular among Blacks in general.

Reparations as Restitution

The problem unearthed by the form of restitution through reparations settled on by the TRC was that it still left the victims unequal, even after reparations were paid by the government. What is not being brought back—perhaps cannot be brought back—is the stolen wealth that would ensure that restitution resulted in social equality. The process of majority rule has resulted in political equality; however, in a capitalist society, it takes the mobilization of resources in order for political equality to become the leverage of power that leads to the equal enjoyment of social position and goods. The model for this was enacted by the Boers in South Africa, who were less affluent than the English commercial class in their country, but who used the leverage of their political power to direct governmental control over private sector industries, setting up "parastatal" companies that were controled by a 51 percent government interest, and thereby creating opportunities in that sector for meaningful participation.

Restitution, then, can only be a negotiated proposition that integrates the interests of those who have the economic resources with those who are seeking justice. As such, the amount agreed upon can only be a symbolic reflection of what was lost. A substantive addition can be made by reparations only if the sum agreed upon is sufficient to make a meaningful difference in the living standards of the group receives them. Otherwise, as argued here, it is important to separate the normal access of Blacks to the programs for which they pay taxes like other groups and individuals, from reparations that may take the form, not of cash, but of special programs and opportunities in various sectors of American society.

Reconciliation

Here, the South African case—as in the other cases that were discussed in the preliminary symposia—is useful because of the implicit assumption that reparations or other restitution would lead to reconciliation. Actually, restitution is only a step toward reconciliation that establishes a moral foundation, a "good faith" gesture to move toward the final stages. Some opponents believe that reparations may prejudice the ability of Blacks to demand social, economic, and political justice, because of the feeling that Blacks had been bought off, that the reparations would set them free from the expectation that the government would engage in any other attempts to address urgent needs. This, however, is a mystifying position, in that none of the other groups who received reparations gave up the right to pursue other social goods, nor was such proposed by the U.S. government when it granted reparations.

In fact, reparations in the United States—as in South Africa—cannot lead to reconciliation in a single step because the economic realm was only one arena of Black subordination. The other factor is racism, and until racism vanishes, there can be no thought that reparations for Blacks will be sufficient to provide racial reconciliation. The expectation that "forgiveness" would lead to reconciliation was always a questionable assumption propounded by Bishop Desmond Tutu, born of the Christian theology that has guided his approach to the struggle against Apartheid and the construction of a post-Apartheid attempt to resolve the racial dilemma. However, as well intended as his concept— "no future without forgiveness"—has been in achieving the reconciliation that would produce a "rainbow nation," it cannot wash away in such a short period and with such a minor process, the deep and abiding effects of Apartheid.[15] Whether the TRC has laid the basis for reconciliation is yet to be seen. It is certain that the same profound conditions obtain in the United States.

While one understands and appreciates the hopefulness of Bishop Tutu's idea—that the cycle of recrimination and violence must broken if there is to be a basis for civil relations—justice contains more elements than a mere sense of moral concession. Tutu points out that with the transition to Black majority rule, many expected a bloodbath, which "did not happen."[16] The reason he infers is that with the ending of Apartheid, there was hope in the coming of a new day, in the stature of Nelson Mandela in the world, and in the progress that the new dispensation might make.

Blacks in America have resorted to protest episodically out of the sense that injustice must be countered, since it is a part of the ever present reality that shapes their living space. They also have had access to hope, both in their version of the Christian religion as a moral force, and in the possibility that slow and steady progress might eventually fulfill the promises enshrined in the founding of the state. Blacks have gone a long way toward forgiveness, extending their trust that the promise of American democracy is reachable; this is evident in the miraculous lack of a crippling malice and resentment toward whites that would have been the seedbed of wholesale revolution. Yes, something beyond forgiveness is necessary: it is the promise that the forgiveness will be reciprocated by extending the promise that a better life will in fact be possible.

Self-Determination

Here we move beyond the assertion that reparations are critical to the process of self-determination. What should be done with the resources? How would self-determination be facilitated by reparations, assuming they are granted? For all of the success that Blacks have had in America, and despite the oppression that they have experienced, they are still in a developmental mode, largely because they live in a dynamic society where successive adjustments to the changes in the state have made it difficult to achieve a straight line of parallel progress. The state changes its approach to racial progress in various eras, moving forward or backward as ideological trends dictate. Then, its actions establish superordinate objectives that take priority over the pursuit of racial reconciliation through restitution, and result in even complicating Black progress by facilitating the introduction into society of competing groups or using resources in ways that deprive the Black communities of the normal resources to remain viable.

What is required is a stable platform of resources and attention to the development of the Black community, a feat that can only be accomplished by Blacks themselves. Therefore, there is a growing consensus among the leadership of the movement that, if reparations were granted, a "check in the mail" format would be counterproductive. Given the past examples of reparations where individual families were given financial resources of some sort, Blacks would also expect the same, as is shown by the current examples of Blacks making unapproved claims for reparations with the Internal Revenue Service.

However, a survey of 250 participants in the "Millions for Reparations" march on August 16, 2002, by the African American Leadership Institute at the University of Maryland, found the following answers to questions posed about this subject, with the highest response among a set of questions noted below:

What are your strongest reasons for reparations?
Slavery—82 percent

Who do you believe is culpable for slavery in the United States?
U.S. government—86.3 percent

If slavery and postslavery racism are evident in today's society, what form does it take?
Poor educational opportunities—76.5 percent

What form should reparations take?
Educational and social programs for *all* African Americans—
74.4 percent

How would reparations change the lives of African Americans, their families and communities? Improve educational opportunities—71.9 percent

As can be seen, there is almost unanimous agreement that the basis of reparations is slavery and that the U.S. government is the most culpable agent. But there is also strong support for the notion of collective reparations with a decided emphasis on making educational opportunities universally available for African Americans.

There is some rough consensus on this issue in the wider population. For whereas most whites disapprove of the general concept of reparations, especially the "check in the mail" model, they generally approve of some scheme of amelioration based on the provision of educational benefits.

Although there is an urgency and seductiveness in the prospect of a check, the question is whether cash or a certain opportunity is a better form of individual restitution. The reclamation of the economic power of Black people according to the AT&T, Ford Motor Company, and Microsoft model cannot be achieved by giving out individual checks, yet this is what we have lost—the ability to stand on the world financial stage with other peoples and, in doing so, to support our own.

The fear is that for many, perhaps most, the delivery of a check would result in the acquisition of momentary material things, while those who have oppressed Blacks in the first place would get richer providing those goods. In a community without a secure and comprehensive financial structure, and with a history as a "pass through" community where money does not stay long, where disproportionate sums are spent for perishable goods, the delivery of a check would not leave Blacks richer. Furthermore, there is a sense that reparations should not be given to those who already have amassed substantial wealth—the Johnnie Cochrans, Michael Jacksons, Russell Simmonses, and Oprah Winfreys—but that reparations should concentrate on the less developed parts of the Black community, seeking ways to improve the living standards of ordinary people and their poorer relatives and friends who may not be able to afford self-determination.

My own view is admittedly ambitious, in assuming that Blacks are the experts in the solution of their own problems and always have been so. They merely have not had the resources to implement whatever solutions they believed were viable. Indeed, there is a long history of such confidence, as witnessed by view of the editors of *The Negro Caravan,* who said that in 1941 that

> the belief as expressed . . . in many publishers' announcements, that white authors know the Negro best is untenable to the editors of this anthology. They believe that the "inside view" is more likely to make possible the essential truth than the "outside." The editors believe . . . that Negro authors, as they mature, must be allowed the privilege and must assume the responsibility of being the ultimate portrayers of their own.[17]

This is a normal assumption by leaders of a people whose population is the size of many nations, who have achieved levels of education and technical sophistication greater than people in most of the Third World, who have significant experience in government administration and in corporate employment and who have lacked only the sums of capital that accompany such development. Below, I suggest some of the activities that might be entertained if such capital should arrive in the form of reparations.

A Plausible Reparations Agenda

Campus.   The first order of business, should adequate financial resources arrive, is to create a thinking place. A place should be created where the best minds in the Black community can routinely grapple with the problems that face Blacks in a variety of sectors of daily living: employment, housing, education, health, family viability, business development, financial management, relations with other peoples of African descent, and the like. The campus would be divided up into issue areas—similar to the National Institutes of Health—where centers of study and planning would be created.

Planning and strategy development.   The objective would be to develop "solutions" or templates that could be used to improve the circumstances in which Black people live, through the application of means and strategies developed by them. Models could be appropriated from communities all over the world, but care should be taken to make them applicable to the special history and culture of African Americans (which includes peoples of African descent living in this country who may be from Africa, Latin America, or the Caribbean). This is important because most of the federal programs that involve Black people, in areas such as health, education, and social relations, are not tailored to them, but to a normative community that is mostly white and middle class. The objective should be strategies for social progress that are tailored to Black experience and that match the Black community as it exists.

Piloting. Reparations would give to the Black community the ability to devise public/private partnerships and mass group solutions to pilot and to create recommendations arrived at in an effort to determine whether or not they would be enhance the Black standard of living.

Deployment of best practices. After determining what some of the best solutions and recommendations might be, as a result of piloting or already grounded experience, they could be displayed or presented and deployed by those communities or groups that accept them—with the emphasis on enhancing the standard of living for the greatest number.

Facilitation. Facilitation of this model requires that whatever resources are received are kept by a trusted collective; perhaps the Council of Presidents of Black Banks or some other group that is already structured to manage large sums of money or another entity structured for this purpose. In any case, facilitation of this will require the kind of trust that has been uncommon in the Black community. If whites did not trust the stock exchange, it would not be possible for trillions of dollars to be invested by the financial services establishment in this country, or if banks or other kinds of financial institutions were not trusted, it would not be possible to entertain the management of financial resources that enable the economy to be viable.

Blacks have confidence in these institutions, but the test is whether they would have the same confidence in institutions run by representatives of their own communities. There is a great prospect that they would not, ironically, because of the damage done to collective trust by slavery and racial manipulation in the postslavery environment. Nevertheless, it would be good to face the test and to be challenged by it as the basis upon which the entire project of Black development might depend.

Reparations and White Interests

As indicated above, white leadership has an important role in considering whether or not to approve reparations, most probably as a legislative program that builds on the findings of H.R. 40. Thus, racial reconciliation cannot be a one-way project, but a mutual contract between equals, with agreement on the terms of the contract—its values, its administration, its longevity, its legitimate parties and their roles, and the like. The mutuality of such a contract raises a question whether racial reconciliation is in the interests of the white majority that would have to cede power in order to make Black self-determination a reality.

In July 2001, I traveled to São Paulo to be a keynote speaker for a conference sponsored by one of the largest Black organizations in the country, Afro Bras. On the way back, I was hosted in Rio by the American consulate at a luncheon involving an expert on the Brazilian census. The principal discussion focused on affirmative action, the subject on which I had been called to speak. I made the argument that it was in the self-interest of all Brazilians—since the Black population was around half of the country—to mobilize all of the human resources of the population for its future growth and development. That this was the only logical strategy to sustain and increase the standard of living of all the Brazilian people.

The census expert said that the main impediment to this argument was that about half of the Brazilian population is developed by all the standards of Western democracies, with respect to the industrialization, business ownership, and personal affluence, all of which identifies a Western-style class structure. Therefore, this developed class sees no need for—and does not have an interest in—expanding this affluence to the rest of society.

In other words, this class does not possess an enlightened view of capitalism that inculcates the intellectual notions of fairness and civil rights with long-term planning for profits, in a way that links to national development. In this sense, they appear to be late colonial bloomers, who have conceived of the nation-state as principally an enabler of their private economic designs and have not yet acquired—because the mechanisms of government regulation are so weak—a mature connection to the state and its wider obligations for all of the citizens of the country.

Similarly, in the United States affirmative action (a euphemism for the mobility of nonwhite peoples in the labor force and within society) as a mechanism that helps to expand the affluent sector to include nonwhites encounters the defensive refutation that it harms the interests of whites—but arguments based in whites' interest are never used. The arguments used are constitutional, that is, "equal protection," buttressed by concepts of fairness such as "reverse racism" and "quotas."

Essentially what we have not appreciated in this case is the strength of the ideology of the "modern racial Herrenvolk" where a democratic ethos exists, and where affluence supports the Herrenvolk class, but where the fruits of modern industrial society are shared within the dominant group culture to sustain its position. Hence, any mechanism that promises to make substantial expansion of these benefits to Blacks and other people of color is viewed as an "encroachment" upon its own preserve of power and privileges.

So there is a paradigm of group relations based on race: racial dominance exists within a range of racial group relations from exclusion to integration or assimilation into aspects of the dominant group preserve. The issue, however, is whether the pattern of dominance is broken down as excluded groups move toward greater levels of integration or whether the essential structure of white dominance holds firm, even with the new adherents. If the latter is the case, this means that the dominant group has a vested interest in the regulation of the rate of entry (integration, assimilation) and the terms on which it takes place.

Change in the nature of the state may come through the increasing diversification of the country's leadership. In the future, the demographics of the country will change to such an extent that nonwhites will constitute a larger share of the effective population, affecting those elements of power that are dependent upon population, such as voting, representation in legislatures, and so on.

Then there is a reliance of the corporate sector on the technical expertise of nonwhite peoples of other countries in real-time economic activities. This reliance, especially upon those who immigrate to the United States, has been encouraged by political leaders as important to the effectiveness of the technological sector of the economy.

The higher education sector also relies on training nonwhite students from other countries, whose presence they depend on for the viability of their programs. In some institutions, Asians, for example, have become the dominant share of students in engineering, medicine, mathematics, and other technical subjects.

The result is that nonwhites will come to constitute a highly mobile and much larger share of the American middle class and become active as leaders in many sectors of American society. In sum, changes in population, in the composition of technological leadership, in the leadership of other sectors of society—finance, higher education, industry, science, and so on—may mean that nonwhites will become a significant part of the leadership of this country. The question is whether, as peoples of color, they will have an enlightened position on racial equality and, beyond that, racial restitution or simply mimic the preexisting attitudes promoted by the white racial hierarchy.

Reparations, then, are necessary as a dynamic way to help correct the moral and material balance within society. Whiteness is a clear advantage, both as an absolute way to organize status and privilege within society and in its relative function to Blacks. The fact that some poor whites do not experience the benefits of whiteness only means that these benefits are not configured as a resource they are able to mobilize against other whites. In competition with Blacks, however, poor whites are able to mobilize or enjoy various forms of advantage simply because of their race. The most vivid example relates to public scrutiny or the presumption of guilt that causes racial profiling in many fields.

How does the nation know that reconciliation has not occurred? Among hundreds of examples, there are these.

> When the social fabric erupts and the majority is shocked at the gaping racial divide, as it was in the aftermath of the O. J. Simpson trial, the Los Angeles Riots over the Rodney King beating, and the Cincinnati uprising of 2001 over white policemen who were absolved of the shooting of unarmed Blacks.
> When there is a call for national unity at moments of crisis, such as with the attack on the World Trade Center and the Pentagon on 9/11, there is the expectation that Blacks will exhibit the same kind of patriotism as others, but Blacks, because of their past, do not respond in the identical way.

Race is always, as we have asserted, part of the tapestry, whether seen or unseen, within which social relations take place. And the illusion carried by many in the white majority (which matches an international naïveté) that, because they do not experience conflict or other forms of effective opposition to their will, it does not exist is patent avoidance of the reality of the primacy of race.

The Price of Racial Reconciliation

The Burden

The burden of reconciliation on racial terms has been placed on Blacks through their willingness to accede to strategies for racial accommodation that have been made by those who have oppressed them in the first place. However, these schemes have always encountered barriers, the failure of integration and the failure of self-development.

One of the largest barriers has been the issue of qualification—to vote, to get a job, to get a mortgage, and so on—which has acted as a tool of modern inferiorization. Affirmative action has been reformulated to demand that those who take advantage of it be "qualified," when the reason for the action has been their lack of qualification. This is loaded concept, for it most often refers to the extent to which Blacks have become socialized to white norms through some test of cultural affiliation. This demand is regulated through the power of the majority not only to acquire the skills or professional qualifications requisite to perform or be hired, but also to be culturally approved. Reconciliation, however, requires an accommodation of interests. Yet willingness to accommodate has declined during the current regime. The political frame of reference that was amenable to considering Black interests has eroded because of the illusory view that white nationalism provides a cultural platform that enables the dominant political actors to ignore such minority interests until they are challenged—and nationalism gives them the power through social consensus to repress such challenges.

The Price

Just as there is a price to the achievement of racial civility, there is a larger price to the achievement of a democratic society. In that sense, what we have in America is a cheap democracy, operationalized within the tolerable limits of the control exercised by the white majority. At the same time it is very expensive democracy, for it costs the achievement of a state that encompasses all American citizens, rather than just those of one color. Racism is a form of undemocratic social control, and to call for its elimination is consistent with democratic expansion of the limits of participation.

Reparations could contribute to the fight against racism by taking away the status motivation of many Americans to believe in Black inferiority. By legitimizing the argument that the source of lower status is the past treatment of Blacks, including the withholding of economic resources, and by restoring those resources, reparations would build the basis for social equality. This addresses the concept that whites are more likely to regard as equals those of like socioeconomic status than those of a lower status.

On the other hand, equalizing the status of Blacks could have the unintended effect of contributing to the growing competition over socioeconomic status among races and ethnic groups, which follows from white insecurities over the decline in their numerical status. Some observers believe that this competition will grow, and that as Blacks, the group least favored by some whites, gain status, some whites may feel that Black progress comes at their expense. This sentiment has fueled the radical conservative movement since the late 1970s and could grow with the grant of reparations. Nevertheless, reparations should not be considered on the basis of difficult-to-predict consequences in an unknown future, but on the positive prospect that they would elevate the human condition of a lower-status, deserving group and thereby achieve the goals of society itself.

One aspect of the price of Black oppression is a substantial degree of Black dependence upon the state. Yet the debate about "dependency" has assumed an immorality in support Blacks have enjoyed from government. Therefore, the argument goes, because through government intervention these groups have become inescapably dependent, that dependency must be broken if independence is to be established. Albert Memi, however, suggests that independence will not be achieved by severing government support. Black dependency cannot be broken in that way because it is configured in a pattern of historical mutual—not singular—dependency between whites and Blacks. His definition is as follows: "Dependence is a relationship with a real or ideal being, object, group or institution that involves more or less accepted compulsion and that is connected with the satisfaction of a need."[18]

Whites have always been dependent upon Blacks, says Tim Wise, a white progressive writer.[19] Whites depended upon Blacks for labor and for validation of white superiority. Today, the latter dependency is still in play to a considerable extent, but more urgently: whites depend upon Blacks, as the most impoverished group, to validate Americanism itself, to go to war for the equality of others while the white elite stays home, to do without while the government shifts resources to private power and into white neighborhoods, to suffer double-digit unemployment befitting a depression as though it were normal, to tolerate the double crime of unjust sentences for petty crimes of poverty, to perform as spokespersons for the oppressive conservative temper of the times and the establishment that supports it. And all the while, the whites who manage the social system depend upon Blacks to suffer in silence, not to revolt, not to shake the foundation to its core, not to object in terms except those that ironically validate the system's goodness. What part of this insupportable structure will collapse, the compulsion of whites to control Blacks for their purposes, or the need for Blacks to achieve real viability in society?

Therefore, Black dependency should not be conceptualized in the popular conservative terms as "dependence on government" as such, but as a manifestation of Black socioeconomic status in relation to American society itself in a context of interdependency with whites. This implies that whites have a substantial unpaid debt to Blacks, not a running series of loans or grants that are undeserved. The acknowledgment of the debt leads to the restoration of the moral currency of the Black condition, which is why, in this age, it has been rejected. Rejecting the dependency of whites upon Blacks is the predicate for rejecting the debt itself.

Governmental Leadership for Reconciliation

The question of racial restitution requires a permanent posture of readiness to assert a claim by the harmed community; neither in South Africa nor in the United States has the attempt to establish mechanisms of racial reconciliation been overwhelmingly approved by the public. And it also requires the acceptance of the claim by leaders of the majority on the basis that it wants racial reconciliation. In fact, although reconciliation is also in the interests of the harmed community, the latter should have as its central objective restitution as the methodology for reaching reconciliation. In this sense, without the substance generated by restitution, reconciliation has a lesser value for the harmed. Thus, both restitution and reconciliation are in the mutual interests of both the majority and harmed Black community.

Accordingly, the goal for reparations is to become a national policy. Therefore, the task of Black leadership is to place reparations on the policy agenda and work to see that they become a priority of the state. The goal is for leaders of the political system to accept this debt repayment as a priority. In this context, social struggle is important in keeping the issue before dominated groups as a mobilizing purpose, and before decision makers as the sine qua non for public policy addressed to the needs of these groups. The American civil rights movement has shown that heavy investment of political resources in the participatory framework of government decision and action can inject Black interests there, but it can stifle group power by making it subject to the rules and behavior of government bodies. A focus on legislation, for example, has at times severely limited strategies of change and, thus, the force of the Black agenda. This argues for the maintenance of a dynamic and autonomous process of group mobilization in which participation in government bodies is one legitimate theater of action, while other strategies are also pursued that may be far more influential. Community-based leadership is important in development, as well as the national organization of indigenous leadership into a coherent group that is autonomously supported and that engages the project of agenda-setting from both the strength of local communities and from an independent national base. As Cobb and Elder have observed, this gives to the character of the agenda the clarity, the force of communication, and the substance that is required for it to be considered within the political system.[20]

In fact, the government of the United States has accepted many projects that seemed outlandish at first, such as Kennedy's goal of going to the Moon. More recently, a commission on American marine resources, appointed by President George Bush in 2001, issued its five-hundred-page report in April 2004, concluding that the oceans were damaged, suffering from overuse and pollution.[21] The report sounded a strong alarm, warning that "the oceans were in trouble" and that the ecosystem's survival and species that inhabit it were at stake. The report called on federal support to improve the oceans, since marine resources contributed $800 billion per year to the nation's economy. The central recommendation was to establish a trust fund, modeled on the Highway Trust Fund, that would contribute $4 billion in federal oil and gas royalties, derived from offshore drilling, to projects to improve the condition of the oceans. The enormity of the task did not dissuade anyone from treating with respect the idea of fixing the seas.

In any case, the history of Blacks in South Africa and in America suggests that the road to racial conciliation is not smooth; since it is not a national priority, there may be periods of unseemly social conflict instead of the progress that might have been made. Perhaps these cycles of racial tension, rather than a rational approach, may be necessary to achieve the ultimate goal, but the expectation of conflict is no reason for either those request restitution, or those who would provide it, to be swayed from the inevitable challenge of achieving social harmony as the basis of national unity.

Finally, it is well worth noting that the process of forgiveness in South Africa was strongly influenced by the fact that the ANC and its supporters, having achieved a dominant role in the politics of the country, also had responsibility for creating a nonracial political and social culture. It is within that context that the liberal values of the TRC must be assessed, values which were adhered to even when they failed to result in fair restitution to victims of Apartheid. In this case, the value of social harmony appeared to supersede the linkage between restitution and racial reconciliation.

The American context, however, is substantially different in that Blacks are not only part of the minority, but its most powerless part. For this reason, racial reconciliation must be a primary goal of those who have responsibility for the American state. Given that they alone exercise state power, they have the means to provide the substantive restitution that could lead to reconciliation. Blacks, however, are in the historical and cultural role of determining whether such restitution is adequate. This has been the substance of their politics.

Conclusion

The thesis that undergirds this work is simple yet profound. It is that memory is central to the identity of social groups, and to the extent that Black memory has been politicized, it calls for healing and restitution by those who control the state. Thus reparations are central to the process of restitution, in that they would provide a critical resource to enable Blacks to overcome both material inequality and the internal damages of oppression. Equality of conditions—not of access—is necessary to the enjoyment of both political and economic democracy in a society where resources determine the ability to achieve self-determination by acquisition of public goods and social status.

Nevertheless, the grant of monetary reparations alone will not resolve the race problem in America, just as it has not resolved the social, political, and economic problems of Native Americans and their unrecognized treaty rights, or Jewish Holocaust survivors, or Hawaiians' continuing disadvantage, or Japanese feelings of continued otherness. Nor would reparations settle the moral and financial debt that the United States owes to Blacks for slavery and postslavery racism. Thus, reparations will not solve the American race problem, since it is wide and deep and encompasses far more than the feelings of Blacks. In fact, since whites are the main perpetrators of racism, on their shoulders rests whether or not reparations are accompanied by other necessary correctives. Specifically, it rests on the degree to which whites are receptive to the claim of Black self-determination. For if whites continue to attempt to resolve problems for the Black community without Blacks' democratic participation, or don't address them at all, then the problems that define race and racism will continue, perhaps even worsen.

The demand for reparations, then, is not simply a request for payment for slavery; it is a demand for something greater, something more difficult to achieve: a major step toward racial reconciliation through the power of Black self-determination. The monetary award of reparations may assist in that endeavor, but it cannot achieve it. That reconciliation is absolutely vital if Blacks are finally to claim their rightful place in America, and feel that it is their rightful place because it is *right.*

Therefore, the moral rightness of reparations is not asserted because they are an additive that might help to improve the normal context of race relations. Nevertheless they are crucial in that respect also, for the "normal context of race relations" involves the attempt by Blacks to improve their socioeconomic status through the mobilization of their resources to influence the distribution of goods and services to their communities through politics and public policy. On the other hand, reparations will require that the national leadership entertain restorative politics as a national question, as an issue relative to the quality of democracy for all Americans. So the demand for reparations is not a substitute for normal politics, but a vital resource in promoting Black self-determination. For self-determination, not government assistance, has been and will continue to be the major means of Black progress.

~♥~

CHAPTER NINE

The Globalization of African Reparations

THE PROJECT OF REPARATIONS IS NOW A GLOBAL PHENOMENON, with campaigns having been initiated in all parts of the international system in countries such as Australia, South Africa, Britain, France, Brazil, and elsewhere. It should be understood that these campaigns have a common origin in events that took place as a part of world history, based on conquest by European states that resulted in African slavery, colonialism, and the continued racism that subordinates African-descendant peoples in many countries around the world. There is, then a "grand narrative" that encompasses this reality and provides the backdrop against which issues of Third World underdevelopment, racial and ethnic conflict, even the remnants of slavery that exist today.

The venerable scholar W. E. B. DuBois in *The World and Africa*,[1] first published in 1946, described what he termed "the rape of Africa" in one of the most succinct, descriptive, and substantive chapters that has been written on slavery and its global effects. From this work we understand that whatever the results of the wealth earned from the rape of Africa,

> Its owners in the main were not royal spendthrifts, nor aristocratic dilettantes; and even if some were, their financial advisers put their funds largely into the safe investments of West Indian slavery and the African slave trade. Thus, an enormous amount of free capital seeking safe investment and permanent income poured into the banks, companies, and new corporations. The powerful British institution of the stock exchange was born.[2]

Citing in support Karl Marx's *Capital,* DuBois points out that the industrial revolution "turned Africa into a warren for the commercial hunting of black-skins, signalized the rosy dawn of the era of capitalist production."[3] He also cites Adam Smith, who averred in his *Wealth of Nations,* "The profits of a sugar plantation in any of our West Indian colonies are generally much greater than those of any other cultivation that is known either in Europe or America."[4] Slavery and the slave trade poured treasure into England, "building her cities, railways and manufacturers, and making her so powerful a country that a defense of the system was fierce."[5] Ultimately, the defense of this system was not only vested in trade, but in the establishment of colonies and their control from the trading country. This system of the social control of Black humanity came to require, as an intellectual defense, an ideology of racism:

> [T]he British empire became the victim of the worst legacy of Negro slavery: the doctrine of race superiority and the color line, which in a later century made civilized man commit suicide in a mad attempt to hold the vast majority of the earth's peoples in thrall to the white race—a goal to which they still cling today, hidden away behind nationalism and power politics.[6]

More recently, the United Nations Educational, Scientific and Cultural Organization initiated a study of the slave trade and its global effects. The summary report concludes that "Africa's losses [from all sources] during the four centuries of the Atlantic slave trade must be put at some 210 million human beings" and that between 15 and 30 million people were actually transported as a part of the slave trade.[7] Despite the record it cites of the scale of the slave trade, its conclusions about the impact on Europe are tentative because of the complexity of associating the slave with the economic development and, essentially because of the novelty of doing so, since it has not been a part of standard calculations of the rise of Europe by scholars.[8] Nevertheless, this work agrees with the inference of DuBois that slavery, the slave trade, and the postslavery use of African labor, both in Africa and in the Diaspora, were substantial factors in the creation of profits used to develop Western civilization. What follows is an outline of a grand narrative on the method by which African peoples were oppressed by various aspects of European control.

European Colonialism and the
Grand Narrative of Oppression

If Lord Acton's dictum that "power corrupts and absolute power corrupts absolutely" is true, then the system by which African people were, in the words of Albert Memi, taken "out of history" was absolutely corrupt. And although the methods by which Africans were taken out of history included slavery and other more benign forms of control of African societies, colonialism was not merely the appropriation of the labor of Africans, but the absolute control of their being—as "possessions" to those who dominated most every human manifestation.

Therefore, the demand for reparations involves, in the first instance, the recognition of the absoluteness of the domination of Europeans over the lives of Africans. At the turn of the twentieth century, one observer said that despite the varying form of colonialism, it involved two dominant characteristics:

(1) . . . a prime consideration that the occupying territory is to be worked like an estate in the interest of the country whose "Possession" it is supposed to be, and (2) the complete subordination of the native interests to those of the occupying power.[9]

Although one does make a specific issue of the economic motive for colonial domination as a basis for reparations, the criterion for understanding the magnitude of the damage done to Africans and their territories is the fact of absolute control itself.

Thus, while the economic ledger of subordination of the African by Europeans is acknowledged to be incalculable, the totality of the damage done to African civilization by the context of total domination is of monumental import. And this does not only refer to the damage to humanity. For example, what is the monetary value of the possession of a strategic portion of the African land mass in the context of European rivalries that set off two world wars?

Second, even though a residual effect of the domination was that it accomplished the contact of Africans with European civilization, the essential direction of this contact was to exercise domination over Africans in order to achieve *European objectives* such as wealth. It is factual that the driving force behind European contacts with Africa was the persistent search for economic benefit, beginning with trade in items of commerce such as salt and gold in the seventeenth century and leading quickly to the enslavement of Africans themselves. And as the trade in humans ebbed in the first half of the nineteenth century, the commodities sought shifted to palm oil, ground nuts, rubber, and other products related to the industrial growth of Europe and America.[10]

In 1915, DuBois observed that part of the roots of World War I was a conflict among European countries for the control of the colonial possessions in Africa and Asia. This analysis had already been proposed by Benjamin Kidd at the end of the previous century.

> The great rivalry of the future is already upon us. It is for the inheritance of the tropics, not indeed for possession in the ordinary sense of the word, for that is an idea beyond which the advanced peoples of the world have moved, but for the control of these regions according to certain standards.[11]

The "standards" Kidd referred to involved the economic conflict among European states, and in that context the importance of the control of territories in the tropics for the propagation of "free trade." Such trade was necessary not only to advance the standard of living in European countries with respect to refined tastes for coffee, cloth, spices, and the like, but a standard that demanded industrial raw materials, as previously noted.

Indeed, in the late 1870s there was a race between France and Britain for the control of the oil-rich area of the Niger delta as one of the most important motivations to colonialism.[12] In some of the French African possessions, the purely economic benefit was small in comparison to both the monopoly of control over the territory (thus, preventing it from being available to potential European competitors), such as in Niger, and the strategic value of the territory itself, such as in Algeria and South Africa.[13] Thus, Kidd saw that at the end of the century, the forces making necessary the conflict that ended in World War I were coming clearly into focus in precisely this direction.

As we know, the conflict among Europeans over the satisfaction of their discrete objectives in Europe was reflected in the Third World and led to a war that had little to do with African objectives. Yet Africans, subject to absolute European control, were forced to participate in the war, indeed both world wars, at the sacrifice of their lives and other precious resources. And while the war reparations were paid to European participant countries, Africans were never reimbursed for the cost of their forced participation in either the First or Second World War.

Third, insofar as the direction of the activity performed under colonial domination was structured narrowly to the benefit of Europeans, it prevented the achievement of the broader social development of Africans, by Africans in line with their own requirements for that period of history and for the future. This involved not only the "objectives" of European states in the most narrow sense, but also the attachment of the subordinated peoples to a dominant state made them party to the political and economic dynamics affecting that state. This is the very definition of dependency.

European dominance shaped the nature of the African economic, political, and social system and, in the first instance, skewed the economic system toward exports to Europe. This export orientation of African economic activity did produce a demand for commodities imported from Europe. It also made necessary the financing of such imports to the point that even before independence considerable amounts of the finances of the territorial governments of Egypt and Tunisia were "in pawn to European bankers."[14]

The investment in West African territories, for example, where the European motivation was likely to be most substantially economic, was likely to be small because independent African producers could provide goods of such quality that there was no need for European intervention in the local economy, and Africans could also provide a political framework within which most of the required functions of colonialism could take place. These elements shaped African culture and politics to be compatible with European dominance.[15]

The classic definition of the way in which European colonialism distorted the development of African civilization was provided by Walter Rodney in *How Europe Underdeveloped Africa.*[16] One of the most poignant examples of the way in which the truncation of African technological development was found in his illustration of the handcrafts industry, such as the making of clothes. His suggestion was that what other writers referred to as a pattern of parallel importation of goods from the colonial country occurred in Africa by the introduction of European clothes, which retarded the African clothing industry. Indeed, he said, the colonial profits from slavery and trading were reinvested by the British in clothes-making technology, achieving an even more profitable cycle when such clothes were bought by colonial subjects.[17] This pattern occurred in many areas of life within the colonial environment.

Most important, Walter Rodney outlines the way in which the development of human capital was retarded by the refusal of Europeans to invest in the technological capacities of Africans themselves. This is evident in the low level of mass education and by the practice of educating primarily the offspring of the elite ruling classes, which was necessary to the smooth functioning of the politics of the colonial system and its administration.[18]

And finally, it should also be recognized that the corruption of African civilization through colonialism bred a system of slavery that deposited Africans all over the world, and that all Diaspora Africans have a claim to share in the benefit of reparations inasmuch as they were all damaged by the corrupting influence of European domination. Slavery in the United States, for example, occurred during a period in which, for most of the time, the United States was a colony of Great Britain and, therefore, subject to its dictates. Thus, for the first 170 years of the American existence as a colony and even for most of the nineteenth century, as an independent state, Britain reaped the benefit of the slave trade in the form of cotton and other agricultural exports from the United States. For example, in 1860 on the eve of the American Civil War, while Britain was importing 205 million pounds of cotton from its other colonial possessions, it was importing more than 1.1 billion pounds from America and although the amount fell during the war, it resumed to high levels afterward.[19] Yet Black people in the United States have little concept of the fact that the reparations demanded of the United States also extends to the recipient of the fruits of much their labor as slaves—Great Britain!

Slavery Practiced under
Writ of International Law

The system of global slavery emerged in the mercantile system as a profitable scheme involving the sale of human beings, their socialization to service for free labor, and the attendant physical brutalization and inferiorization of their humanity. As such the participants in the slave trade, slavery, and colonialism were states who at every point in the process, provided the legal authority for citizens to participate in this commerce. By authorizing their citizens to practice slavery as a legitimate form of economic activity, those states acquired many of the elements characteristic of the impact of slavery.

The Asiento of March 26, 1713, between the king of Spain and government of Great Britain allowed the British (who paid a duty of thirty-three pieces of eight per head to the Spanish Crown) to import Africans into certain Spanish territories in America. Similarly, the Asiento of July 13, 1713, between Spain and Great Britain, France, and Ireland made possible the introduction of Africans into other Spanish territories in the Americas. In 1808, the U.S. government legally abolished the slave trade; in 1807 the British had taken similar action. Afterward the United States and Britain, at the Treaty of Ghent in 1814, agreed to work to eliminate the slave trade, indicating that they were aware of the crime against African humanity and the basic norms of human rights. In fact, article 10 of that treaty held,

> Whereas the Traffic in Slaves is irreconcilable with the principles of humanity and justice, and whereas both His Majesty and the United States are desirous of continuing efforts to promote its entire abolition, it is hereby agreed that both the contracting parties shall use their best endeavors to accomplish so desirable an object.[20]

African Colonialism

The point one makes about the development of colonialism is consistent with the paradigm described by George M. Weston as an internal process of regional pauperization within the United States. If one substitutes the rich planter class for the European powers, the African slaves in America for African slaves under European colonialism in Africa, and the whites in the southern part of the United States for the white settlers in Africa, all of the ingredients exist that explain the poverty and the arrested development in Africa as the result of slavery and colonialism.

This integrated system of racial oppression managed by western European states, with the tacit support of relatively powerless African chiefs, led to the modern divide between the life circumstances and the opportunity structure that provides the environment within which

African peoples live today. In fact, the legacy of victimization from the triple crimes of slavery, colonialism, and racism is that Africans have entered modern global system experiencing multiple aspects of oppression.

The Western states that have had a substantial, largely dependent population of peoples of African descent and those that have inherited such populations since World War II have believed that they have attempted to make restitution to peoples living within their state through targeted public policies as a response to the agitation of African-descendant people themselves.

In addition, many of the states of Africa came into existence through the African independence movement and have received developmental assistance from European powers since that point, administered on such terms and in such modest amounts that, in most cases, the arrangement resembles the former official colonial relationship.

The question that must be addressed to the global community is whether, in either case, of Africans living in European, American, and Latin American states or on the African continent, the magnitude of the economic, social, and political assistance has been sufficient to close the divide between Africans and African-descendant peoples with Europeans or European-descendant peoples.

One answer is that it is unlikely as long as the Africans living in those states continue to be subject to the unequal treatment of having some victims of European oppression accorded reparations and the African rejected. An example is seen in the little-discussed reparations payment by the German government of $68 million to Greece in the 1960s for the consequences of Nazi occupation in World War II.[21] This, however, did not prevent the children of victims of a Nazi massacre of two hundred Greek citizens sixty miles northwest of Athens in June 1944 from taking their claim to the highest German court for further restitution.

Yet Africans were also killed in World War II, as they served in the hundreds of thousands for the British and the French in a program of mandatory labor, but "the British Empire became the main user of African military manpower, both black and white."[22]

By May 1945, the total number of Africans serving in the regular British military units, combatants as well as ancillary, amounted to about 374,000. British soldiers from all colonies

. . . totaled about 473,000. The combined losses of the British colonies totaled 21,085.[23]

The Senegalese, however, slaughtered by the Germans in World War II, were also the unfortunate victims of the German gas ovens, as they also were considered inferior human beings by the Nazi racist ideology.

Africa and Global Racism

Global racism is a social, economic, and political process of human subordination, characterized by slavery, colonialism, and modern racial discrimination, visited extensively upon African peoples, among other peoples in the world, for centuries. As a crime against humanity, the impact of these processes have prevented African peoples from achieving their rightful place in the global system with material equality and cultural dignity, within states and between African states and the Western system. In short, it has created a substantial distance between the racial groups who benefited from these global processes and those who were its victims. Fair restitution has never been made in a manner that has matched the depth and scope of this crime; in particular, states have not done enough to replace the economic infrastructure that was lost, without which the project of mass racial equality will never be achieved. The primary consequence is human suffering will persist and prevail and most important, the construction of true democratic society will continue to be abated as the developed states maintain dominance over African peoples through an ideology and a social practice of white racial supremacy.

The consequence of racism, both in the Americas and in Europe, placed Africans "outside of history" and prevented them from amassing the resources that would have made it possible for them to become captains of industry, builders of national and international institutions, masters of their own individual destiny on par with other peoples. In short, what was taken away was the ability to create, new personal situations, even new worlds consistent with their imagination, something that cannot be quantified.

This feature of Western colonialism in Africa was one of the major preoccupations of African and African-descendant intellectuals in the 1920s, who had begun to challenge colonialism and its damage to

African peoples, forming the negritude movement in France and its counterpart, the Council on African Affairs, in the United States.[24] One component of thought was that Europe owed to Africa a monumental debt for its development, since it occurred partially at the expense of African resources, both human and material. This belief guides the modern concept that the notion of an "African debt" to European countries is merely a continuation of the immorality of colonial occupation, transferred to the semi-independent status of African countries. Thus, the notion of a debt, together with the lack of direct investment and the exposure to higher terms of trade set by developed countries, means that Africa in the modern world has still enjoyed less equal treatment than other countries with respect to its access to the fair share of economic resources.

Modest Amelioration of Africa

Economic Assistance

The first phase of modest amelioration of the debt that Europeans owe to Africa has been their provision of economic assistance to various African countries, in most cases the former colonial territories of the donor state. This phase has been only modestly successful on the whole, both because of the lack of capital possessed by African countries and by the interposition marginally successful economic development plans by European countries and international agencies for African agriculture and other sectors of society. Most especially, as pointed out, the continuing lack of localized control of such economies means that they have existed, since the independence era, largely as dependent territories on a subsistence level that only recently have begun to achieve autonomous levels of significant economic growth. In this way, billions of dollars have been wrongly spent, both by African governments and by external actors.

In 2000, the United Nations announced the Millennium program aimed at African countries with development goals, set on a fifteen-year time line, for substantially increasing assistance to African states in critical areas such as national development strategies, financing for development, trade, and debt relief. Other attendant problems such as

HIV/AIDS, environmental stability, migration, and security are also issues that may be addressed through the success of the primary foci.

While Great Britain has proposed a response to the Millennium program of $25 billion by 2010 and another $25 billion by 2015, the U.S. commitment was much smaller, $15 billion by 2010. But while a Millennium Challenge Corporation has been established to administer the increases, the pace of funding by Congress has not met the goal set by the Bush administration.[25]

African Growth through Trade?

On an international level, the financial and development assistance strategies and operation of former colonial states have had a minimal impact on the economic distance between Africa and the Western state system. Their policies have not resulted in genuine economic independence by any existing African state. In fact, the legalization of such dependence is achieved through the development of the World Trade Organization and through investment treaties that give the competitive advantage to Western corporations rather than to Africans.

An example is the African Growth and Opportunity Act (AGOA) passed in 2000 by Congress with strong bipartisan support and the support of the African states. This legislation intervenes unnecessarily in African affairs, urges the elimination of protective features of African economies—in contravention to studies by the United Nations Conference on Trade and Development, and, in any case, does not contain the financial resources to support serious levels of African trade and investment with the United States.[26]

In any case, by late 2003, studies by the International Monetary Fund showed that Africa stood to gain modestly from the AGOA, but could not take full advantage from the expansion of trade since the United States limited its access to its market for apparel by imposing restrictive rules of origin. Although African exports to the United States grew 8 percent between 1998 and 2003, since AGOA was adopted the African countries who have qualified to use it will come under considerable competition from other exporters of apparel in 2005 as quotas maintained on their exports expire.[27] Thus, for all of the extraordinary expectations for the outcome of the AGOA, the results are exceedingly modest.

"Debt" Relief

Another modest program of amelioration in Africa has been attempts by progressive groups such as Jubilee 2000 to cancel the so-called African debt to Europe and America. The notion that Africa would owe a debt to Europe is a fatuous and ahistorical concept on its face and only represents the fact that African countries came into independence at a time when the services they needed had been monetized by the international financial system. In any case, the missing part of the independence movement was a commitment to heal the land by programs that rebuilt infrastructure, reeducated people, and provided capital for large-scale business education and development. In other words, the missing part of the independence movement was the grant of immediate reparations to African countries for the hundreds of years of colonial control that decimated their resources and their ability to produce on the level of modern countries.

African slavery was Europe's first Marshall Plan, and now there needs to be a reverse gift back to those who originally provided the labor power, free of charge, to lift the minerals out of the ground that went to Europe, America, and Latin America to fuel the economic development of those regions. The fair notion of a debt is one that balances the resources taken from a country from the funds that it has been given. In this sense, Africa has undergone a double process of oppression, once through the process of colonialism and again through having to borrow funds and thus become financially indebted to survive in a monetized world that took its resources in the first place.

However, the notion of an African debt has been pursued in the eyes of the world as though it were fair, a manifestation of the continuing power of the European former colonial powers to enforce their postcolonial extraction of financial resources from the African continent. And it is simultaneously a manifestation of the powerlessness of African states to refuse to pay the so-called debt.

African Reparations for Slavery and Genocide

The African reparations movement is not as robust in Africa as it is outside of the continent. Still, some actions have been taken by the Organization of African Unity in the past. For example, in December 1990 a conference on reparations was held, after which the OAU established a "Group of Eminent Persons" (GEP) in June 1992 to plan for a larger meeting, under the leadership of Chief Moshood K. O. Abiola, then a candidate for the presidency of Nigeria.[28] The planning group included such distinguished leaders from the Diaspora as Dudley Thompson, Jacob Ade Ajayi, and Ali Mazrui. A meeting of the First Pan-African Conference on Reparations was held in Abuja, Nigeria, April 27–29, 1993.

The meeting was important, as over 250 delegates from Africa and the Diaspora grappled with issues attendant to this problem. Who would pay? What about the time line of colonialism, slavery, and racism? What about the culpability of African leaders? How would it be possible to organize the reparations movements that were then emerging? And there were many other questions.

The format was the presentation of papers and debate, but no hard-and-fast decisions were reached. The conference declaration noted,

> The damage sustained by African peoples is not a "thing of the past" but is painfully manifest in the damaged lives of contemporary Africans from Harlem to Harare, in the damaged economies of the Black World from Guinea to Guyana, from Somalia to Surinam.

Thus, the declaration

> calls upon the international community to recognize that there is a unique and unprecedented moral debt owed to the African peoples which has yet to be paid—the debt of compensation to the Africans as the most humiliated and exploited people of the last four centuries of modern history.

The Abuja conference apparently lit the fuse of some interests in various countries, including Britain. The British reparations movement, begun by a Black member of Parliament, Bernie Grant, challenged the British Government to consider payment to African descendants for the oppression of slavery and colonialism that affected many British immigrants, principally from Africa and the Caribbean. The British Reparations Committee supported African governments in demanding the return of many artifacts such as the famous Benin Bronzes and a

substantial list of other items that were looted from the African continent and housed in British museums.

Some steps were taken after the Abuja conference to organize a
movement, as indicated by the fact that in Kenya, the Pan African
Reparations Movement, headed by Dennis Akumu, longtime trade
union activist, has been registered as an organization. It seeks reparations from the British government for atrocities that Kenyans suffered
under colonialism and joins activists already organized in Uganda and
Tanzania. Akumu has said:

> We will finally move to seek an international apology for
> slavery and colonial oppression. We are now a legal entity in
> this country and are embarking on a rigorous pursuit of
> claims from people who distorted our lives and insulted our
> dignity.[29]

Akumu and his colleagues are beginning to give substance to the
initiative that began in 1993. However, there needs to be a more forth-
right unified and global demand developed by the new African Union,
which superseded the Organization of African Unity, to serve as a platform and legitimizing base for the wider reparations movement in the
Diaspora. In the aftermath of the World Conference against Racism
that had taken place in Durban, South Africa, and at a time when the
new African Union (AU) was just beginning to establish its agenda, it
is fitting to ask whether to present the reparation issue to the UN. I will
comment first on the Durban conference and then on the adoption of
this mandate by the AU.

The Challenge of Durban

In late July 2002, the United Nations sponsored the World Conference
against Racism in Durban, South Africa. It was an international gath-
ering that drew thousands of delegates from all over the world and provided both sympathetic governments as well as activists and NGO representatives with a global opportunity to solidify the reparations
campaigns begun in the various countries.

The United States, however, voiced its opposition to attending this
meeting, ostensibly because of the potential denunciation of Israel by

the Palestinian delegation and its supporters and the emergence of reparations for African slavery as an issue with substantial international support. The planning meetings had signaled that the United States would be hostile to the conference not only because of the Israeli issue, but because of its opposition to the call for reparations by the U.S. NGO delegation and others. Thus, by the time the decision was to be made regarding whether the United States would attend, the official position was that the United States would send an exploratory delegation to hold low-level negotiations in order to eliminate the offending issues from consideration by the conference. Having failed to obtain such agreement, largely because of the commitment of some African states to the issue of slavery and its consequences, the United States did not attend.

It should be noted that the concerns of the U.S. and Israeli delegations appear to be misplaced, as there not a generally hostile atmosphere exhibited either toward Israel or Jews in particular. In fact, the Final Declaration of the conference noted (no. 58), "We recall that the Holocaust must never be forgotten." Then, a few items later (no. 61), noted: "We recognize with deep concern the increase in anti-Semitism and Islamophobia in various parts of the world as well as the emergence of racial and violent movements based on racism and discriminatory ideas against Jewish, Muslim and Arab communities." These concerns were voiced both by governmental delegations from Europe and other quarters of the globe, as well as by a strong delegation of Jewish delegates from the United States and other countries who participated in the conference.

Nevertheless, there was also a widespread feeling among many delegates that the United States had not wished to attend because the embarrassing topic of slavery and slavery reparations were also going to be dynamic issues, as indicated by the preparatory meetings. The Durban meeting was successful in drawing a substantial delegation of African-descendant peoples who formed a caucus with which to negotiate with official representatives to have language emerge from the conference that would legitimize slavery as a "crime against humanity."[30] It is this specific eventuality that the United States wanted to avoid, in light of the prospect that it would be sued by reparations activists in the United States. In fact, suits had been initiated by the Adrian Farmer-Paellmann group, and the Reparations Coordinating Committee had announced it would suit the United States at some point.

After the Durban conference, a Working Group of Experts on People of African Descent was created by the United Nations Commission on Human Rights. However, opposition to the results of the Durban conference persisted as the United States and the European Union block of states boycotted the meeting of the Working Group held in February 2003 in Geneva. Nevertheless, many countries attended from Africa, the Caribbean, Latin America, Asia, and even Europe; however, the European countries, including Greece, which held the rotating presidency of the European Union, attended as individual countries only. Another form of boycott had occurred at the first meeting of the Working Group in November 2002: the United States and European countries were supposed to contribute experts, but they failed to do so.

At a subsequent session of the UN Commission on Human Rights, delegates from western Europe argued against continuing the Working Group. Nevertheless, the delegate from Asia, George Jabbour, acting chairman of the Working Group, said at the Geneva meeting that although reparations were not in the final document of the World Conference against Racism, there was a "silent consensus" that "reparations for slavery is in harmony with the simple sense of justice and with the basic tenets of international law."[31] He suggested that there were three parties to the relationship: the slave descendants, descendants of slave traders, and the public authority. However, he also noted that while the public authority (or the government) had, for example, benefited when in 1848, France offered recompense to slave owners but not to the freed slaves; and while in 1824 Haiti was made to pay France $100 million francs for war reparations for its independence, the United States promised freed African slaves forty acres and a mule, but had not fulfilled this promise.[32]

The African Union and
Leadership on Reparations

The legacy of African leadership on reparations is a legitimate issue in light of its role in the global grand narrative of the oppression of people from that continent and the linkages to their status in other countries. In this sense, it is puzzling that in the aftermath of the Durban conference, a search of 283 online documents of the organizations in August

2004 found no substantive mention of the term and no discussion of the concept of reparations.

The African Union was born from an idea proposed by President Mu'ammar Gadhafi at the Fourth Extraordinary Session of the OAU that he hosted in Sirte, Libya, in September 1999. Secretary of State Colin Powell expressed the anxiety of his country that Gadhafi would be seen to be the leader of such an effort; nevertheless, he had the support of the OAU.[33] By the summer of 2000, the new idea had taken official form and the Constitutive Act of the African Union was ratified by fifty of the fifty-three countries on the continent by July 11. Article 14 of that document lists the various "Specialized Technical Committees" that were established on appropriate subjects such as agriculture, finance, trade and immigration, transport and communication, health, labor, education and social matters, and others. The mandate leaves open the possibility that other appropriate committees may be established by the organization and administered by its executive council.

Reparations, as indicated above, had surfaced on the agenda of the OAU, and were the subject of a world conference held on African soil. Moreover, individual countries such as Nigeria, Namibia, Uganda, and others have had occasion to demand consideration of reparations from various European countries. One of the most important cases in this regard is that of Namibia. In 1904, as part of its colonial occupation of what was then called South West Africa, the General Lothar von Trotha of Germany gave the orders to break the resistance of the Herero tribal peoples with armed force. The result was that sixty-five thousand of the Herero people, an estimated 75 percent of that group, were massacred, a fact that was the subject of a lawsuits in American courts demanding $4 billion in reparations. In 2001, the Herero Peoples Reparation Corporation also sought $2 billion for atrocities committed under German colonialism from German companies such as Deutsche Bank, mining company Terex Corporation (former Orenstein-Koppel), and the shipping company Deutsche Afrika Linie (former Woermann Linie).[34] To mark the one hundredth anniversary of that event, there was a national demonstration in Namibia reaffirming the demand. The German government, however, sent a message asking for "forgiveness" from the Herero peoples that was summarily rejected in light of the court case that asked for material redress. Herero paramount chief Kuaima Riru suggested that there could be room for negotiation of the lawsuit, but that since "the Germans are guilty," the guilty should not determine the terms on which the case should be withdrawn.[35]

The role of Germany in colonial Africa preceded its activities in World War II by thirty-five years and therefore, the contrast between its generous approach to Jewish reparations and its opposition to Black reparations is another object lesson in the disparate treatment of Blacks. Moreover, with respect to World War II, the direct issue of reparations for Africans by Germany is raised by the presence of Africans in the Nazi camps, survivors of which still exist, as indicated in a 1994 documentary film by Serge Bile, a Martinican filmmaker. Some researchers have put the number of Africans who died in Nazi camps at appropriately two thousand.[36]

Given the magnitude of this struggle, which includes, as indicated, efforts by Nigeria and other countries to reclaim valuable antiques that were looted and deposited in European museums, the AU should begin to provide significant collective leadership on the issue of reparations. A serious campaign could educate citizens in many countries of the role that their banking community, which now asserts that Africans have a debt to it, have played in the process of financing enterprises in Africa that have returned enormous profits to the banks and therefore to those very citizens. But leadership by the AU would also support the various campaigns that are underway in many countries, all of which have for their origin the original repression suffered by those people taken out of the African continent.

As an important adjunct to this initiative, the research component initiated by the UNESCO, to understand more clearly the impact of slavery and African subordination on world history, might be renewed, as well as the research efforts begun at the Abuja conference sponsored by the OAU Eminent Persons Group. Such an intellectual grounding is important in light of the statement by former OAU secretary general Salim Salim on July 9, 2001: "We have seen the total eradication of colonialism as well as institutionalized racism." There are doubtless many African intellectuals who would disagree with this statement. But to the extent that it represents an opinion that exists in official circles, it constitutes a basis for the continued devaluation of the global struggle for reparations by those who were most damaged by global racism and who are most in need of redress.

Conclusion: Pan-African Reparations

Many countries in Africa are at the stage of attempting to consolidate their national integration, while the most advanced countries in the world are superseding the state and building regional or continental entities that afford them greater economic power and leverage in the global system. Africa, then, should use its newly reformulated Pan-Africanism to take seriously the building of a stronger continental identity through regional and continental structures and projects, affording them the capacity to transcend the trap of struggling only for national sovereignty. The damage was done to Africa by European colonial powers that exercised sway over territories in Africa larger than individual countries. Thus restitution should take place on a regional and continental basis. However, it will not occur as long as this issue is at the bottom of the African agenda in its relationship with the European powers. There is a reason for the poverty of Africa, and to fail to force the global system to face up to the history that created African poverty is to occupy permanently the place of a footstool in the international system.

Postscript

As a political scientist, I am aware of the theorists of identity politics who have evaluated the demand for reparations and found a surfeit of complex problems. Such responses are typified by Wendy Brown's work.[1] Brown notes that the demand for reparations may turn in upon itself in unintended ways as, plumbing the vortex of blame and victimization as "sovereign identifies" that reinforce status positions, demanding rectification from the state that participated in the crime that begs relief, and projecting revenge through the instrument of payment that evokes punishment upon the provider. These and many more complexities are offered as the risk that reparations will become an oppressive force. However, Lawrie Balfour meticulously examines the attendant risks and concludes that Brown's "swift dismissal of reparations is unconvincing":

> While Brown's account of the traps that can ensnare the reparations movement ought to give its advocates pause, her assumption that they must do so is symptomatic of a more general tendency among political theorists to reproduce a white perspective in the course of the analysis.[2]

Symptomatic of oppositional views of a different character from theorists are those of Adolph Reed who, from a Marxist perspective, offers a surprisingly moderate current of criticism, which holds that the corrective proposals for the injustice experienced by Blacks in America may be attended to by more practical strategies involving broad coalition politics that are often rejected by the strain of Black nationalism inherent in proposals for reparations.[3] Moreover, Reed reflects the feelings of more conservative scholars and Africa American leaders who are concerned that the energy invested in the reparations movement could better be expended in more practical policy pursuits.[4] Indeed, a host of theoretical concerns have evolved that cumulatively lead some to reject the notion of reparations as ultimately unworkable and unachievable.

However, Thomas McCarthy, who confronted such issues in his study of the Holocaust, cautions that the introduction of objective issues into an analysis of the history of the Holocaust might have been interfered with by the assertion of what was essentially a question of power.

> Another issue in the Historikerstreit was the extent to which historical scholarship can and should inform the politics of memory in the public sphere by, among other things, introducing an element of objectivity into what might otherwise become simply a matter of power.[5]

In other words, it is necessary in constructing the *full force* of an argument for the moral essence of the crime against one group in society to leverage an argument that privileges that suffering and its origins in order to give practical weight to the perspective of the injustice. To move the location of the analysis to the space between the oppressed and the oppressor and accord each with a moral force destroys the moral value of the historical act of oppression. Once the moral weight of the crime has been established, it becomes the foundation that allows the formation of strategies based on practical considerations that resolve it. One of the problems of racial reconciliation is that the repression of the full force of the argument persists, by both friend and foe for different reasons, but both privileging a civility that masks a historically rancourous truth.

Perhaps it is theorists' concerns with the linkage between the concrete historical events experienced by Blacks and the structural forms of racism in a given era that re-defines and thus, recenters the notion of the "risk" involved in supporting the concept of reparations. It continually poses the question: are the progressive ends that restore the wholeness of a people and contributes to the richness of democracy in the process?

Thus, my view holds, first, that the practicality of reparations rests upon real historical precedents showing that other groups have been accorded recognition, their historical claim legitimized, and material resources given to the aggrieved group because of verifiable instances of their past oppression. Therefore, the demand for reparations appears to be impractical because it is tendered by African Americans—an analysis that acknowledges that their race, class, and power position are insufficient to achieve the attention due to the subject. Not to raise this question—an act of unfairness bounded bt a selective distribution of reward based on race—would be to ignore a historical error of massive proportions, an error especially egregious when committed by those whose ancestors suffered such oppression and whose descendants still do.

Second, there are important tactical considerations. Given the difficulty of initiating social movements, as opposed to discrete organizational or issue-oriented mobilizations, one respects the moment when certain factors come into existence that accidentally spark the elevation of an issue to a national level. Such was the case with the reparations movement. The dramatic elevation of this issue from its languishing state to the attention of political culture—which involved notice by important elites, high-profile legal cases against major corporations; units of government passing laws related to the reparations, and other manifestations—meant that the supporters of the cause had no option but to respond.

But as indicated above, there is also a degree to which the demand for reparations is a tactical response to the closure of the opportunity structure by the rise of conservatism. As noted by Charles Henry, this writer, and others, the seedbed for the restoration of the discussion about reparations was fueled by a series of executive, legislative, and court decisions that have restricted the full implementation of the intent of the civil rights laws and social legislation passed in the 1960s.[6] In this sense, the tactical counter was to raise the stakes of achieving racial justice by leveraging the full bill of particulars involved in the entire history of racial oppression of Blacks in America.

Third, one rejects the assumption that the education of Americans about the damage done to Blacks is a restorative psychological palliative with vengeance as a motive, as Brown indicated, or that the education about the scope and meaning of Black suffering is ever sufficient. To be sure, the restorative project is partly psychological; we have discussed here the concept of psychological damage to Black identity and the need to restore racial integrity and the dignity of the Black personality. This is based on the proposition that there can be no genuine achievement of equality for individuals or the group to which they belong if they do not believe that they have a right to justice and equality. Thus, there is a psychological dimension to the demand for reparations, but it is not predominantly associated with that aspect of Black humanity.

Detailed knowledge of the damage done to Black Americans exists in a realm accessible substantially to experts, but unfortunately it is not emphasized as frequently as necessary in the realms of general education or public affairs. Indeed, in the view of Nathan Irwin Huggins, the "master narrative" of American history is "largely unshaken" with respect to the paradigm of a nation being shaped on the founders' ideas rather than their actions, many as slaveholders.[7] This set the stage for a persistent lag in the politics of the public memory of slavery and the exploits of those enslaved and their place in the construction of American life. In fact, this lag is not benign since there has been a dedicated attempt to repress a reminder of the brutalities meted out by the majority against Blacks as the foundation of the demand for reparations. Indeed, some Blacks and whites are often mystified by the demand, since their socialization to the history of race conflict has been based on a vague memory of slavery and an assertion that modern racial discrimination amounts to modest race prejudice, allowing some whites to make the absurd proposition that they have been the subject of race oppression in the attempt of society to effect mild correctives for Blacks. So, if slavery is regarded as the primary rationale for the distance between the Black experience of democracy and that of the majority group, then, the full measure of restorative justice for Blacks is necessary to the achievement of democracy for society itself.

Fourth, I have not written this work with the understanding that a practical program of reparations will be achievable in my lifetime. Rather, I believe that regardless of the success of the demand, it is both intellectually honest and politically sound to develop a substantive discussion of the subject. It is intellectually honest because it addresses an issue that has a monumental base in supportive data and conceptualizations, but relatively little attention to the direct policy implications of the corrective of reparations. In this sense, my effort is to present a forceful, but "objective" rendering of the case for restorative treatment of Blacks by the mechanism of restitution that matches the scope of the oppression suffered. Such an analysis is politically sound because it assumes that the issue of reparations will continue to maintain its currency as long as it remains unaddressed. Therefore, the arrival of a moment in history that allows it to be seriously entertained may find that such analyses provide illustrative and useful arguments.

My rendering of this subject has been based in the perspective of the dominant attitude among African Americans that reparations are a just cause. In this sense it acquires an objective character rooted in Black thought and culture. Other attitudes may be valid as representative of majority opinion, but they emanate from a position outside mainstream of the Black community, outside of the realm of the historically injured group and thus have less legitimacy, even though they have equal intellectual currency.

Given the example of the Truth and Reconciliation Commission and other restorative efforts by governments in other countries, I offer what will be considered a bold assumption in this work, that the restorative project for African Americans, the most damaged and unrequitted group in society, is as germane to the quality of American democracy as any other. The force of memory is a germinating ingredient for social unrest, the rise of social movements, the lack of confidence in institutions, and perceptions of the value of citizenship. The achievement of a truly democratic state involves the ongoing rehabilitation of the historical condition of damaged groups of every stripe. That is why, regardless of the theoretical risks involved in calling attention to the complicity of the state in the ongoing suffering of Blacks, the state must be confronted both with the crimes that it allowed in the past and with the demand for correction in the present and future.

Finally, an appreciation of the unique history of African Americans will find that some of the most audacious past demands for redress were at the time considered "impractical." How could Frederick Douglass believe that the demand for the elimination of slavery would be fulfilled in his lifetime? How could A. Philip Randolph believe that the March on Washington would actually challenge President Roosevelt to pen an executive order outlawing racial discrimination in the war industries? How could the NAACP know, when it decided to attack racial discrimination full force, that the doctrine of "separate but equal" would be undone by *Brown v. Board of Education*? And how could Dr. Martin Luther King, Jr. know that the civil rights movement would usher in the most extensive regime of civil rights legislation since the post–Civil War amendments to the Constitution? This litany demonstrates that the timing of the effort by Blacks in the context of social movements, together with changes in the majority group's sentiments and in political institutions, brought about unanticipated, fundamental change. Considering the historical expectations of generations of African Americans—and others in American society who value justice—what right do we have to refuse to make perhaps the most righteous demands for redress in the history of America?

Appendix

TABLE A1.   Monthly Wages in South Africa for Racial Groups by Industry (1967, 1968)

Industry	White	Coloured	Asian	African
Mining (1967)	396	83	98	24
Construction (1968)	357	142	172	61
Manufacturing (1968)	340	87	93	64
Public Service (1967)	208	74	93	33
Average	325	97	114	45

Source: Survey of Race Relations in South Africa, 1968. Reported in Africa Research Group, *Race to Power: The Struggle for South Africa* (New York: Anchor/Doubleday, 1974), p. 26. Author's calculations.
Note: Wages in U.S. dollars.

TABLE A2.   Persons Killed by the Police in South Africa (1980, 1981)

Group	1980		1981	
	Adults	Juvenile	Adults	Juvenile
Indian	—	—	—	—
Coloured	40	12	46	8
African	206	29	210	28
White	2	—	4	—

Source: Restructured data, Alfred Moleah, *South Africa: Colonialism, Apartheid, and African Dispossession* (Wilmington, DE: Disa Press, 1993), 474.

TABLE A3.   Persons Wounded by the Police in South Africa (1980, 1981)

Group	1980		1981	
	Adults	Juvenile	Adults	Juvenile
Indian	—	2	5	—
Coloured	161	41	158	38
African	467	50	615	92
White	17	2	11	—

Source: Restructured data, Alfred Moleah, *South Africa: Colonialism, Apartheid, and African Dispossession* (Wilmington, DE: Disa Press, 1993), 474.

TABLE A4.   Death Sentences Carried Out in South Africa, 1975–84

	Executed
1975	68
1976	61
1977	90
1978	132
1979	133
1980	130
1981	96
1982	100
1983	90
1984	115
Total	1,015

Source: Alfred Moleah, *South Africa: Colonialism, Apartheid, and African Dispossession* (Wilmington, DE: Disa Press, 1993), 475.

TABLE A5.   Adjusted Monthly Death Toll in South Africa, 1993–95

Run-up to the elections (July 1993 to April 1994)	452
Postelection months (May 1994 to December 1994)	106
Year of 1995 (January to December)	75

Source: Max Coleman, ed., *A Crime against Humanity: Analysing the Repression of the Apartheid State* (Cape Town: David Philips, 1998), 235.

TABLE A6.   Lynchings in America, 1940–65

Year	Number
1940	4
1941	4
1942	7
1943[a]	7
1944	2
1945	1
1946	9
1947	14
1948	2
1949	3
1950	6
1951	5
1954	1
1955	7
1956	13
1957	3
1958	2
1959	4
1962	1
1963	7
1964	7
1965	5

Source: "The Lynching Century: 1865–1965: African Americans Who Died in Racial Violence in the United States, Chronology: Dates of Death, 1940–1965." In Michael Newton and Judy Ann Newton, *Racial and Religious Violence in America: A Chronology* (New York: Garland, 1991), 688–705.

[a]For 1943, in addition to 7 lynchings, there were 25 unidentified blacks murdered in Detroit.

TABLE A7.   Black Population as a Percentage of the Total Population in Selected States

	1910	1940	1960
California	1	2	6
Illinois	2	5	10
Michigan	1	4	9
New York	1	4	8
Ohio	2	5	8
Pennsylvania	3	5	8

Source: Bureau of the Census, U.S. Department of Commerce, *The Social and Economic Status of the Black Population in the United States, 1790-1978* (Washington, DC: GPO, 1979), 17.

TABLE A8. Higher Education Degrees Completed by Race, 2000–2001

Degree	Total	Blacks	Whites	Hispanics	Asians	Native American
Associate	578,865	11.0	71.0	9.8	4.9	0.01
Bachelor	1,244,171	8.9	74.5	6.2	6.3	0.007
Masters	468,476	8.1	68.4	4.6	5.2	0.005
Doctorate	44,904	4.9	61.1	3.3	5.7	0.003
Professional	79,707	6.7	73.5	4.7	11.6	0.005

Source: "Degrees Conferred by Racial and Ethnic Group, 2000," *Chronicle of Higher Education*, August 29, 2003, 19.

Note: These data do not include "nonresident aliens." Data by race are in percentages.

TABLE A9. Minority Businesses in the United States, 1997

Race	Firms	Sales and Receipts (millions of dollars)
Hispanics	1,199,896	186,275
Asians	912,960	306,933
Blacks	823,499	71,215
Native Americans	197,300	34,334

Source: "Minority Owned Business Enterprises," U. S. Census Bureau, 1997 Economic Census, table A, "Comparison of Business Ownership by Minority Group: 1997."

TABLE A10. Life Expectancy for Blacks and Whites in the United States, Selected Years

	Black	White
1900–1902	32.5 years	48.2 years
1919–21	47.1	56.3

Source: Bureau of the Census, U.S. Department of Commerce, *The Social and Economic Status of the Black Population in the United States, 1790–1978* (Washington, DC: GPO, 1979), 113–32.

NOTES

Preface

1. See also Ronald W. Walters, "Comparative Politics of Public Policy in the African Diaspora," Occasional Paper Series of the William Monroe Trotter Institute at University of Massachusetts, Boston, 23. Then, most recently, an article, "The African Growth and Opportunity Act: A Renaissance for Whom?" in *Black Renaissance* 2, no. 2 (1999): 161–69. My article, "U. S.—Africa Relations" will appear in the next edition of *Oxford Companion to the Politics of the World*, 2nd ed (New York: Oxford University Press).

Chapter 1

1. James Cox, "Aetna, CSX, FleetBoston Face Slave Reparations Suit," *USA Today*, March 24, 2002, 1.
2. Randall Robinson, *The Debt: What America Owes to Blacks* (New York: Penguin Putnam/Dutton, 2000).
3. "The Case for Reparations," transcript, TransAfrica Forum, Washington, DC, January 2000, Transafricaforum.org. Also see Julie Foster, "Slavery Reparations Lawsuit Brewing," WorldNetDaily, January 31, 2001, WorldNetDaily.com. The article mentions the "legal dream team": Johnnie Cochran of O. J. Simpson fame, Alexander Pires, who won a suit against the U.S. Department of Agriculture because the department had denied loans to Black farmers, tobacco industry lawsuit victor Richard Scruggs, and Dennis C. Sweet III, who won the "fen-phen" diet drug case. Others included Willie Gary, Adjoa Ayietoro, lawyer for NCOBRA, and social scientists such as Cornel West, Manning Marable, and James Comer.
4. The resolution offered in the City Council of the City of Chicago, for instance, was presented by Alderman Dorothy Tillman from Ward 3 in 2000, and hearings took place in March 2004. See document no. PR2000–2, available at http://www.chicityclerk.com/legislation.
5. Mark Sappenfield, "California Tests Racial Boundaries," *Christian Science Monitor*, May 6, 2002, 1.
6. DeNeen L. Brown, "A Whitewashing of History," *Washington Post*, February 17, 2001, A29.
7. Eric M. Yamamoto, *Interracial Justice: Conflict and Reconciliation in Post–Civil Rights America* (New York: New York University Press, 1999), 11.

8. Avishai Margalit, *The Ethics of Memory* (Cambridge: Harvard University Press, 2003), 51.

9. Ibid., 30–31.

10. Jeffrey Zaslow. "Civil War Veterans Are Gone, but Kids Have Stories to Tell," *Wall Street Journal,* May 28, 2004, 1.

11. Ibid.

12. Ibid.

13. "Civil War Battle Lines Drawn Again: Spotsylvania's Re-enactors Not Just a Band of Brothers," *Free Lance-Star* (Fredericksburg, VA), May 9, 2004, 1.

14. "Proposed Outer Connector Beltway at Chancellorsville Is Defeated," press release, Coalition to Save Chancellorsville Battlefield, Chancellorsville, Virginia, January 22, 2004.

15. "Civil War Preservation Trust Unveils Most Endangered Battlefield Report," press release, Civil War Preservation Trust, Washington, DC, February 24, 2004.

16. John Taliaferro, *The Great White Fathers* (New York: Public Affairs Press, 2002), 240.

17. Ibid., 157.

18. Ibid., 186–89.

19. Ibid., 192.

20. Ibid., 407.

21. A. W. James Booth, "The Unforgotten: Memories of Justice," *American Political Science Review* 95, no. 4 (2001): 777–92.

22. Ueno Chizuko, "The Politics of Memory," *History and Memory* 11, no. 2 (1999): 138.

23. Ibid., 142.

24. "Memory, Identity, and Political Action: An Interview with Professors Larry J. Griffin, William James Booth, and Michael Kreyling," *Letters* (Robert Penn Warren Center for the Humanities), 10, no. 1 (2001): 2.

25. Ibid., 3.

26. Ibid., 6.

27. W. James Booth, "Communities of Memory: On Identity, Memory, and Debt," *American Political Science Review* 93, no. 2 (1999): 252.

28. Robert Sandler, "Spokanes Want What Colvilles Got: Grand Coulee Dam Changed Tribal Life Forever, Member Says in Asking Congress for Reparations," *Spokesman Review,* October 3, 2003, A1.

29. Dale M. King, "Bitter Compensation: Holocaust Survivors Find Little Solace in Money Paid to Them," *Bocanews* (Boca Raton, FL), August 4, 2004.

30. Ibid.

31. Ibid., 129–52.

32. C. Eric Lincoln, *Coming Through the Fire: Surviving Race and Place in America* (Durham, NC: Duke University Press, 1996), 41.

33. Arnold J. Heidenbeimer, Hugh Heclo, and Carolyn Teich Adams, *Comparative Public Policy* (New York: St. Martins Press, 1990), 3.

34. Gabriel A. Almond and G. Bingham Powell Jr., *Comparative Politics: A Developmental Approach* (Boston: Little, Brown, 1966), 128–62.

35. Ronald W. Walters, *Pan Africanism in the African Diaspora* (Detroit: Wayne State University Press, 1993), 1–13.

36. Michael Brown, "The Viability of Racism," *Philosophical Forum,* special double issue on racism in South Africa, 18, nos. 2–3 (1987): 260.

37. Ibid., 261.

CHAPTER 2

1. Max Coleman, ed., *A Crime against Humanity: Analysing the Repression of the Apartheid State* (Cape Town: David Philips, 1998), 1.

2. Alfred Moleah, *South Africa: Colonialism, Apartheid, and African Dispossession* (Wilmington, DE: Disa Press, 1993), 112.

3. Ibid., 114.

4. Ibid., 116.

5. Ibid., 281.

6. Ibid., 286.

7. Ian Goldin, *Making Race: The Politics and Economics of Coloured Identity in South Africa* (New York: Longman, 1987), 1–9.

8. Ernest Harsch, *South Africa: White Rule, Black Revolt* (New York: Monad Press, 1980), 42.

9. Moleah, *South Africa,* 286.

10. Ibid., 297.

11. Harsch, *South Africa,* 42.

12. Nigel Worden, *The Making of Modern South Africa: Conquest, Segregation, and Apartheid* (Cambridge: Blackwell, 1994), 41.

13. Renfrew Christie, *Electricity, Industry, and Class in South Africa* (Albany: State University of New York Press, 1984), 138.

14. Ibid., 139.

15. Reported in Africa Research Group, *Race to Power: The Struggle for South Africa* (New York: Anchor/Doubleday, 1974), 26.

16. Robert Ross, *A Concise History of South Africa* (Cambridge: Cambridge University Press, 1999), 132.

17. Ibid., 116.

18. Ibid.

19. Ibid., 121.

20. Essy M. Letsoalo, *Land Reform in South Africa* (Johannesburg: Skotaville, 1987), 44.

21. Moleah, *South Africa,* 428.

22. Robert A. Denemark and Howard P. Lehman, "The Political Economy of Repression and Reform in South Africa," *Africa Today* 29, no. 3 (1982): 10.

23. Andre Odendaal, *Black Protest Politics in South Africa to 1912* (Totowa, NJ: Barnes and Noble, 1984), 273.

24. Harsch, *South Africa,* 238.

25. Ibid., 243–44.

26. Muriel Horrell, *Action, Reaction, and Counter-Action* (Johannesburg: Institute of Race Relations, 1971), 40.

27. Dale T. McKinley, *The ANC and the Liberation Struggle: A Critical Biography* (Chicago: Pluto Press, 1997), 27.

28. *Speeches of Mangaliso Sobukwe from 1949–1959 and Other Documents of the Pan-Africanist Congress of Azania* (New York: PAC Observer Mission to the UN, n.d.), 8.

29. Richard Leonard, *South Africa at War: White Power and the Crisis in Southern Africa* (Westport, CT: Lawrence Hill, 1983), 28–35.

30. McKinley, *ANC and Liberation Struggle*, 25–41.

31. Africa Research Group, *Race to Power*, 36.

32. Leonard, *South Africa at War*, 118.

33. Africa Research Group, *Race to Power*, 37.

34. Harsch, *South Africa*, 130.

35. Ibid., 132.

36. Ibid., 131.

37. Ibid., 129.

38. Leonard, *South Africa at War*, 119.

39. John Kane-Berman, *Soweto: Black Revolt, White Reaction* (Johannesburg: Ravan Press, 1978), 39.

40. Cited in Leonard, *South Africa at War*, 121.

41. Gordon Winter, *Inside BOSS* (New York: Penguin, 1981), 580–606.

42. Moleah, *South Africa*, 476.

43. Robert M. Price, *The Apartheid State in Crisis: Political Transformation in South Africa, 1975–1990* (New York: Oxford University Press, 1991), 215.

44. Jeremy Seekings, *The UDF: A History of the United Democratic Front in South Africa, 1983–1991* (Athens: Ohio University Press, 2000), 169, 193. This idea was similar to the slogan From Protest to Politics coined by American civil rights activist and theorist Bayard Rustin as the goal of the civil rights movement in the 1960s.

45. Seekings, *The UDF*, 196.

46. Price, *Apartheid State in Crisis*, 268.

47. Seekings, *The UDF*, 203.

48. Price, *Apartheid State in Crisis*, 267.

49. Coleman, *A Crime against Humanity*, epilogue, 243–70.

50. Gitanjali Maharaj, ed., *Between University and Diversity: Essays on Nation-Building in Post-Apartheid South Africa* (Cape Town: David Philips, 1999), 96.

51. Ibid., 97.

52. John Kane-Berman, *Political Violence in South Africa* (Johannesburg: South African Institute of Race Relations, 1993), 30.

53. Ibid., 34.

54. Ibid., 41.

55. Price, *Apartheid State in Crisis*, 216.

CHAPTER 3

1. Bonny Schoonakker, "12,000 Memories," *Sunday Times* (South Africa), August 24, 2003, 15.

2. Heribert Adam and Kanya Adam, "The Politics of Memory in Divided Societies," in *After the TRC: Reflections on Truth and Reconciliation in South Africa*, ed. Wilmot James and Linda van de Vijver (Athens: Ohio University Press, 2001), 32. For Asmal, see Kader Asmal, Louise Asmal, and Ronald Suresh Roberts, *Reconciliation through Truth: A Reckoning of Apartheid's Criminal Governance* (New York: St. Martin's Press, 1997), 10.

3. *Truth and Reconciliation Commission of South Africa Report*, 7 vols. (Cape Town: The Commission, 1998–2003), 49.

4. Amal, Asmal, and Roberts, *Reconciliation through Truth*, 10.

5. Alex Boraine, Janet Levy, and Ronel Scheffer, *Dealing with the Past: Truth and Reconciliation in South Africa* (Cape Town: IDASA, 1997), 3.

6. Ibid., 10.

7. Truth and Reconciliation Commission, 1997 seminar series, January 24, 1997, unpublished transcript.

8. Ibid., March 12, 1997, unpublished transcript.

9. Ibid.

10. Ibid.

11. Ibid.

12. Boraine, Levy, and Scheffer, *Dealing with the Past*, 79.

13. James and van de Vijver, *After the TRC*, 69.

14. Boraine, Levy, and Scheffer, *Dealing with the Past*, 99.

15. Roy Brooks, "What Price Reconciliation," in *When Sorry Isn't Enough*, ed. Roy Brooks (New York: New York University Press, 1999), 445.

16. Boraine, Levy, and Scheffer, *Dealing with the Past*, 115.

17. Truth and Reconciliation Commission, 1997 seminar series, May 6, 1997, unpublished transcript, p. 1.

18. Ibid., March 12, 1997, unpublished transcript, p. 1.

19. Ibid., p. 3.

20. Boraine, Levy, and Scheffer, *Dealing with the Past*, 144.

21. Ibid., 130.

CHAPTER 4

1. *Truth and Reconciliation Commission Report*, 5:171.

2. Ibid., 178.

3. Clarie Keeton, "Parliament Must Act on Reparations," *Sowetan*, August 16, 1999.

4. Ibid.

5. Ido Lekota, "Apartheid Victims Ignored—TRC," *Sowetan*, September 3, 1999.

6. Ibid.

7. Adrian Hadland, "Nation's Ship of Reconciliation Drifts Rudderless," *The Star*, October 12, 1999.

8. Adrian Hadland, "Red Tape Ruins Reconciliation," *The Star*, October 11, 1999.

9. Adrian Hadland, "Much Given but Reconciliation Denied," *The Star*, October 11, 1999, 1.

10. Desmond Tutu, *No Future without Forgiveness* (New York: Random House, 1999).

11. Sekola Sello, "Apartheid Victims: The Pain Is Not Over," *Sowetan*, October 11, 1999, 1.

12. *Cape Times*, February 25, 2000, 1.

13. Heather Robinson, "Red Tape on the Long and Rocky Road to Reparation," *Sunday Times*, February 2, 2000, 1.

14. Ibid.

15. "The TRC Could Find Itself in Hot Water," *Ekapa News, City Press,* March 12, 2000, 4.

16. Robert Brand, "NGOs to Pressure Govt on Reparations," *Cape Times,* March 27, 2000.

17. Ibid.

18. Paul Setsetse, "The TRC Was about More Than Paying Reparations," *City Press,* May 21, 2000)

19. Ibid.

20. Themba Molefe, "Eikenhof 3 Appeal for Retrial Starts," *Sowetan,* August 30, 1999.

21. Themba wa Sepotokele, Chimaimba Banda, and Sapa, "Williamson: Fury as Killer Spy Gets Off," *The Star,* June 2, 2000, 1.

22. *Sowetan,* June 5, 2000, 8.

23. Susan Daley, "Panel Denies Amnesty for Four Officers in Steve Biko's Death," *New York Times,* February 17, 1999, A4.

24. *Truth and Reconciliation Commission Report,* 5:409.

25. Ibid., 402.

26. Ivor Powell, "Heat Rises over Arms Deal," *Mail and Guardian,* June 2, 2000, 8.

27. "From Excellence in Destruction to Excellence in Construction," Cease Fire Campaign, Johannesburg, November 16, 1998.

28. Ibid.

29. Ibid.

30. Rob Thompson, "The Defense Budget and Some Alternatives," in *From Development to Defense: Redirecting Military Resources in South Africa,* ed. Jacklyn Cock and Penny Mckenzie (Claremont, South Africa: David Philips, 1998), 37.

31. *Truth and Reconciliation Commission Report,* 5:252.

32. Ibid., 434.

33. Ibid., 180.

34. Ibid., 178.

35. Marj Brown, Justin Erasmus, Rosalie Kingwill, Colin Murray, and Monty Roodt, *Land Restitution in South Africa: A Long Way Home* (Cape Town: IDASA, 1998), 1.

36. Ibid., 17.

37. Ibid., 66.

38. Ibid., 109.

39. "Land Issue: The Legacy since 1980 . . . Why Mugabe Has Waited Till Now," *New African,* June 2000, 20–21.

40. "The Land Claims Court of South Africa," http://www.law.wits.ac.za/lcc/Rules/index.html.

41. "ANC Submission to the Truth and Reconciliation Commission," Executive Summary, August 1996, http://www.anc.org.za/ancdocs/misc/trcsum.html.

42. Ibid., 15.

43. AC-Nielsen's Market Research Africa, reported in "TRC Has Harmed Race Relations: Survey," South African Press Association, Johannesburg, July 27, 1998. http://www.doj.gov.za/trc/media/1998/9807/s980727a.htm.

44. Ridwan Laher Nytagodien, "The ANC and White Accommodation," *Juluka,* February–March 1998, 8.

45. "Mbeki Urged to Speed Up TRC Reparations," South African Broadcasting Corporation, August 15, 2002.

46. "Mbeki to Approve Apartheid Reparations," South African Broadcasting Corporation, August 16, 2002.

47. Ibid.

48. Meron Tesfa Michael, "Moment of Truth: South Africa's Truth and Reconciliation Commission Closes Its Doors," *Worldpress,* May 2, 2003. http://www.world press.org/Africa/1077.cfm.

49. Gershwin Wanneburg and Wambui Chee, "South Africa to Pay Apartheid Victims," *Tiscali News,* March 15, 2003, http://www.tiscali.co.uk/news/.

50. "Mbeki Urged."

51. "South Africa: Parliamentary Committee on Apartheid Reparations," Southern Africa Documentation and Cooperation Centre, June 6, 2003. http://www.sadocc .at/news/2003_161.shtml.

52. "Jubilee South Africa Statement on Reparations," statement, July 24, 2003, www.pambazuka.org.

CHAPTER 5

1. Sterling A. Paige, "The Poverty Story": A House without a Stove to Cook On," *Baltimore Afro-American,* June 20, 1964, reprinted, February 15, 2003, February 21, 2003, D4.

2. Gunnar Myrdal, *An American Dilemma: The Negro Problem and Modern Democracy,* vol. 1 (New York: Harper Torchbooks, 1944), 28–29.

3. Dinesh D'Souza, *The End of Racism* (New York: Free Press, 1999), 245–88.

4. Benjamin Quarles, *The Negro in the Making of America* (New York: Collier-Macmillan, 1969), 33–61.

5. D'Souza, *The End of Racism,* 80, 83.

6. Ann M. Pescatello, *The African in Latin America* (New York: Random House, 1975), 152.

7. William Safire, *Lend Me Your Ears: Great Speeches in History* (New York: Norton, 1992), 541–55.

8. Paul Finkelman, "Garrison's Constitution," prologue, National Archives, Washington, DC, Winter 2000, 233.

9. Robert W. Fogel and Stanley L. Engerman, *Time on the Cross* (Boston: Little, Brown, 1974), 179.

10. Richard J. Herrenstein and Charles Murray, *The Bell Curve: Intelligence and Class Structure in American Life* (New York: Free Press, 1994).

11. W. D. Wright, *Racism Matters* (Westport, CT: Greenwood Press, 1998), 182.

12. George M. Weston, *The Progress of Slavery in the United States* (New York: Negro Universities Press, 1969).

13. John Elliott Cairnes, *The Slave Power* (New York: Harper Torchbooks, 1969), 76.

14. Frank Tannenbaum, *Slave and Citizen* (Boston: Beacon Press, 1992), 10.

15. Richard Bardolph, *The Civil Rights Record: Black Americans and the Law, 1849–1970* (New York: Thomas Y. Crowell, 1970), 61.

16. Ibid.

17. V. O. Key, *Southern Politics* (New York: Knopf, 1949), 555.

18. David McKean, *Party and Pressure Politics* (New York: Houghton Mifflin, 1949), 66.

19. Mark Sullivan, *Our Times: The United States, 1900–1925* (New York: Charles Scribner's Sons, 1926), 590.

20. Quarles, *Negro*, 142–43, cited in Bardolph, *The Civil Rights Record*, 59.

21. Ibid.

22. Ibid.

23. John E. Ashford; Mettie Ann Strong—Peon, Federal Bureau of Investigation, File 50–145, March 18, 1939, Justice Department Peonage Files, Manuscript Division, Library of Congress, Reels 22–25.

24. Nellie Echols; A. Leslie Wilkes, Federal Bureau of Investigation, File 50–34, October 27, 1943, Justice Department Peonage Files, Manuscript Division, Library of Congress, reels 22–25.

25. Royce Green; Federal Bureau of Investigation, file No. 50–52, October 19, 1943, Justice Department Peonage Files, Manuscript Division, Library of Congress, reels 22–25.

26. Len Cooper, "The Damned: Slavery Did Not End with the Civil War; One Man's Odyssey into a Nation's Secret Shame," *Washington Post*, June 16, 1996, F1.

27. Daniel Novak, *The Wheel of Servitude: Black Forced Labor after Slavery* (Lexington: University of Kentucky Press, 1978), 83.

28. James E. Cutler, *Lynch-Law: An Investigation into the History of Lynching in the United States* (New York: Longmans, Green, 1905), 1.

29. Myrdal, *An American Dilemma*, 560–61.

30. Ida B. Wells-Barnett, *On Lynchings* (New York: Humanity Books, 2002), 30.

31. Ibid., 48.

32. Ibid., 78.

33. Table 6, "Lynching by Year and Race, 1882–1959," United States Commission on Civil Rights, *Annual Report* (Washington, DC: GPO, 1961), 268.

34. Ibid., table 13: Referral Sources of Police Brutality Matters Received by the Department of Justice, Negro and Other Minority Group Victims, 272.

35. *The Selected Writings of John Jay Chapman*, ed. Jacques Barzun (New York: Farrar, Straus and Cudahy, 1957), v.

36. Ibid., 256, 257.

37. James Gilbert Cassedy, "African Americans and the American Labor Movement," *Federal Records and African American History* 29, no. 2 (1997): 4.

38. Aldred L. Brophy, *Reconstructing the Dreamland: The Tulsa Riot of 1921* (New York: Oxford University Press, 2002.)

39. Ibid., 24–62.

40. Stanley Norvell, "Bloody Smear in the Promised Land," in *Afro American History: Primary Sources*, ed. Thomas R. Frazier (New York: Harcourt, Brace and World, 1970), 261–67.

41. "A Praiseworthy Lynching," *Chicago Chronicle*, in *Literary Digest*, June 19, 1897.

42. "Strength of Race Prejudice," *Mobile Register*, in *Literary Digest*, June 19, 1897.

43. Charles Hamilton, Lynn Huntley, Neville Alexander, Antonio Sergio, Alfredo Guimaraes, and Wilmot James, eds., *Beyond Racism: Race and Inequality in Brazil South Africa, and the United States* (London: Lynne Rienner, 2001), 9.

CHAPTER 6

1. Franklin Raines, "What Equality Would Look Like: Reflections on the Past, Present and Future," presented at the Annual Conference of the National Urban League, August 2001, prepared by Lawrence Q. Newton and Maria E. Ugincius, Editorial Research Service, August 1, 2001.

2. "African Americans' Status Is 73% of Whites Says New 'State of Black America' 2004 Report," *News,* n.d., press release, www.nul.org/news/soba.html, downloaded March 5, 2004.

3. Carter G. Woodson, *Mis-Education of the Negro* (1933; Trenton, NJ: African World Press, 1998).

4. *Public Papers of the Presidents of the United States,* Lyndon Baines Johnson, June 1965.

5. Philip Hauser, "Demographic Factors in the Integration of the Negro," in *The Negro American,* ed. Talcott Parsons and Kenneth B. Clark (Boston: Beacon Press, 1966), 71.

6. St. Clair Drake, "The Social and Economic Status of the Negro in the United States," in Talcot Parsons and Kenneth Clark, ed., *The Negro American* (Boston: Beacon Press, 1966), 40–41.

7. Kenneth Clark, *The Pathos of Power* (New York: Harper and Row, 1974), 28.

8. *A Testament of Hope: The Essential Writings of Martin Luther King, Jr.,* ed. James Washington, Jr. (New York: Harper and Row, 1986), 118.

9. Ibid., 100–101.

10. Martin Luther King, Jr., *Where Do We Go from Here: Chaos or Community?* (Boston: Beacon Press, 1968), 6.

11. William J. Clinton, commencement address at University of California at San Diego, La Jolla, CA, June 14, 1997.

12. Steven Holmes, "Clinton Panel on Race Urges a Variety of Modest Measures," *New York Times,* September 18, 1998, 1.

13. Bureau of the Census, U.S. Department of Commerce, *The Social and Economic Status of the Black Population in the United States, 1790–1978* (Washington, DC: GPO, 1979), 14.

14. Joseph V. Stefko, "Residential Segregation and Job Loss in Cities," 5, http://www.acsu.buffalo.edu/%7Ejstefko/UNLppr2000.pdf, downloaded June 16, 2007.

15. William Julius Wilson, *The Truly Disadvantaged: The Inner City, the Underclass, and Public Policy* (Chicago: University of Chicago Press, 1987), 46–48; Marc Settles, "The Perpetuation of Residential Racial Segregation in America: Historical Discrimination, Modern Forms of Exclusion and Inclusionary Remedies," *Journal of Land Use and Environmental Law* 14 (fall 1998). http://www.law.fsu.edu/Journals/Landuse/vol141/seit.htm.

16. Benjamin F. Bobo, *Locked in and Locked out: The Impact at Urban Land Use Policy and Market Forces on African Americans* (Westport, CT: Praeger, 2001), 85.

17. Raymond Winbush, ed., *Should America Pay?* (New York: HarperCollins, 2003), 48–49.

18. Federation of Southern Cooperatives Land Assistance Fund, Federation of Southern Cooperatives, www.federationsoutherncoop.com.

19. Bureau of the Census, *Status of Black Population,* 83–96.

20. Roderick Harrison, "Census Shows Despite a Decade of Economic Gains, Race and Gender Gaps Persist," *The Crisis* (National Association of Colored People), July–August 2003, 17.

21. "Housing Discrimination Study: Synthesis," Urban Institute, Washington, DC, 1989.

22. Douglas S. Massey, "Shrugging Off Racism: When Proof of Housing Discrimination Arrived, the Administration Didn't Care," *Washington Post,* May 17, 1992, C2.

23. Barbara Ruben, "Fair Is Fair, or Is It? Discrimination Claims by Buyers and Renters Are on the Upswing," *New York Times,* August 2, 2003, F1.

24. Ibid.

25. Matthew Mosk, "Blacks See Bias in a Pricier Neighborhood; Buyers, Researchers Allege Housing Discrimination in the Outer Suburbs," *Washington Post,* September 2, 2001, C1.

26. Ibid.

27. H. Jane Lehman, "Study: Race Factor in Loan Rejections," *Washington Post,* October 24, 1992, F1.

28. Ann Mariano, *Washington Post,* in *The West County Times* (San Francisco), June 14, 1992.

29. Jonathan D. Glater, "Fed Finds Disparities in Mortgage Denials: Lending Rose in 1993; OTS Chief Draws Flak," *Washington Post,* October 27, 1994, B10; also Don Finefrock, "Barnett Banks Denies Loan Bias Accusations," *Miami Herald,* March 20, 1995.

30. Jonathan D. Glater, "Black and White Become Gray Areas in Loan Study to Critics; 'Cultural Affinity' Is Code for 'Bias,'" *Washington Post,* July 18, 1995, D01.

31. H. Jane Lehman, "Insurance Study Finds Racial Disparity," *Washington Post,* February 6, 1993, F1.

32. Raines, "What Equality Would Look Like," 17.

33. Harrison, "Census Shows," 16.

34. Raines, "What Equality Would Look Like," 15.

35. David Swinton, "The Economic Status of African Americans," in *The State of Black America, 1992* (New York: National Urban League, 1992), 16–17.

36. William A. Darity, Jr. and Samuel L. Meyers, Jr., "Racial Earnings Inequality in the 21st Century," National Urban League, *State of Black America,* 119–39.

37. Paul Burstein, *Discrimination, Jobs, and Politics: The Struggle for Equal Employment Opportunity in the United States since the New Deal* (Chicago: University of Chicago Press, 1985).

38. "Opportunity Denied, Opportunity Diminished," Urban Institute, Washington, DC, 1991.

39. Lynette Clemetson, "Treasury Dept. Faces Suit by Minority Agents," *New York Times,* May 17, 2002, A21.

40. Stephen Barr, "OPM Finds Blacks Fired at Higher Rate," *Washington Post,* April 19, 1995, A01.

41. Alam B. Krueger, "Economic Scene: Sticks and Stones Can Break Bones, but the Wrong Name Can Make a Job Hard to Find," *New York Times,* December 12, 2002, C2.

42. Fred Blumrosen and Ruth Blumrosen, "The Realities of Intentional Job Discrimination," Center for Law and Justice, Rutgers School of Law, Rutgers University, July 2002, http://law.Newark.Rutgers.edu/Blumrosen-eeo.html.

43. Ibid.

44. "Blacks Less Likely to Get Medical Advances," *Washington Post/Health*, January 17, 1989, 11.

45. Isabel Wilkerson, "Blacks Assail Ethics in Medical Testing," *New York Times*, June 2, 1991, A12.

46. Sheryl Gay Stolberg, "Race Gap Seen in Health Care of Equally Insured Patients," *New York Times*, March 21, 2002, A1.

47. Ibid.

48. Sheryl Gay Stolberg, "Race Gap in Health Care," *New York Times*, March 24, 2002, sec. 4, p. 2.

49. David Crocker, "Retribution and Reconciliation," Institute for Philosophy and Public Policy," School of Public Affairs, University of Maryland, 5, http://www.puaf.umd.edu/IPPP/Winter-Spring00/retribution_and_reconciliation .htm.

50. Steven A. Holmes, "Race Analysis Cites Disparity in Sentencing for Narcotics," *New York Times*, June 8, 2000, A14.

51. Ibid.

52. Fox Butterworth, "Study Finds Big Increase in Black Men as Inmates since 1980," *New York Times*, August 28, 2002, A14.

53. Fox Butterworth, "U.S. Expands Its Lead in the Rate of Imprisonment," *New York Times*, February 11, 1992, A16.

54. "40% on Death Row Are Black, New Figures Show," *New York Times*, September 30, 1991, A15.

55. Adam Liptak, "Number of Inmates on Death Row Declines as Challenges to Justice System Rise," *New York Times*, January 11, 2003, A13.

56. Jerry Gray, "Panel Says Courts Are 'Infested with Racism'," *New York Times*, June 5, 1991, B1.

57. Mary Tabor, "Judge Finds Bias against Minority Inmates," *New York Times*, October 3, 1992, B1.

58. Richard Perez-Pena, "3 on High Court Fault Peremptory Challenges," *New York Times*, March 20, 2002, B2.

59. David Stout, "Attorney General Says Report Shows No Racial and Ethnic Bias in Federal Death Sentences," *New York Times*, June 7, 2001, A29; Robin Toner, "President of Urban League Calls for Review of Inequality," *New York Times*, July 30, 2001, A10.

60. Lena Williams, "When Blacks Shop, Bias Often Accompanies the Sale," *New York Times*, April 30, 1991, A1.

61. "Quicker Not to Dicker," *USA Today*, August 4, 1992, A12.

62. Jonathan D. Glater, "Nissan Settles Bias Suit by Minority Buyers," *New York Times*, February 21, 2003, C3.

63. Walter E. Goodman, "Missing Middle-Class Blacks in TV News," *New York Times*, May 22, 1990, C18.

64. Ellis Cose, "Rape in the News: Mainly about Whites," *New York Times*, May 7, 1989, editorial.

65. Ishmael Reed, "Tuning Out Network Bias," *New York Times,* April 9, 1991, 23.

66. Garry Pierre-Pierre, "Black Family's Car Is Torched in Brooklyn," *New York Times,* July 20, 1995, B5.

67. Sue Anne Pressley, "A New Residence and a Tragedy Forced Out of One Texas Town, Black Man Is Killed on Street," *Washington Post,* September 3, 1993, A4.

68. Anthony Ewell, "The Color of His Skin," *New York Times,* June 10, 1991, A17.

69. Kirk Jonson, "A New Generation of Racism Seen," *New York Times,* August 27, 1991.

70. "Whites Who Set Black Man Afire Arrested," *The Challenger* (Buffalo), January 20, 1993, 18.

71. Andy Stapp, "24 Lynchings Feared in Mississippi," *The Challenger* (Buffalo), November 25, 1992, 18.

72. Carol Marie Cropper, "Black Man Fatally Dragged in a Possible Racial Killing," *New York Times,* June 10, A16.

73. "A Third Car-Dragging Incident Is Reported," *New York Times,* June 15, 1998, A14.

74. "Black Man Found Hanged in Florida Is Ruled a Suicide," *New York Times,* July 30, 2003, A15.

75. "Man Hanging from Tree Investigated," *Montgomery Advertiser,* August 19, 2004, 1.

76. Press conference, statement of Ari Fleischer, August 1, 2001, *Public Papers of the President of the United States.*

77. CNN/USA Today/Gallup Poll, January 25–27, 2002.

78. "Race in America," Gallup Poll, January 4–February 28, 1997.

79. "Bush: Slavery One of History"s 'Greatest Crimes,'" CNN.com/World, July 8, 2003.

80. World Conference against Racism, Racial Discrimination, Xenophobia and Related Intolerance Declaration, United Nations, August 31–September 8, 2003, Durban, South Africa.

81. "Money Income of Families—Percent Distribution by Income Level, Race, and Hispanic Origin, in Constant (1999) dollars: 1980–1999," table 668, Bureau of the Census, Department of Commerce, 2001.

82. Reynolds Farley, and Walter R. Allen, *The Color Line and the Quality of Life in America* (New York: Russell Sage Foundation, 1987), table 10.3, "Median Net Worth of Households by Race, Monthly Income," 290.

83. Gerald David Jaynes and Robin M. Williams, Jr., eds., *A Common Destiny: Blacks and American Society* (Washington, DC: National Academy Press, 1987), 292.

CHAPTER 7

1. Ronald W. Walters, *White Nationalism, Black Interests* (Detroit: Wayne State University Press, 2003).

2. Quoted from Bess Beatty, *A Revolution Gone Backward: The Black Response to National Politics, 1876–1896* (Westport, CT: Greenwood Press, 1987).

3. Ibid.

4. R. W. Apple, Jr., "Clinton to Conclude Contrite Tour at Notorious Slavery Site," *New York Times,* April 1, 1998, online.

5. Remarks of Rep. Sheila Jackson-Lee, U.S. House of Representatives, March 31, 1998.

6. Mirta Ojito, "Clinton Trip Evokes Strong Feelings from African-Americans," *New York Times,* March 26, 1998, online.

7. J. Angelo Corlett, *Race, Racism, and Reparations* (Ithaca: Cornell University Press, 2003), 65.

8. Ibid., 69.

9. David G. Payne and Jason M. Blackwell, "Truth in Memory: Caveat Emptor," in *Truth in Memory,* ed. Steven Jay Lynn and Kevin M. McConkey (New York: Guilford Press, 1998), 32, 403.

10. Ralph Underwager and Hollida Wakefield, "Recovered Memories in the Courtroom," in Lynn and McConkey, *Truth in Memory,* 410.

11. Angelyn Mitchell, *The Freedom to Remember: Narrative, Slavery, and Gender in Contemporary Black Women's Fiction* (New Brunswick, NJ: Rutgers University Press, 2002), 147.

12. Ibid., 12. Mitchell attributes the concept of rememory to Toni Morrison.

13. John F. Kihlstrom, "Exhumed Memory," in Lynn and McConkey, *Truth in Memory,* 18.

14. Woodson, *Mis-Education of the Negro,* 24.

15. Alicia L. Young, "Class Struggle," review of Stephen Kendrick and Paul Kendrick, *Sarah's Long Walk: The Free Blacks of Boston and How Their Struggle for Equality Changed America* (Boston: Beacon Press, 2004), *Washington Post Book World,* April 24, 2005, 13.

16. Margalit, *The Ethics of Memory,* 47.

17. Molly Secours, "Riding the Reparations Bandwagon," in Winbush, *Should America Pay?* 287–89.

18. Ronald Roach, "Taking Supreme Action, *Black Issues in Higher Education,* April 24, 2003, 22.

19. Judith Roof and Robyn Wiegman, eds., *Who Can Speak? Authority and Critical Identity* (Urbana: University of Illinois Press, 1995), 6–17.

20. Quoted in ibid., 8.

21. Ibid., 10.

22. Ibid., 9.

23. Ibid.

24. Matthew O. Hunt, "The Individual, Society, or Both? A Comparison of Black, Latino, and White Beliefs about the Causes of Poverty," *Social Forces* 75, no. 1 (1996): 313.

25. Mary Beth Marklein, "On Campus: Free Speech for You but Not for Me?" *USA Today,* November 3, 2003, 11.

26. Dinesh D'Souza, *What's So Great about America* (Washington, DC: Regnery, 2002), 47, 118.

27. Philip Dray, *At the Hands of Persons Unknown* (New York: Modern Library, 2003), ix.

28. Lynda Richardson, "For Civil Rights Lawyer, the Fight Is Far from Over," *New York Times,* July 5, 2002, B2.

29. Ibid.

30. Ibid.

31. Ibid.

32. Susan Sontag, *Regarding the Pain of Others* (New York: Farrar, Straus and Giroux, 2003).

33. Ibid., 86.

34. Ibid., 87.

35. Ibid., 88.

36. Ibid.

37. E. Franklin Frazier, *The Negro Church in America* (New York: Schocken, 1964), 6–11.

38. Philip S. Foner and Yuval Taylor, eds., *Frederick Douglass: Selected Speeches and Writings* (Chicago: Lawrence Hill Books, 1999), 347.

39. Underwager and Wakefield, "Recovered Memories," 409.

40. Jeffrey Gardere, *Love Prescription: Ending the War between Black Men and Women* (New York: Kensington, 2002).

41. Na'im Akbar, *Breaking the Chains of Psychological Slavery* (Tallahassee, FL: Mind Productions and Associates, 1996).

42. Dawn K. Wilson, Wendy Kliewer, Laura Plybon, and Domenic A. Sica, "Socioeconomic Status and Blood Pressure Reactivity in Health Black Adolescents," *Hypertension* 35 (2000): 496.

43. B. R. Gump, K. A. Matthews, and K. Raikkonen, "Modeling Relationships among Socioeconomic Status, Hostility, Cardiovascular Reactivity and Left Ventricular Mass in African American and White Children," *Health Psychology* 18 (1999): 140–50; R. W. Jackson, F. A. Treiber, J. R. Turner, H. Davis, and W. B. Stong, "Effects of Race, Sex, and Socioeconomic Status upon Cardiovascular Stress Responsivity and Recovery in Youth," *International Journal of Psychophysiology* 31 (1993): 111–19, cited in Wilson et al., "Socioeconomic Status," 496. The disparate result is probably accounted for by the fact that family resources were not taken into account and where they have previously been found to be crucial to such a result (Wilson et al., 496).

44. Kathleen C. Light, Kimberly A. Barowniey; J. Rick Turner; Alan L. Hinderliter; Susan S. Girdler; Andrew Sherwood, and Norman B. Anderson, "Job Status and High-Effort Coping Influence Work Blood Pressure in Women and Blacks," *Hypertension* 25 (1995): 554–59.

45. Ibid.

46. Melissa C. Stoppler, "Doctors Show Victims of Racism Have Elevated Blood Pressure," *Newswire*, October 20, 2003.

47. Richard L. Armitage, "Remarks to the Holocaust Education Task Force," Washington, DC, May 14, 2003, http://www.state.gov/s/d/former/armitage/remarks/20634.htm, downloaded June 12, 2007.

48. Ibid.

49. Sherry Ricchiardi, "Exposing Genocide . . . for What?" *American Journalism Review* 15, no. 5 (1993).

50. James M. Washington, ed., *A Testament of Hope: The Essential Writings of Martin Luther King, Jr.* (San Francisco: Harper & Row, 1986), 233.

51. Cited in Yamamoto, *Interracial Justice*, 272.

52. Stephanie M. Wildman and Adrienne Davis, "Making Systems of White Privilege Visible," in *White Privilege: Essential Readings on the Other Side of Racism*, ed. Paula S. Rothenberg (New York: Worth, 2002), 89.

53. Peggy McIntosh, "White Privilege: Unpacking the Invisible Knapsack," in Rothenberg, *White Privilege*, 97.

54. Tim Wise, "Whiteness: The Power of Its Privileges," in Rothenberg, *White Privilege,* 108.

55. Ibid.

CHAPTER 8

1. Mitchell, *The Freedom to Remember,* 4.

2. Corlett, *Race, Racism, and Reparations,* 220.

3. This number has been estimated at between $1 and $4 trillion by various researchers.

4. Michael Z. Wise, "Reparations," *Atlantic Monthly,* October 1993, 4.

5. Stuart Eizenstat and Sheldon Kirshner, "The Unfinished Business of Restitution (Imperfect Justice)," *Canadian Jewish News,* June 12, 2003.

6. Ibid.

7. "Race Relations," Gallup Poll, January 4–February 28, 1997.

8. Author's meeting notes, Reparations Coordinating Committee, Washington, DC, January 11, 2000.

9. John M. Blum, Bruce Catton, Edmund S. Morgan, Arthur Schlesinger Jr, Kenneth M. Stamp, and C. Vann Woodward, *The National Experience* (New York: Harcourt, Brace & World, 1963), 562.

10. "Slave Narratives," Federal Writers Project, Austin, Texas, Austin History Center, Austin Public Library.

11. Margalit, *The Ethics of Memory,* 111.

12. Ibid., 114.

13. Joseph Berger, "After Pain beyond Price, Feeling Shortchanged," *New York Times,* May 8, 2005, 25.

14. Robert Westley, "Many Billions Gone: Is It Time to Reconsider the Case for Black Reparations?" in Winbush, *Should America Pay?* 109–34.

15. Tutu, *No Future without Forgiveness.*

16. Ibid., 206–33.

17. Sterling Brown, Arthur P. Davis, and Ulysses Lee, eds., *The Negro Caravan* (New York: Citadel Press, in arrangement with the Dryden Press, 1941), 4.

18. Albert Memi, *The Colonizer and the Colonized* (Boston: Beacon Press, 1965), 119, 140.

19. Tim Wise, "Breaking the Cycle of White Dependence and the Call for Majority Self-Sufficiency, ZNET Daily Commentaries, May 19, 2001, http://www.zmag .org/sustainers/content/2001-05/19wise.htm.

20. Roger Cobb and Charles Elder, *Participation in American Politics: The Dynamics of Agenda-Building* (Boston: Allyn and Bacon, 1972), 110–20.

21. Juliet Eilperin, "Committee Proposes Trust Fund to Aid Oceans," *Washington Post,* April 21, 2004, A3.

CHAPTER 9

1. W. E. B. DuBois, *The World and Africa: An Inquiry into the Part Which Africa Has Played in World History* (New York: International Publishers, 1985).

2. Ibid., 56.

3. Ibid.

4. Ibid., 59.

5. Ibid., 64.

6. Ibid., 66.

7. *The African Slave Trade from the Fifteenth to the Nineteenth Century: Reports and Papers of a Meeting of Experts Organized by Unesco at Port-au-Prince, Haiti, 31 January to 4 February 1978* (Paris: UNESCO, 1979), 211.

8. Ibid., 18.

9. Benjamin Kidd, *The Control of the Tropics* (London: Macmillan, 1898), 23.

10. Mary Townsend, *European Colonial Expansion since 1871* (New York: J. B. Lippincott, 1941), 64–65.

11. Kidd, *Control of the Tropics*, 3.

12. D. K. Fieldhouse, *Economics and Empire, 1830–1914* (Ithaca: Cornell University Press, 1973), 144–45.

13. Ibid.

14. Ibid., 146.

15. Ibid., 147.

16. Walter Rodney, *How Europe Underdeveloped Africa* (Washington, DC: Howard University Press, 1982).

17. Ibid., 112–23.

18. Ibid., 263–86.

19. Alleyne Ireland, *Tropical Colonization* (London: Macmillan, 1899), 94.

20. Treaty of Ghent, 1814, Article 10, Avalon Project at Yale University, http://www.yale.edu/lawweb/avalon/diplomacy/britain/ghent.htm, downloaded June 17, 2007.

21. "Greeks Take Compensation Claim for 1944 Nazi Killings to Highest German Court," Associated Press Worldstream, August 24, 2003.

22. L. H. Gann and Peter Duignan, *Colonialism in Africa, 1870–1960,* vol. 2 (Cambridge: Cambridge University Press, 1970), 18.

23. Ibid., 19.

24. Georges Ngal, *Discours sur le Colonialisme* (Paris: Presence Africaine, 1994), 14.

25. See the Hearings by the International Relations Committee of the House of Representatives, especially, Testimony by Paul V. Applegarth, Chief Executive Officer, Millennium Challenge Corporation, House Committee on International Relations, May 19, 2004.

26. Ronald W. Walters, "The African Growth and Opportunity Act: Changing Foreign Policy Priorities toward Africa in a Conservative Political Culture," in *Foreign Policy and the Black (Inter)national Interest,* ed. Charles P. Henry (Albany: SUNY Press, 2000), 17–36.

27. Aaditya Mattoo, Devesh Roy, and Arvind Subramanian, "The African Growth and Opportunity Act and Its Rules of Origin: Generosity Undermined?" IMF Working Paper, WP/02/158, International Monetary Fund, September 2002, 14–18.

28. Moshood Abiola was a true Pan-Africanist who invited the author to serve as the chair of the American delegation to the Abuja conference. He was jailed after it appeared that he had won the general election in Nigeria in 1993, and he eventually assassinated by the regime of General Ibrahim Babangida.

29. "Kenya Legalises Body Pushing for Slavery Compensation," Daily News Wire, *PanAfrican News Agency,* November 23, 2003.

30. "Durban Conference against Racism from the Birthplace of Passive Resistance, a Call for Tolerance," *United Nations Chronicle,* online edition. http://www.un .org/Pubs/Chronicle/2001/issue4/0104p53.html.

31. Gustavo Capdevita, "World Powers 'Boycott' U.N. Afro-Descendants Group," Special to the NNPA, *Baltimore Afro-American,* February 15–21, 2003, D9.

32. Ibid.

33. Charles Cobb, Jr., "Africa Union Announced as U.S. Official Denounces Foremost Promoter," May 25, 2001, allAfrica.com. http://allAfrica.com/stories/printable/200105250411.html.

34. "Namibia: Germany Rules Out Reparations but Offers Aid," United Nations Integrated Regional Information Networks, August 16, 2004, allAfrica.com. http:/www.panapress.com/dossindexlat.asp?code=eng005.

35. Petros Kuteeue, "Hereros Insist Apology Must Come with Compensation," *The Namibian* (Windhoek), August 20, 2004, allAfrica.com. http://www.irinnews.org/report.asp?ReportID=42694.

36. Ibrahim Seaga Shaw, *The Independent* (Banjul), July 19, 2004, allAfrica.com. http://allAfrica.com/stories/200407191478.html supplemental result.

POSTSCRIPT

1. Wendy Brown, *States of Injury: Power and Freedom in Late Modernity* (Princeton: Princeton University Press, 1995), 27.

2. Lawrie Balfour, "Reparations after Identity Politics, *Political Theory* 33, no. 6 (2005): 789.

3. Adolph Reed, "The Case against Reparations," *The Progressive,* December 2000, 16–17.

4. Such criticisms from a more conservative perspective are rendered by prominent Black commentators and intellectuals Armstrong Williams, John McWhorter, and Shelby Steele in Winbush, *Should America Pay?* 165–99.

5. Thomas McCarthy, "*Vergangenheitsbewaltigung* in the USA: On the Politics of the Memory of Slavery," *Political Theory* 30, no. 5 (2002): 623–48.

6. Charles Henry, "The Rise of Racial Reparations," *Journal of Black Studies* 34, no. 2 (2003): 131–52.

7. Cited in McCarthy, "*Vergangenheitsbewaltigung* in the USA," 635.

INDEX

Text design by Mary H. Sexton
Typesetting by Delmastype, Ann Arbor, Michigan
Text Font: Adobe Caslon

William Caslon released his first typefaces in 1722.
Caslon's types were based on seventeenth-century Dutch old
style designs. Because of their remarkable practicality, Caslon's
designs met with instant success. Printer Benjamin Franklin
hardly used any other typeface. The first printings of the
American Declaration of Independence and the Constitution
were set in Caslon. For her Caslon revival, designer
Carol Twombly studied specimen pages printed by
William Caslon between 1734 and 1770.
—courtesy myfonts.com